DATE DUE

9/27/11			

Muslim Modernities

Muslim Modernities

Expressions of the Civil Imagination

Edited by

AMYN B. SAJOO

I.B. Tauris *Publishers*
LONDON • NEW YORK
in association with
The Institute of Ismaili Studies
London, 2008

Published in 2008 by I.B.Tauris & Co. Ltd
6 Salem Road, London W2 4BU
175 Fifth Avenue, New York, NY 10010
www.ibtauris.com

in association with The Institute of Ismaili Studies
42–44 Grosvenor Gardens, London SW1W 0EB
www.iis.ac.uk

In the United States of America and Canada distributed by Palgrave Macmillan,
a division of St Martin's Press, 175 Fifth Avenue, New York, NY 10010

ISBN: 978 1 84511 872 3

A full CIP record for this book is available from the British Library
A full CIP record for this book is available from the Library of Congress

Library of Congress catalog card: available

Typeset in Minion Tra for The Institute of Ismaili Studies
Printed and bound in Great Britain by TJ International Ltd, Padstow, Cornwall

The Institute of Ismaili Studies

The Institute of Ismaili Studies was established in 1977 with the object of promoting scholarship and learning on Islam, in the historical as well as contemporary contexts, and a better understanding of its relationship with other societies and faiths.

The Institute's programmes encourage a perspective which is not confined to the theological and religious heritage of Islam, but seeks to explore the relationship of religious ideas to broader dimensions of society and culture. The programmes thus encourage an interdisciplinary approach to the materials of Islamic history and thought. Particular attention is also given to issues of modernity that arise as Muslims seek to relate their heritage to the contemporary situation.

Within the Islamic tradition, the Institute's programmes promote research on those areas which have, to date, received relatively little attention from scholars. These include the intellectual and literary expressions of Shi'ism in general, and Ismailism in particular.

In the context of Islamic societies, the Institute's programmes are informed by the full range and diversity of cultures in which Islam is practised today, from the Middle East, South and Central Asia, and Africa to the industrialized societies of the West, thus taking into consideration the variety of contexts which shape the ideals, beliefs and practices of the faith.

These objectives are realised through concrete programmes and activities organized and implemented by various departments of the Institute. The Institute also collaborates periodically, on a programme-specific basis, with other institutions of learning in the United Kingdom and abroad.

The Institute's academic publications fall into a number of inter-related categories:

1. Occasional papers or essays addressing broad themes of the relationship between religion and society, with special reference to Islam.
2. Monographs exploring specific aspects of Islamic faith and culture, or the contributions of individual Muslim thinkers or writers.
3. Editions or translations of significant primary or secondary texts.
4. Translations of poetic or literary texts which illustrate the rich heritage of spiritual, devotional and symbolic expressions in Muslim history.
5. Works on Ismaili history and thought, and the relationship of the Ismailis to other traditions, communities and schools of thought in Islam.
6. Proceedings of conferences and seminars sponsored by the Institute.
7. Bibliographical works and catalogues which document manuscripts, printed texts and other source materials.

This book falls into category two listed above.

In facilitating these and other publications, the Institute's sole aim is to encourage original research and analysis of relevant issues. While every effort is made to ensure that the publications are of a high academic standard, there is naturally bound to be a diversity of views, ideas and interpretations. As such, the opinions expressed in these publications must be understood as belonging to their authors alone.

Contents

Acknowledgements   ix

About the Contributors   xi

1. Introduction
   AMYN B. SAJOO   1

2. Scripture, History and Modernity:
   Readings of the Qur'an
   BRUCE B. LAWRENCE   25

3. Heroic Themes: An Invitation to Muslim Worlds
   JOHN RENARD   51

4. An Andalusian Modernity in Narratives of Women
   HASNA LEBBADY   73

5. Civil Sounds: The Aga Khan Music Initiative
   in Central Asia
   THEODORE LEVIN AND
   FAIROUZ R. NISHANOVA   93

6. Forbidden Modernities: Islam in Public
   NILÜFER GÖLE   119

7. Revivalism and the Enclave Society
    BRYAN S. TURNER   137

8. Modern Citizenship, Multiple Identities
    EVA SCHUBERT   161

9. Globalization, Civil Imagination and
    Islamic Movements
    KEVIN McDONALD   183

10. Reimagining the Civil: Pluralism
    and Its Discontents
    AMYN B. SAJOO   207

Notes   227
Select Bibliography   259
Index   271

Acknowledgements

A visiting fellowship from the University of Cambridge gave impetus to this volume in the spring of 2005. What until then were fairly raw ideas built around Charles Taylor's gem of a study, *Modern Social Imaginaries* (2004)*, began to shape themselves in conversations, formal and social, at the Centre for Research in the Arts, Social Sciences & Humanities (CRASSH). I am grateful to Ludmilla Jordanova as director and to an assortment of visiting fellows whose generosity of intellect made my sojourn so fertile.

Credit for endorsing an early incarnation of this project – and for staying with it to culmination – is due to the Institute of Ismaili Studies (IIS) in London. Azim Nanji as director and Farhad Daftary as head of research and publications gave invaluable support. Kutub Kassam lent the benefit of his creative patience as friend and editorial chief from the outset, with fine technical assistance from Nadia Holmes. Equally congenial were our publishers, I.B.Tauris.

As the project evolved into an exploration of the Muslim civil imagination in the making of plural modernities, the collaborative energies of Bruce Lawrence, Nilüfer Göle, Bryan Turner, Hasna Lebbady and Eva Schubert were crucial. With John Renard, Fairouz Nishanova, Ted Levin and Kevin McDonald coming on board, the worthiness of our pursuit was assured. What they wrought has for me as editor been inspiring, especially in the unfolding aftermath of September 11, 2001.

Amyn B. Sajoo
London, October, 2007

* Since subsumed into his opus, *A Secular Age* (Cambridge, MA, 2007).

About the Contributors

Nilüfer Göle is professor of sociology at the Ecole des Hautes Etudes, Paris, and a leading authority on the political movement of today's educated, urbanized, religious Muslim women. She is the author of *The Forbidden Modern: Civilization and Veiling* (1996). Her sociological approach – which includes extensive personal interviews and case studies of young Turkish women turning to the tenets of fundamental Islamic gender codes – has produced a broad critique of Eurocentrism with regard to emerging Muslim identities. An earlier version of her chapter here appeared in *Public Culture*, 14 (2002); the journal's permission to draw upon that material is appreciated.

Bruce B. Lawrence is the Nancy and Jeffrey Marcus Humanities Professor at Duke University, where he also directs the Duke Islamic Studies Center. His research ranges from institutional Islam to Indo-Persian Sufism, from Morocco to Borneo; it also encompasses the comparative study of religious movements. His recent books include *Messages to the World: The Statements of Osama Bin Laden* (2005); *The Quran – A Biography* (2006), which his chapter here draws upon, and *Muslim Networks from Hajj to Hip Hop* (2005, with Miriam Cooke).

Hasna Lebbady is professor of English at Mohammed V University, Rabat, Morocco. Her involvement in the culture and development research units as well as women's studies in that department has enabled her to advance a particular concern for the status of women in Morocco (and their representation in Western discourse). She is especially engaged with the oral literature of women in the north of Morocco, on which she is presently writing a book. An earlier version of her chapter here appeared in *The Muslim World*, 2 (2005); the journal's permission to use that material is appreciated.

Theodore Levin is professor of music at Dartmouth College and senior project consultant to the Aga Khan Music Initiative in Central Asia. His musical fieldwork in Central Asia, Siberia, Morocco and Bosnia spans three decades, and has resulted in more than twenty ethnographic recordings and two books, *The Hundred Thousand Fools of God: Musical Travels in Central Asia (and Queens, New York)* (1996) and *Where Rivers and Mountains Sing: Sound, Music, and Nomadism in Tuva and Beyond* (2006). He has also been active as a curator of concerts, festivals and international cultural initiatives on behalf of emerging artists from the developing world.

Kevin McDonald is associate professor in the school of political science, sociology and criminology at the University of Melbourne, and visiting research fellow in the department of sociology, Goldsmiths College London. He is associated with the 'sociology of action' tradition founded by Alain Touraine at the Ecole des Haute Etudes en Science Sociale, Paris, and is the author of *Global Movements: Action and Culture* (2006), upon which he draws in his chapter here. He is currently undertaking a comparative study of emerging Islamic movements in Australia, Spain and the United Kingdom.

Fairouz R. Nishanova is director of the Aga Khan Music Initiative in Central Asia. She is also involved with the new University of Central Asia, the world's first internationally chartered institution of higher education created to foster economic and social development in the mountain regions of Central Asia. She joined the Aga Khan Development Network in 2000 as a specialist and programme officer for initiatives in the CIS and Central Asia. Prior to this, she served as a regional expert with the United Nations Economic Commission for Europe.

John Renard is professor of theological studies at St. Louis University, Missouri, where he specialises in Islamic Studies. His publications include *Knowledge of God in Classical Sufism: Foundations of Islamic Mystical Theology* (2004, with Ahmet Karamustafa), *Windows on the House of Islam: Muslim Sources of Spirituality and Religious Life* (1988), and *Islam and the Heroic Image: Themes in Literature and the Visual Arts* (1993), upon which he draws in his chapter in this volume.

Amyn B. Sajoo lectured at Simon Fraser University in Canada on human rights, civil society and Islamic social and intellectual history, before joining the Institute of Ismaili Studies in 2007. He has held visiting appointments at Cambridge and McGill universities, and the Institute of Southeast Asian Studies in Singapore, having also served as an advisor with the Foreign Affairs and Justice departments in Canada. His books include *Pluralism in Old Societies and New States* (1994), *Muslim Ethics* (2004), and the edited volume, *Civil Society in the Muslim World* (2002).

Eva Schubert is currently with the Department of Academic Research and Publications at the Institute of Ismaili Studies. She was previously Humanities Fellow at Simon Fraser University, specialising in the interplay of citizenship and religion. She has also served as a lecturer at Beijing's University of Science and Technology, in 2004–05.

Bryan S. Turner is professor of sociology at the National University of Singapore, and research leader on religion and globalisation at the Asia Research Institute. He was professor of sociology at the University of Cambridge from 1998 to 2005. His latest publications include *Vulnerability and Human Rights* (2006), and an edited volume with Patrick Baert on *Pragmatism in European Social Theory* (2007). He is the founding editor of the journal *Citizenship Studies*, edited the *Cambridge Dictionary of Sociology*, and is writing a study of the sociology of religion for Cambridge University Press.

Introduction

Amyn B. Sajoo

Modernity has many guises. In Jafar Panahi's acclaimed 2003 film, *Crimson Gold*,[1] the protagonist (Hossein) is a stolid, blue-collar veteran of the Iran–Iraq war who delivers pizzas in Tehran. This exposes him to the full spectrum of urban sprawl, from clogged traffic to privileged suburbs whose inhabitants might as well be in Las Vegas. In a poignant encounter at the end of the film, Hossein finds himself in the lavish quarters of the Other: a client who is lean, loquacious, wealthy and worldly. This occurs on the heels of a delivery impeded by police who have cordoned off the decadent young guests at a late-night party. It all conspires to drive Hossein to extremes, though he is generous enough to dole out pizza slices to the policemen who thwart his delivery.

Crimson Gold interrogates more than the 1979 Iranian Revolution's cry of *mustaz'afin*, 'solidarity with the oppressed'. Certainly, there is plenty of blame to go around. If the theocratic state stifles personal freedoms that youths crave, we are reminded of the class complications by a policeman who says of rich and indulgent party-goers, 'Their kind sleeps during the day.' If the wealthy are awash in new technology, what frustrates Hossein is a broken elevator that compels him to climb four flights of stairs. The traffic chokes, yet Hossein is a participant on his sizable motor-cycle. Avarice is everywhere: 'If you want to arrest a thief, you'll have to arrest the world', offers a common felon. It is the human condition that *Crimson Gold* engages with plaintively, in the spirit of contemporary Iranian cinema spearheaded by Panahi's mentor, Abbas Kiarostami, and Samira Makhmalbaf, among others.[2] We are invited not merely to observe the sins and blessings of onscreen characters but to reflect on the culture, ethics and political reality in which individuals and communities find themselves – on the outcomes of choices made by an ever-widening circle of people that finally encompasses history itself.

Cinema as a medium lends itself especially well to such an exploration. Its technology allows the flow of images that purport to represent humans and their environment in narratives of varying complexity and depth. Theatre, of course, does this too, and with the advantage of 'presence' that the stage offers, but without quite the range of depictive power that the camera commands. Surely this has much to do with the politically transgressive power of cinema, which keeps censors busy in every society. *Crimson Gold* was banned in Iran – even as Jafar Panahi and several fellow directors have been denied permission to enter the United States. That transgressive power is not only about *what* the images convey but also *how* they do so. For cinema captures the visual 'flattening' of time, rendering it in a domain that is profane, mundane, stolen from the realm of the sacred as surely as the fire of Prometheus. It is in this sense that Charles Baudelaire's *The Painter of Modern Life* (1860) draws our attention to the sheer scope of the narrative power of images. To that essay is ascribed the first use of the term 'modernity' (though 'modern' can be traced back much earlier).[3] Baudelaire sought to depict the everyday with its 'crowds and incognitos',[4] from which he sought to extract significance, rather like Panahi's roving camera. He found much to embrace and disdain in the here and now, but what is distinctive is Baudelaire's persistent quest 'for a furtive yet eternal present'.[5] Distinctive because it is about the appreciation and measure of time that we have come to regard as the quintessence of modernity.

Time, technology, the cherishing of individual subjectivity amid class difference, civil society and a heightened consciousness of the presence of the state, all these give substance to the varying guises of modernity. The ways in which they do so may appear inevitable, much like the anarchic traffic in which Hossein is routinely enmeshed on his pizza deliveries – or the weekend city flocking of trendy men and women in 19th-century Paris amid the ascent of the middle class. But these disparate outcomes of a myriad choices, advertent and otherwise, are hardly inevitable; nor do they bear the same significance, emerging out of histories that are both shared and distinct. Baudelaire's obsession with the here and now was integral both to the secular as a new historical phenomenon, and to secularism as a European socio-political doctrine. Panahi's obsession with urban time also harkens to the secular, but is located in a cultural space that seeks alternatives to European secularism. It is here, in realities that are overlapping yet distinctive, that we find expressions of the civil which make for modernities in the plural.

Modernities in Perspective

It is hardly a surprise that definitions of something as diffuse as 'the modern' and its cognates often stretch the boundaries of coherence. Indeed, scholars readily acknowledge the elusiveness of the subject, with allusions to its constant transience and expansive character. Marilyn Ivy in her *Discourses of the Vanishing* is illustrative on this score:

> What I mean by the modern – as if one could simply define it – indicates not only urban energies, capitalist structures of life, and mechanical and electrical forms of reproduction . . . the problem of the nation-state and its correlation with a capitalist colonialism . . . a global geopolitical matrix from the mid-nineteenth century on. It indicates as well the changes effected in identities and subjectivities, through the emergence of individualism and new modes of interiority; in relationships to temporality, through the emergence of 'tradition' as the background against which progressive history could be situated; and in institutional procedures, through what Foucault has called individualization and totalization: bureaucratic rationalisms . . . novel forms of image representation, mass media, scientific disciplines. In their historical specificity, these modes, procedures, and apparatuses constitute a discursive complex which I think of as modern.[6]

Or consider Marshall Berman's influential account in *All that is Solid Melts into Air*. It offers a critical Marxist reading of Western socio-economic and ideological impulses projected on to a shrinking global landscape:

> The maelstrom of modern life has been fed from many sources: great discoveries in the physical sciences, changing our images of the universe and our place in it; the industrialisation of production, which transforms scientific knowledge into technology, creates new human environments and destroys old ones, speeds up the whole tempo of life, generates new forms of corporate power and class struggle; immense demographic upheavals, severing millions of people from their ancestral habitats . . . systems of mass communication, dynamic in their development, enveloping and binding together the most diverse people and societies; increasingly powerful national states, bureaucratically structured and operated, constantly striving to expand their powers; mass social movements of people, and peoples, challenging their political and economic rules, striving to gain some control over their lives; finally, bearing and driving all these people and institutions along, an ever-expanding, drastically fluctuating capitalist world market.[7]

In these accounts the modern is an all-encompassing force, not only contagious and pervasive but also singular in its momentum through time and space. The sprawling language only heightens those qualities, teeming like an orientalist's bazaar. Others have sought to highlight the sense of rupture as an essential feature. 'Modernity is often characterised', for Michel Foucault, 'in terms of consciousness of the discontinuity of time: a break with tradition.'[8] For Tilo Schabert, modernity privileges an 'aimless dynamism' that fosters a 'truth gap' between past and present: ever fresh prizes of scientific enquiry always trump tradition.[9] Hence, the tension between new and old becomes a defining trope: constancy of change engenders a longing for stability and reinventions of tradition. Even programmes of modernisation tend to find a 'traditional justification for doing the modern thing.'[10] However, while this approach to modernity may evade the sprawl of the all-encompassing, it risks reducing complexity to a single vector or pivot. It also invites a binary view – past vs. present, science vs. wisdom – that is unhelpful.

Indeed, the anthropologist John Kelly rejects the very concept of modernity as a useful analytical category, because it cannot be delimited and must therefore be evoked. This makes it what he calls a 'sublime', along with ideas like 'God or terror, nature, justice, or love'.[11] For Kelly, the magnitude of what is being evoked distracts us from the need to focus on the particularities of context that press for attention – as with 'civilization', another sublime category that lends itself to ideological games. We are urged instead to consider 'the specificities of recent global history', most notably the impact of United States power since World War II, made all the more urgent by the events of September 11, 2001.[12] Kelly's critique serves as a welcome admonition about the need to ground our claims in *contingencies*. Enquiring about the locales, historical settings and political realities where the encounters with modernity occur, and their practical outcomes, can keep us from lapsing into discourses (especially of the postcolonial variety) that seem to become semantic ends in themselves.[13] But our enquiry must go beyond Kelly's concern about the 'imperial' gaze, in terms of its wider historical context and implications, and the realities of other lifeworlds.[14] Only if we subscribe to a singular modernity are we trapped in a lifeworld that pivots exclusively on the hegemony of United States power, conspicuous as it may be.

How then do we balance complexity and essence, particularity and overlap, in our approach? Clearly, the idea of modernities implies that there are 'variations on some invariant theme or set of themes'.[15] What are the shared elements or themes? For Marshall Hodgson in *The Venture of Islam*, 'Modernity has been not simply rational emancipation from custom, nor has it been simply the further unfolding of a bent for progress peculiar to the Western tradition; it has been a cultural transformation *sui generis*.'[16] In seeking to offer a coherent account of what it is that we are talking about, and why it is thought to be uniquely transformative, an unpacking is required of key premises that attend our reflections and claims on the subject. I propose to single out five themes that are located in historical and contemporary political contexts. These themes are not intended as definitive markers or as 'constitutive' of modernity. Rather, they serve as a platform for salient lines of enquiry both here and in the chapters that follow.

1. **Rationalism**: Max Weber (1864–1920)'s extensive sociology provides what is generally taken as a hallmark of the emergence of modernity in the public sphere, in the *differentiation* of various sectors according to their functions, from the economy and governance to culture and religion. Science and technology were the raw sites for the emergence of the rationalism celebrated by the 18th-century European Enlightenment. While Marx drew out the economic and social threads in the wake of the Industrial Revolution, it was Weber's opus, *The Protestant Ethic and the Spirit of Capitalism* (1905), that provided the most detailed account of the cultural and social convergences taken to be formative in Western modernity, which in turn dominated and shaped the non-West. Jürgen Habermas is perhaps the most ardent proponent of Weberian rationality as the essence not only of a Western but a universal public sphere of communication, one that best supports the freedom of individual lifeworlds, most broadly in his *The Philosophical Discourse of Modernity* (1985).[17]

2. **Secularism**: A major result of the rational differentiation of the public sphere was the clearer delineation of boundaries between Church and State. In the breach arose the 19th-century doctrine of secularisation, built on the older though shifting idea of the secular that came to be opposed to the sacred. Émile Durkheim (1858–1917) was the principal chronicler of the new doctrine and its ramifications, wedded as it was to both the nation state and the economy as a symbol of political modernity.[18] *Anomie* or alienation was for Durkheim integral to the human condition in the midst of secularisation. Time in this account is quintessentially profane, distinguished from the 'vertical' trajectory of sacred time that is linked to events outside human agency; as such, secularism is commonly associated

with the cognates of rationality – the capacity and agency for change.[19] The resources of modernity in terms of institutions and the ethos of citizenship are in Western liberalism anchored in the secular domain.

3. **Individualism and Human Rights:** Human agency in the context of the emerging nation state required fresh emphasis on the ethics as well as the politics of individual autonomy, given the sheer asymmetry in power between citizen and state.[20] The idea that human vulnerability required institutionalised protection was hardly new: precursors included Magna Carta, the Muslim shari'a and Hammurabi's Code. But the social contract between citizen and state raised the stakes; the *legitimacy* of national sovereignty came to be tied to respect for individual autonomy. When the Universal Declaration of Human Rights (1948) was proclaimed by the nascent United Nations, it staked its claim on 'the inherent dignity' and 'equal and inalienable rights' of all under the rule of law; every individual was 'entitled to a social and international order . . . in which this Declaration can be realised'.[21] Contemporary forms of vulnerability have demanded that the scope of human rights extend far beyond that envisaged in early modernity by John Locke, Tom Paine and Mary Wollstonecraft – to include refugees, marginalised social groups and prisoners in assorted ideological conflicts.[22]

4. **Democratic Governance:** A vital political shift in the advent of modernity is the claim that newly sovereign nation-states are *accountable* to their citizens. This did not follow inevitably from rationalism: functional differentiation and bureaucratisation can also serve authoritarian rule. But it did follow from the conditionality of the social contract on respect for citizen autonomy as a marker of political legitimacy – also honoured in the breach by authoritarians who insist on the rhetoric of democracy. Modern citizenship is empty outside the bounds of democracy, constitutionalism and the rule of law (as value, not mere procedure).[23] This is not to deny the historical

enlargement of what constitutes democracy: the Greek ideal was as fraught with exclusion (women, slaves, aliens) as Euro-American citizenship practices in early modernity. But Alexis de Tocqueville was prescient in tying the democratic ideal of balancing liberty and equality not only with individualism but also with associations of civil society[24] – now seen as essential to accountable governance.[25]

5. **Globalism:** Capitalism as driving the growth of the public sphere, coupled with the expansion of the state's political control and military capacity, could hardly remain a local phenomenon. The projection of modernity in its hegemonial forms was made inevitable by colonialism and is intensified by new information technologies. For Anthony Giddens, the outcome is a 'disembedding' from the local and a challenge to stable identity and trust in the traditional sense; we now rely on shifting and multiple expressions of the self, and on abstract systems of time and space that stretch across borders.[26] The cultural effects of globalism are essayed by Arjun Appadurai in *Modernity at Large* (1996), which holds that our 'overlapping, disjunctive order' cannot be grasped in terms of old centre-periphery thinking. To capture the fluidity of this cultural economy, he posits 'scapes' – amorphous flows of media, technology, people, finance and ideology – as bearers of agency in today's diasporic public spheres.[27] Yet this leaves open old hegemonies, even if expressed through such 'scapes', in a post-September 11 world where trust is in short supply.[28]

The narratives and impulses in these themes play a foundational role in any discussion of modernity and its cognates, such as modernisation. Clearly, the scientific, industrial and political revolutions that were the crucibles in which these themes emerged were Western, which is not to say that they lacked crucial non-Western influences, most particularly from China, India and the Muslim world. From the physical and natural sciences to architecture, art, commerce and social thought, Western accomplishment is inextricably linked to those Others, unpalatable though this may be to the 'clash of civilisations' warriors.[29] Still, the revolutions that impelled (and were set off by) economic, techno-scientific and civic modernity occurred in the West. At the same time, modernity has come to be distinguished by its *plurality*, that is, the multiple sites where it is produced, the diversity of those who produce it and the variant processes that are involved, all contest the idea of a unitary modern.[30] The globalism that pervades modernity is by its very nature multifarious in form and substance; local responses to global forces only add to that plurality. The implications of this challenge to a hegemonial modernity have been significant.

For some, modernity's association with the universalist claims of the Enlightenment could not survive the sins of the West as capitalist, colonial and genocidal – and as implicated in the commodification of knowledge. In the postmodern critique of Michel Foucault, knowledge attached to power requires us to excavate 'subjugated knowledges'.[31] The fragmentation of authority, identity and reality meant that the only tenable position was relativist, and that Habermas's project of a rationalist public sphere was simply illusory.[32] The ideological roots of modernisation as a development strategy applied to the 'Third World' were also cast as fatal to aspirations of progress in the mould of a West unworthy of emulation.[33] Yet the notion of a rupture with modernity implicit in the term postmodern was soon felt to be untenable: the fragmentations on hand were seen as integral to the modern condition. More broadly, the assertion of a seismic rupture in social thought was decried by Bernard Yack's *The Fetishism of Modernities* (1997): 'Why is it that contemporary intellectuals cannot uncover a new or hidden development without declaring the coming of a new epoch in human experience?'[34] Pragmatically, if all knowledge and public institutions were relativised, where would this leave us? Would citizenship be tenable? What about the return of religion to the public square, often with singular truth-claims?

There is no denying, however, that public authority and identity in the late modern period are far more fractured and layered than before. Further, mass migration with its diasporic public spheres has altered what 'local' and 'global' stand for, and how they interface. Yet with the growing intrusion of state power into the private domain of individuals and communities – through channels of bureaucracy, surveillance and administrative/legal control – the civil protections of human rights and citizenship are ever more vital. Civil society in its local as well as global forms still matters, in terms of institutions as well as informal webs of solidarity (secular and religious). Evidently, then, we are challenged to accommodate strong opposing pulls: toward civil and socio-economic centres and institutions and away from them, towards the continuity and stability of traditions and away from them. Amid these tensions, Giddens argues that what allows individuals, communities and societies to negotiate and reform their situations is the 'reflexive monitoring of action', which stems from the social impulse and capacity to constantly remain in contact.[35] This 'reflexivity' is felt to rescue human agency from the regimes of technology and power.

> To the Enlightenment thinkers, and many of their successors, it appeared that increasing information about the natural and social worlds would bring increasing control over them. For many, such control was the key to human happiness ... [M]ore pessimistic observers connected knowledge and control. Max Weber's 'steel hard cage' – in which he thought humanity was condemned to live for the foreseeable future – is a prison-house of technical knowledge; we are all, to alter the metaphor, to be small cogs in the gigantic machine of technical and bureaucratic reason. Yet neither image comes close to capturing the world of high modernity, which is more and more open and contingent than any such image suggests – and is so precisely *because* of, not in spite of, the knowledge that we have accumulated about ourselves and about the material environment.[36]

In making a virtue of the fractures and technocracies of our time, this view rests on bold assumptions. Is the problem of social trust that Giddens raised earlier resolved merely by knowledge and communicative action? Can the self-correcting power of reflexivity address the problems of unequal access to information and communicative action, within and beyond the West? The evidence of the post-September 11 world lends scant support to such confidence. What emerges here seems complacent and oblivious of the non-West, harkening back to a modernity that is hegemonial.[37] A perspective more attuned to the tensions outlined above, and pluralist in the understanding of the key themes of the modern, is required. Alternatives *to* modernity seem untenable: history and political economy are too far gone, and seeking such alternatives only re-centres what is being rejected. It is the idea of *plural modernities* that holds promise, coming to terms with the present yet aware of the ethical and practical limits of the hegemonial narrative. Plural or multiple modernities partake of the 'founding' narratives that are Eurocentric (though not exclusively Western), for their influence is obvious, a *fait accompli*. They insist, however, on the plurality of ways in which to construct the key themes of the modern, within the broad nexus between past and present. The legitimacy of vernaculars is asserted.

Plural modernities are not marked out solely on the basis of culture, geography, religion or ideology. To speak of African, Chinese, Indian or Muslim modernities is to accept also the vernaculars within these settings, local inflections of what it means to be traditional or progressive.[38] Plural modernities are distinctive but also overlapping. While they relativise the claims of Eurocentric modernity, they do not deny the universality of certain truth-claims or values. Their pluralism does not perforce amount to relativism.[39] Otherwise, one risks squandering hard-won gains, including those of the sciences, human rights and democratic governance merely because some may see them as occidental. The ,perils of doing so after September 11 are plain. To illustrate the usefulness of this conception of plural modernities, consider how 'civil society' – attached in Western vernaculars to secularism – is differently anchored elsewhere. For Ernest Gellner and Şerif Mardin, societies with affinities like those of the Muslim *umma* (community) fall outside 'the' narrative of civil society.[40] Yet the social capital generated by religious and secular vectors in associational life is today recognised in the Muslim world as well as in North America.[41] Plural modernities accommodate this reality, in which the shared value of civic solidarity is coupled with local difference in praxis. A unitary modernity fails to recognise shared values, at high cost. For the ability to foster an 'overlapping consensus' among citizens that John Rawls has cast as imperative for modern democratic culture[42] is no less important at the transnational level. Accountable global governance is impossible without such consensus on shared interests and values, amid difference.[43]

The drawing out of plural modernities requires, however, more than a tactical or strategic rationale. After all, the historical narratives of modernity are not only about fresh ways of perceiving reality, but also about being in the world. There is an ethos at stake, expressed in the discursive themes listed earlier. For Charles Taylor, the self-understandings that constitute this ethos are framed in a 'social imaginary', which is more than a collection of ideas. It is the 'common understanding that makes possible common practices and a widely shared sense of legitimacy' – and is carried not in theories but in 'images, stories and legends'.[44] Crucially, it is about shared expectations of what is right: a sense of *moral order* that forms the background to the practices of the civil order. While such practices are nourished in a daily 'habitus', they are expressed in the social imaginary in symbolic terms; this is how the practices gain meaning and legitimacy.[45] Taylor maps the contours of the social imaginary of Euro-American modernity, as what he hopes will be a step toward coming to terms with multiple modernities.[46] If this is becoming more likely, it is less because of academics or elites than the practical reality of ordinary citizens. Thus Appadurai ties 'the imagination as social practice' to the ongoing 'negotiation between sites of agency (individuals) and globally defined fields of possibilities'.[47] The imagination here is tool and canvas; it enables and is enabled by the exercise of personal and collective choices that constitute modernity in each locale.

Plural modernities unfold as moral orders that are embodied in social practices, no longer confined to sovereign or cultural boundaries. This approach to the modern is not merely useful as a way of seeing and casting reality, but also in recognising where and who we are in the civic order, as individuals, citizens and communities. A single, hegemonic modernity subjugates (to recall

Foucault) the social imaginaries of those outside its privileged narratives and many within them. In effect, this amounts to colonialism by other means; it calls for appropriate resistance as well as re-engagement. Plural modernities map out the realities of the Other – and finally render Western maps as also 'alternative' modernities. This volume's subtitle calls attention to the role of the civil imagination, past and present, in that process. The expressions of that imagination shed light, we would hope, on questions about what it is to be Muslim and how this impacts the ongoing shaping of the modern.

Muslim Modernities

It should be evident at this stage that the contributors to our volume treat Muslim social imaginaries as, for all their differences, partaking of the modern. Not surprisingly, dominant and strident Western narratives have spurred an industry in robust counter-assertions of identity, of difference as 'essential'. The talk of authenticity figures prominently in the postmodern critique, in response to the overdetermination of identity by hegemons, real or perceived.[48] In Muslim contexts, this has found expression in the insistence of a 'return', usually to a pristine original – of text, historical period or practice – cast as authentic. It is mirrored by Western commentators for whom the distinctiveness of Islam and Muslims is expedient. In both instances, this 'othering' can serve political ends, where it is not exoticisation for its own sake.[49] Aziz Al-Azmeh puts it thus in *Islams and Modernities* (1993),

> The theme of 'return' has become a discursive *topos* which facilitates the elision of history, of society, and of polity, and is one which not only sustains this segregationist discourse in the West, but is also a prime instrument of the totalitarian Islamist political claim . . . Like its counterpart in Western writing, it subsists in a discourse of authenticity whose primary epistemological instrument is the recognition and registration of difference, and where the sacralization of politics is regarded not as a disguise, but as an unveiling.[50]

Al-Azmeh pits historicity against the rhetoric of authenticity, including that of nationalists and orientalists, in order to avoid 'exceptionalising' Islam. Ibn Khaldun (1332–1406) would no doubt approve! But Al-Azmeh does not directly link this to the nature or making of plural modernities. Mohammed Arkoun is somewhat more explicit, tying the historical role of the *imaginaire* in managing 'symbolic capital' to claims of authenticity.[51] However, it is the religious imaginary of Islam and the Judaeo-Christian traditions that chiefly concerns Arkoun, rather than the broader social imaginary that occupies us here.[52]

Historicism of a special sort – sacralisation – feeds the talk of authenticity in revivalist (*salafi*) trends, which feature prominently in the chapters that follow. 'Tradition' here is cast in binary opposition to 'modernity', as is often the case in Western narratives. Yet it is on a continuum between old and new, past and present, that individuals and communities locate themselves in practice. This is evident when secularism is considered – perhaps the single most critical issue in debates about modernity within and beyond the Muslim world.[53] Secularism as a doctrine of separation between religion and politics plays itself out very differently in republican Turkey, postcolonial Pakistan, and post-revolutionary Iran. In all these instances, however, the distinction between *institutional* separation as a political arrangement, and an *ethic* of separation of sacred and secular, is all but lost. Although no society embraces a pure version of either, appeals to the authenticity of 'secular constitutionalism/nationalism' (France, Turkey) or of 'Islam' (Iran, Afghanistan under the Taliban) are rife. In the bid for legitimacy, political and religious, where each side portrays the other as betraying modernity or tradition, the fertile middle ground is best found in the *imaginaire* of ordinary citizens, which rarely sits at either extreme. The secular, notes Andrew Davison, loses usefulness as an idea when 'stripped of its concern with creating (context-specific) conditions that will ensure the fullest expression for the human conscience'.[54]

Our contributors variously address expressions of Muslim identity and citizenship, piety and protest, music and modes of dress, as social expressions that bear on the making and remaking of modern public spheres. In what sense are these 'Muslim' expressions, when secular 'rationalism' and science – refracted through the lens of colonial/postcolonial encounters with the West – are so pervasive? How can religiosity and identity adapt to such presences while holding on to their integrity (itself a shifting notion)? Bruce Lawrence's chapter looks at how three Muslims have centred their responses to these questions on what the Qur'an means in everyday terms. Sayyid Ahmed Khan (1817–1898) and Muhammad Iqbal (1873–1938) shared a passion for both rationalism and scripture in colonial India. Both were ardent social reformers who grappled alike with religious orthodoxy and the secular claims of Darwinist scientism, mindful no doubt of the glories of medieval 'Islamic science'.[55] Iqbal had an additional outlet in Urdu poetry, whose place in the social imaginary looms as large as his opus, *Reconstruction of Religious Life in Islam,* which affirmed republican political institutions as fully consistent with Islam and necessary 'in view of the new forces that are set free'.[56] One recalls that while Fazlur Rahman in his *Islam and Modernity* (1982) also advocated a reconstructive reading of the Qur'an, his was a more theocentric liberalism. All this is sacrilege for Lawrence's third interlocutor, Osama bin Laden (1957–), who deploys religious texts in the service of a message that is not 'fundamentalist' but simply anarchist. The upshot for Lawrence is that the Qur'an is unavoidably 'plurivocal', and that shari'a and secularism alike are needed for the collective good, 'yet neither is the natural, or easeful, companion of the other.'

Yet sacred and secular motifs travel cordially in the cultural spaces of epics, folk-tales, music and architecture. These are among the formative elements in the identity and ethos of individuals, communities, nations, and civilisations – often more penetratingly than formal creeds, doctrines and ideologies. The enduring sway of *The Thousand and One Nights,* the songs of Oum Kalthoum, and the site of the Alhambra in Granada attests to this: they don't merely captivate but also shape how ordinary Muslims and non-Muslims see the world and themselves.[57] In the richly illustrated *Hamzanama* (Adventures of Hamza), a collection of heroic narratives about the Prophet Muhammad's uncle, imaginative courage serves virtue: nature is celebrated, political power is mocked, females are empowered, saints are playful.[58] How and why such tales and themes have endured, and what they tell us about religio-cultural unity and diversity in the Muslim world, is the burden of John Renard's chapter. 'Heroic themes' in Malay, Persian and Central Asian languages are shown to educate, socialise and refresh devotion. Above all, local narratives indigenise values associated with Islam, whether through icons such as Hamza, 'Ali, cousin and son-in-law of Muhammad, and Iskandar, the Hellenic Alexander – or through local figures. The local acts vitally to update values and themes, to reinvent tradition, in 'integrating the deepest aspirations of a people's culture', observes Renard.

Formidable 'other modernities' can obstruct local ones, as post-Soviet Central Asia has found. A socio-spiritual heritage shaped by thirteen centuries of indigenised Islam struggles to find expression today within political boundaries that served Soviet ideology after the 1917 revolution with no regard to ethno-cultural realities.[59] 'Nationalist in form, Socialist in content' was the slogan in the Marxist-Leninist ejection of tradition, especially of the non-Slavic kind, in the race to match Western modernity. Assorted national versions of that posture fed just the sort of rivalries that suited Moscow, rather than meaningful citizenship at home. How the new Central Asia is finding its locus on the continuum of past and present is explored in the chapter by Theodore Levin and Fairouz Nishanova – not in broad strokes, but rather through the particulars of the Music Initiative launched in 2000 by the Aga Khan Development Network. Fresh approaches to old performance styles and music education, revitalised genres and instruments, and networks that integrate the region into the global music marketplace are what the programmes are about. What they are *not* about is forced separateness from Soviet or Western modes through law or public policy. For the aim is a 'reimagination of traditional musical culture within a cosmopolitan and pluralistic Central Asian modernity'.

Hasna Lebbady offers a sobering reminder of the challenges and rewards of such reimagining in her chapter on the narrative traditions of a strikingly successful civilisation, that of Al-Andalus or Muslim Spain.[60] Its musical and poetic legacy is today familiar through genres such flamenco, *ra'i*, *Muwashah* and *Zajal*. But it is the complementary oral tradition of women's tales (which influenced Europe's courtly practices of storytelling) that provides for Lebbady a potent 'imagined community' of narrators, often in exile. She singles out for interpretation a popular and canonical narrative of travel and unveiling, *The Female Camel*, linking it to the status of women in socio-economic and religious settings, as well as to the pain of exile. Her inferences are trenchant and provocative. 'The religious domain did not exclude matters such as sexuality that Westerners consigned to a separate space', despite later developments in Muslim law and society. Further, the vernacular Arabic in which women's tales were rendered lost its popular place amid the growing preference for classical Arabic, a development that Lebbady finds to have serious alienating implications for ordinary citizens. In the Maghreb, and specifically in her native Morocco, an Andalusian tradition widely lauded for its pluralism and inclusion must contest – and help reconfigure – a modernity that turns out to be considerably less so.

By itself, a reconfiguration on vernacular lines can hardly assure esteem for the civic values of pluralism and accountable governance. Particular claims tied to power, secular or religious, readily trump those cast as the Other. Kemal Atatürk's brand of cultural and political modernity, with its faith in secular republicanism, has been severely tested of late and found wanting by many as insufficiently democratic or tolerant. Nilüfer Göle's chapter sees new forms of public Islam in Turkey as going to the heart of what it means to be modern, especially when it comes to women's 'participation in public life, corporeal visibility, and social mixing'. Whether it is Merve Kavakçı seeking to take her place in Parliament while wearing a headscarf,[61] or the insistence of female university students, television journalists or opera-goers on wearing 'Islamic dress', the social imaginary of the public sphere as implicitly secular is recast. For Göle, the conscious exercise of agency by educated citizens separates these acts as different from 'grandmother's headscarf' with its aura of traditionalism, and puts them in the realm of 'the forbidden modern'. They are also a public assertion of legitimate citizenship. As such, they raise the question as to whether one might have an 'excess of secularism' not on grounds of civility, but 'as a fetish of modernity'. Civility as shared citizenship, however, is at stake for Bryan S. Turner in essaying the implications of religious revivalism. For him, this worldwide trend rides on 'rituals of intimacy', which are 'everyday norms that are important for defining religious differences, sustaining group identities and maintaining the continuity of the group'. Rituals of intimacy enact a 'wall of virtue' – an enclave in which believers may dress, eat, associate and pray without secular intrusion. Citing evidence from Southeast Asia, Turner argues that enclave societies – often marked not only by religion but also ethnicity – take issue with basic assumptions of liberal democratic order. 'What is the relationship between state and society when civil society is an ensemble of separate enclaves?' Further, such enclaves have no obvious interest in the idea of an 'overlapping consensus' as the lifeblood of civic culture. Turner finds promise in the cosmopolitanism of the Andalusian Muslim philosopher and mystic Ibn al-'Arabi (1165–1240), who affirmed the 'Unity of Religions' and the diversity of customs and laws, without espousing cultural relativism or an overarching universalism.[62] Ibn al-'Arabi also recognised that 'communities need to believe that their laws and political structures are not simply arbitrary', a grounded pluralism that for Turner supports the overlapping social consensus required today. Indeed, recent readings of the cosmopolitanism of Kant – whose universalism is often linked to a singular modernity – likewise stress the pluralist yet non-relativist aspects of his thought.[63]

Eva Schubert and Kevin McDonald in their respective chapters take up key tensions broached by Göle and Turner, notably within the supposed clash of identity-based and civic modernities. In Schubert's account of citizenship as 'transcendent ethical code' that demands agency and engagement beyond personal gain, excluding religio-cultural actors is neither prudent nor coherent. Creating a stake for all segments in a pluralist civil society is more likely to make it viable. And the notion that religious identity is 'subsuming and perhaps incapable of integration' ignores the sheer multiplicity of markers that form an individual's identity. This 'denies the vital role of individual reasoning and choice in assigning importance to some markers over others', and feeds what Amartya Sen calls the 'illusion of destiny'.[64] Civic secularism is commonly justified on grounds of state neutrality, as in France and Turkey; yet Schubert notes that the French model which so influenced Kemalist Turkey stems from a specific ethno-cultural trajectory and history, most obviously in relation to the role of the Catholic Church. In both countries a modernity attached to a fixed set of cultural features and dependent on them has been used to exclude Muslims *as Muslims* from equal public standing. Not all values and interests merit equal treatment; but hegemonic exclusion of peaceful engagement feeds the risks it wishes to avoid.

That exclusion, argues McDonald, is integral to a modern liberal imaginary whose version of cosmopolitanism is an abstract view of agency and subjectivity grounded in the ideal of autonomy, which thrives on its binary opposite, fundamentalism. While the cosmopolitan individual is everywhere at home and welcomes the unknown, the fundamentalist is confined by tradition. The former is curious and open to change, the latter fears and opposes it in tribal anti-modernism.[65] This imaginary fails to grasp what McDonald calls 'religious grammars' outside the secularised personal Christianity of Europe, even though such grammars have been critical within the West as 'sources of the self' that ushered in new kinds of public culture.[66] In Muslim and non-Muslim settings alike, older state-centric movements like the Muslim Brotherhood must contend with newer globalised forms of religiosity linked to mobility and diaspora. Some religious movements are violent, others entirely peaceful; but there is more to either than identity politics or resistance to globalism. For McDonald, post-secular understandings of agency, ethics and responsibility are needed, as 'autonomy and sovereignty (of the state and the individual) may be less and less able to respond to the questions confronting the civil'.

In the concluding chapter, I probe some of those post-secular understandings in Muslim-majority as well as diasporic settings, where the evidence is plentiful of the 'entwining of particularist and universalist readings of texts, gender and minority inclusion, and a renewed commitment to ethics beyond traditional rule-bound understandings'. While enclaving by 'rituals of intimacy' can be real enough, such rituals today have a globalised ambivalence: dietary choices, trendy headscarves and devotional modes draw on overlapping imaginaries of sacred and secular. Militant Wahhabis or the Taliban may hanker for an austere exclusive code (as do some Hindus, Jews and Protestants), but they must contend with a growing Muslim activism that prizes pluralist ethics and human rights[67] – a 'religious cosmopolitanism' with deep historical roots. This is readily obscured in the post-September 11 landscape with its either/or attitudes, which I explore in contexts from Afghanistan, India and Turkey to Britain and Canada. If our collective record on access to justice, distributive equity, expressive freedoms and gender/minority rights is to improve, civil society and the state must navigate the perils of secular as well as religious absolutism – which puts us in the realm of an imaginative citizenship of the spirit, beyond confines of culture and territory.

An underlying theme in all the chapters is the role of the ethical imagination in the making and expressions of the civil. This interplay is evident in plural Qur'anic understandings, in cultural narratives as sources of the self, in Islamist motivations, and in practices of citizenship and civil society. It may be extended to numerous other aspects of the civic domain, past and present. Consider, for example, the struggle of Jamal al-Din al-Afghani (1838–1897) in 'reconciling' scientific rationalism and religiosity amid the politics of Western colonial hegemony; his encounters with leading European, Middle Eastern and South Asian figures generated rich debates on the consequences of post-Enlightenment modernity.[68] No less intriguing, surely, would be an enquiry into the implications here of Abu Hamid al-Ghazali (1058–1111)'s notion of a 'threshold' (*dihliz*) of mind and soul from which to negotiate the shifting currents of social as well as personal change.[69] Again, our grappling with the values at stake in new reproductive technologies and genetic therapies offers a fertile field of appreciation of civic complexity, as do problems of poverty and social justice in the global market economy.[70] If social imaginaries are finally about moral orders that attend our practices and identities, then the ethics enfolded in tradition lay fair claim to continuity and vitality in our own time.

*   *   *

When the city of Cairo became host in 2005 to Al-Azhar Park, a 74-acre green space in what was once its poorest locale, it came to embody historic, ecological and social renewal amid urban overcrowding and decay.[71] It was the culmination of over twenty years of consultative planning, excavation, rehabilitation and restoration, home upgrading, tree planting and urban design – in the midst of Egypt's 1,000 year old capital with 17 million densely packed people. A site whose harshly saline soil served as a repository for debris and fill during the past five centuries was radically refreshed and endowed with three water reservoirs and tens of thousands of trees. Residents of the Darb al-Ahmar neighbourhood with its appalling housing conditions and massive un- and under-employment were fully engaged in its renewal of housing, health, work and credit resources. They were also integral to the archaeological initiative that recovered the 12th-century Ayyubid Wall with its towers and crenellated battlements, among other historic landmarks.[72] Spectacular vistas now accompany a transformation in the locale's quality of life, making Darb Al-Ahmar a major attraction for Egyptians as well as foreigners.

Led by the Aga Khan Trust for Culture (AKTC) in conjunction with domestic and international partners, the Al-Azhar Park project aspires to an alternative to standard approaches to development in declining historic locales.[73] These have tended to privilege monuments at the expense of neighbourhoods where residents are commonly displaced, often by force; commercial development then follows along laissez-faire lines. The critique of neoliberal modernisation ideology has much to do with such postcolonial schemes, where corporate and technocratic priorities hold sway.[74] By contrast, the AKTC has sought to ensure that among the stakeholders in this project are Darb Al-Ahmar's residents, from the original planning stage onwards. Training in proficiencies that range from masonry and carpentry to computers, automobile electronics and telephony is under way. Various segments of Egypt's public and private sectors, including non-governmental organisations, will remain engaged with the AKTC in shaping the project's future. The Park also serves as an evolving template for non-profit projects of historic and urban renewal across the Muslim world, from Afghanistan to Mali and Zanzibar.

Beyond its symbolism for alternative urban planning and social development, Al-Azhar Park serves to mould a wider cultural memory and sense of civic belonging, of continuity rather than rupture.[75] It harkens to a momentous past that includes the Fatimid Shi'a caliphs (969–1171) who founded Cairo and its Al-Azhar University, the world's oldest continuously functioning seat of learning, as well as Saladin Ayyubi (r.1171–1193), who duelled gracefully with Richard the Lionheart. The Park also invokes the particular locus of public gardens in Muslim civilisations, from Cordoba, Marrakesh and Damascus to Isfahan, Lahore and Delhi.[76] Indeed, the Qur'an offers no less than 120 references to the idea of *jannat al-firdaus* or 'gardens of paradise', ranging in purpose from blissful retreat to secure refuge – woven into an enduring social imaginary through art, narrative and architectural design. Finally, the park site is integrated with that of the adjacent 'Urban Plaza' comprising the new Museum of Historic Cairo along with commercial and parking spaces, sponsored by the AKTC in part-nership with the host country.

As such, Al-Azhar Park sits congruently with the civic visions of two of the most influential designers of modern public space, Frederick Law Olmsted (1822–1923) and Hassan Fathy (1900–1989). For Olmsted, landscapes that framed park spaces were key to urban civility;[77] his work includes North America's greatest public sites, including New York's Central Park. Fathy insisted on socially respon-sible buildings sensitive to the needs of less privileged rural and urban citizens;[78] his 'architecture for the poor' across Egypt won global acclaim, including from the AKTC. The Olmsted–Fathy conjunction also offers a departure from the orientalist 'segregated Islamic city' of tradition that is contrasted with modernity's inte-grated city.[79] In embodying the ideals of both Fathy and Olmsted,

Al-Azhar Park signals a modernity that is also Muslim. It reimagines the civil in ways that set new standards for vernaculars, Western and otherwise – rather like the innovative Iranian cinema of Jafar Panahi, Abbas Kiarostami and Samira Makhmalbaf.

2

Scripture, History and Modernity: Readings of the Qur'an

Bruce B. Lawrence

I

Commenting on Wittgenstein's dictum that 'language is a labyrinth of paths',[1] a modern philosopher of religion notes that '[f]rontal attack on a troublesome word may be a less effective means of disenchantment than a patient exposition of its versatility.'[2]

There are actually two troublesome words that confront those who want to make sense of Muslim modernities. One is shari'a, the other is secularism. Each is used to complicate and also regulate the other. To paraphrase from Wittgenstein's exemplar, Leo Tolstoy, shari'a without secularism is religious tyranny, or theocracy, while secularism without shari'a is social anomie, or moral anarchy'.[3] Both shari'a and secularism are needed for collective well being or public good (*maslaha*) in the contemporary Muslim world, yet neither is the natural, or easeful, companion of the other.

Of the two concepts, secularism is the better known in the contemporary academy. It operates in tandem with other key words: public reason, pluralism, human rights, civil society, citizenship. Public reason has been developed in both Rawlsian and Habermasian models of secularism, not least because it implies autonomy from subjective influences and undeclared motivations, yet the analytic power of public reason wobbles once it is contrasted with private faith. 'If the nobility of secularism resides in its quest to enable multiple faiths to exist in the same public space', argues William Connolly, 'its shallowness resides in the hubris of its distinction between private faith and public reason.'[4] It is precisely the metaphysical shallowness of public reason that requires its admixture with faith. 'To participate in the public realm,' explains Connolly, 'does not require you to leave your faith at home in the interests of secular reason [glossed for Connolly as equivalent to public reason]; it involves mixing into the relational practice of faith itself a preliminary readiness to negotiate with presumptive generosity and forbearance in those numerous situations where recourse to the porous rules of commonality across faiths, public procedure, reason, or deliberation are insufficient to the issue at hand.'[5]

Faith in Islam almost always becomes nestled within some consideration of shari'a. And shari'a projects the truth claims of an Abrahamic metaphysics channelled through multiple scriptural nodes – from Torah to Bible to Qur'an – that are felt to be required for modernday citizenship in majority Muslim polities. Indeed, can modernday citizenship ever be defined apart from religious categories? No, for if Charles Taylor is correct, 'religious language is the one in which people find it meaningful to code their strong moral and political experience.'[6] How believers code their experience politically will depend on available instruments of technology; so much so that many social scientists, hoping to avoid the pitfalls of interpretation, confine themselves to the instrumental definition of secularization and modernization in the Muslim world.

Dale Eickelman, for example, looks at symbolic politics in general and Muslim politics in particular as not just the domain but also the showcase of technological change. 'In country after country since the 1950s, mass education and mass communication, particularly the proliferation of media and the means by which people communicate, profoundly influence how people think about the language of religious and political authority throughout the Muslim world.' The upshot, for Eickelman, is 'a constructive fragmentation':

> With the advent of mass higher education has come an objec-
> tification of Islamic tradition in the eyes of many believers, so
> that questions such as "What is Islam?" "How does it apply to
> the conduct of my life?" and "What are the principles of faith?"

are foregrounded in the consciousness of many believers and explicitly discussed. [The result] is a 'democratization' of the politics of religious authority and the development of a standardized language inculcated by mass higher education, the mass media, travel, and labor migration. This has led to an opening up of the political process and heightened competition for the mantles of political and religious authority . . . Indeed, one can now speak of an emerging Muslim public sphere. If that seems to empower the religious intellectuals, it also restricts their impact. Even the idea of Islamic law, the shari'a, once a matter entrusted to specialists, now involves large numbers of people – and not just a scholastically trained religious elite – who debate its meaning and application.[7]

Nowhere has this debate within Muslim circles become more acute than in reading and reciting, reflecting and projecting the Noble Qur'an as the lodestone from the seventh to the 21st century. If there is to be an Islamic reformation, or if it has already taken place and is yet to be recognized, its hallmark must be fresh interpretations of the Qur'an and *sunna* (exemplary conduct of the Prophet as preserved in traditions traceable to his companions among the first generation of Muslims). Despite Eickelman's optimism about competing authorities, fresh interpretations of the Qur'an and *sunna* face many obstacles, not least from state institutions and the ideological allegiances they foster. Whether they be linked to ruling elites or to large-scale movements, Muslim institutions can make religious identities into holistic markers, at once subservient to the interests of their custodians and usurping all other possible identities. This is especially challenging since the postcolonial state and its hegemonic institutions are insinuated into the daily lives of all citizens in majority Muslim states.[8] The paramount need, as Abdullahi An-Na'im has argued, is to make constitutionalism and human rights protection into more than media slogans. 'The safeguards of separating Islam from the state and regulating the political role of Islam through constitutionalism and the protection of human rights are necessary to ensure freedom and security for Muslims so that they can participate in proposing and debating fresh interpretations of foundational sources (i.e., the Qur'an and *sunna*).[9]

Into the arena of debate will come pluralist notions of the Qur'an. While the Qur'an is authoritative as a whole, its content must be applied to particular contexts. What aspect of the Qur'an applies and where? When does it apply and for whom? These are questions that probe coherence and selectivity at two levels. First, why are some but not all passages of the Qur'an of special value at different times and places? And secondly, how do changes in context impart special value to particular verses or chapters?[10]

No context can exceed the text or limit its further potential. Yet every context shows how human agents channel their understanding of the Qur'an for specific, pragmatic ends. The pivotal category is history. Attached to history, the Qur'an becomes *a* Book of Signs, multilayered in its meanings and interactive with its audiences. Detached from history, the Qur'an becomes *the* Book of Signs, singular in its meaning, applicable across time and place, unchanging, univocal.

Among devout Muslims who have understood the issues at stake in this debate are two South Asian public intellectuals. Sir Sayyid Ahmad Khan, the 19th-century rationalist, welcomed the pragmatic values of the British, especially in governance and education. To the extent that modern science embodied the metaphysical values of modern Europe, however, Sir Sayyid challenged its superiority. He countered with an alternative modernity based on the rigorous retrieval of Qur'anic values. In this sense, he was the precursor to Muhammad Iqbal, the most famous Indian, then Pakistani interpreter of Islam in the 20th century. A poet-philosopher, Iqbal was not a Qur'an interpreter, either by intention or by reputation. Yet he was a child of the Qur'an. While he engaged both European philosophy and modern science as twins, each reinforcing the authority of the other, he saw them as inseparable from the larger message of Islam over time that was presented in the Qur'an. Iqbal was also a citizen of the modern world. Defiantly Muslim, he projected in verse a perception of Qur'anic truth at once pervasive and superior to all other truths, including modern philosophy.

But is the Qur'an plurivocal, as Khan and Iqbal assert, or is it univocal, as some traditionalists and their modernday successors, assert? Only God knows! At the least, one can say, and one must say, that those who assert that it is univocal are fully Muslim; they occupy one perspective within the interpretive community of Qur'an users. They are not fundamentalists but absolutists, since they see the Qur'an, and by extension Islam, as primordial. For them, it is above time and beyond history; it remains untouched by human temperament or by temporal change. The absolutists exist in different eras. Osama bin Laden had his precursors in the seventh century Khawarij, early Muslims who rejected any human mediation of God's Word. In common with the Khawarij, Bin Laden decries the departure of Muslims from a single, 'true' interpretation of Qur'anic revelation and social action. An Islamist, he claims to speak on behalf of eternal Qur'anic values.

Yet neither Bin Laden nor other absolutists speak for all Muslims. Absolutist Muslims remain a fractious minority who stress the confrontational aspect of monotheistic faith. While not all absolutists are militant, all militants are absolutist. For the militant Muslim minority, the necessary sequel to professing the faith is defending the faith. Instead of daily prayer, almsgiving, fasting or pilgrimage – all deemed to be essential practices, or pillars of piety, for most Muslims – the very next step required of all believers, in the view of militants, is to wage all-out war, jihad: one must be prepared to sacrifice oneself for one's faith. Militants claim as their proof text justifying jihad as all-out or holy war certain passages from the Qur'an. In what follows I will offer a perspective on these three committed yet conflicting interpreters of the Noble Qur'an as the yardstick for both Muslim identity and collective solidarity.

II

One must begin where many believers find themselves in the age of modern science: how does one reconcile the claims of modern science with the counterclaims of religion? Believers from every major religious tradition have tried to answer this question since science became the key to technological progress, economic success, social prestige and, most importantly, political/military dominance. It is impossible to imagine the emergence of Western Europe, North America or more recently Japan without crediting the instrumental power of modern science.

The Judaeo-Christian world pegged the problem of science on the work of Charles Darwin, and especially on the concept of evolution. Instead of an active agent shaping the world and humankind, Darwin offered an innate law of nature that was neither an intelligent first cause nor an interventionist benign creator. Instead he posited a long-term evolutionary process to explain both the continuity and change observable in the world of phenomena. The Islamic world faced the crisis of modern science not through Darwinian logic but through European presence. Since the age of discovery (16th–17th centuries) Western Europe had expanded beyond its borders, and by the 19th century both France and England became major powers in parts of Africa and Asia with Muslim majorities.

One such place was India. Among Muslim elites subjected to British rule in Northern India none was more renowned, or more reviled, than Sir Sayyid Ahmad Khan (1817–1898). Sir Sayyid, as he was most often known, since he was both descended from the Prophet Muhammad's family and honoured by the Queen of England, gained the stature of the leading public intellectual of pre-Partition India. His energy was prodigious, his activities numerous and his achievements astonishing. He formed a scientific society for the translation of European scientific writings into Urdu, the literary language of North Indian Muslims at the end of the 19th century. He also co-founded a major university for Muslim elites, Aligarh, which became the benchmark for vilifying as well as praising him. Aligarh's claim to modernity had much to do with the fact that its faculty, many of them initially Europeans, used English (not Urdu or Arabic or Persian, all Muslim languages of North India) to teach the subjects deemed important for science.

If Sir Sayyid was engaged by science, he was also mindful of the demands of religion. He saw that the British administration of India abetted, even if it did not directly support, Christian missionary activities aimed at all groups, but especially at Muslims. European scientific researchers also challenged Islam. Known as orientalists because they studied Islamic texts from the Orient, they learned Arabic and Persian (and occasionally Urdu) not to become Muslims but to assess the accuracy of Muslim claims about the sources of their belief and ritual, their law and practice. Caught between missionary polemicists and academic orientalists, Sir Sayyid sought a middle way.

The middle way was to stress the sources as essential, above all the Qur'an. The Bible was also deemed important, and Sir Sayyid produced a unique, if partial, commentary on the Gospels (*Tabyin al-Kalam*, 1862). In later years, however, he turned his attention to a new, and scientific, study of the Qur'an (1880–1895). He laid out principles for his modern commentary and used them as a guidepost for the future that was also a buffer against the past. He critiqued the traditional commentators, such as Tabari, Razi and Zamakhshari, as preoccupied with secondary problems. While they framed the Qur'an with reference to law or theology, and defended its eloquence against poetry and other works of rhetorical excellence, these were not issues of critical import in the modern age. What was paramount now was attention to foundational principles. It was these that had to be clarified, then applied to the range of evidence in the Qur'an. For Sir Sayyid there were fifteen basic principles. They informed his commentary, and he argued, by extension, that they should inform all future, 'modern' commentaries:

1 God is all Powerful and all Prescient; He alone is the Creator of all that is;
2 God has sent prophets, including Muhammad, to guide humankind;
3 The Qur'an is the authentic revelation of God's eternal Word;
4 The Qur'an was revealed to Muhammad by divine inspiration (with or without an angelic intermediary like Gabriel);
5 Nothing in the Qur'an could be wrong or incorrect or ahistorical;
6 The Divine attributes exist only in their essence;

7 The Divine attributes are identical with God's Self and are also eternal;

8 Though the attributes have no limits, God created the laws of nature and through them channelled His Wisdom and His Power;

9 Nothing in the Qur'an can be contrary to the laws of nature;

10 The present text of the Qur'an is at once complete and final;

11 Every Chapter and every verse in every Chapter follow a chronological order;

12 There is no such thing as abrogation (*naskh*), using a later text to trump an earlier one with which it seems to disagree;

13 The revelatory process of the Qur'an developed in stages;

14 Major teachings of the Qur'an – the End of Time, the Realm of Angels, the Role of Demons and the Structure of the Universe – cannot be contrary to the laws of nature, or the teachings of modern science; they must be interpreted in light of these 'recent' truths;

15 Both the direct and indirect expressions in Qur'anic language point to the possibilities of development in human society, and must be studied for their relevance to contemporary social life.[11]

On the basis of these fifteen principles, Sir Sayyid divided all Qur'anic verses into two categories. It was certainly not the clear or ambiguous dyad known to Tabari (828–923) as *muhkamat* and *mutashabihat*, those that are not just clear but binding, and those others that require extensive reflection and may never be clear, at least to human interpreters. Instead, Sir Sayyid framed verses as either essential or symbolic. The essential offered the irreducible core of faith, while the symbolic were open to multiple interpretations, allowing the believer to explain ages and circumstances far removed from those of the Prophet Muhammad in early 7th-century Arabia.

If Sir Sayyid distanced himself from classical commentators, he also alienated their contemporary successors, the *'ulama*, or learned scholars. They openly opposed him, especially after he began to publish his Qur'an commentary serially, making each section available to an expanded reading public. Through the printed press, Sir Sayyid disseminated blistering attacks on his critics. Not just the standard commentaries on the Qur'an but also the classical collections of hadith withered under the lens of his rationalist review. Many of them in his view were demonstrable fabrications, but even more, they were based on the reliability of individuals rather than a logical critique of the text. Sir Sayyid did not accept collections of hadith as a basis for true religion. At most, he argued, they could offer an historical reflection on the ideas and attitudes of the first generations of Muslims. (On this point, as on others, his view elided with those of European scientizers, the textual orientalists.)

In all his endeavours Sir Sayyid was trying to demythologize and to rationalize. Miracles have no place in his approach to the Qur'an. The account of Muhammad's Night Journey and his conversation before the Divine Throne, for instance, are not to be taken at face value. They are neither physical nor spiritual experiences but instead a dream. No man, even a prophet, can have a direct vision of God. What mystics depict is due to their spiritual intensity, not to supranatural powers or the interruption of nature.

A graphic example of Sir Sayyid's militantly rationalist approach to the Qur'an comes in his view of the chapter titled 'Muhammad.' The key phrase is 'Set them free, whether as a favour or through ransom.'

The phrase occurs in a passage (Q 47:5) that refers to the disposition of unbelievers whom the Muslims have fought (and defeated):

> So when you meet in battle those who disbelieve,
> smite their necks;
> then when you have overcome them,
> make them prisoners
> but afterwards set them free,
> whether as a favour or through ransom,
> so that the toils of war may be ended.

For Sir Sayyid, this verse amounts not just to a limit on the treatment of prisoners of war but to a categorical denial of all servitude.

Implicit in this revelation is a call for the liberation of slaves. Because the verse occurred near the end of the Prophet's lifetime, when he had just re-entered Mecca in the famous peace pilgrimage, Sir Sayyid calls it *Ayah hurriya* (the verse of liberation). He regards its message as applicable for all Muslims in all periods. The fact that it was not always observed as such is not the fault of the Qur'an but of previous generations of Muslims – or unenlightened readers in his own generation. It is they who have failed to grasp the revelatory import of the Qur'an.

Similarly, with reference to the age-old question of polygamy, Sir Sayyid did not accede to either the missionary onslaught or the orientalist critique of Muslim practice. Instead, he showed that the key element for a valid Muslim interpretation, at once rationalist and modernist, lay in the opening verses of the Chapter on Women (Q 4:3):

> And if you fear you cannot
> do justice by the orphans,
> then marry women who please you,
> two, three, or four;
> but if you fear you won't be equitable,
> then one, or a legitimate bondmaid of yours,
> that way it is easier for you not to go wrong.

Emphasizing the phrase 'if you fear you won't be equitable', he argues that the basis for Muslim marriage is not love but justice. Since a man cannot treat more than one woman equitably, polygamy is inherently impossible and unIslamic. Devout Muslims, in marriage as in ownership, must always strive to be just.

Whether interpreting the Qur'an to oppose slavery or to show the limits on polygamy, Sir Sayyid argues time and again that the work of God can never be in conflict with the word of God. Since nature and its laws are divinely sanctioned, the Qur'an will always undergird the principles and practices of modern science. And science extends to religion. During a speech that he gave in Lahore, the former seat of Mughal glory, in the Padshahi Mosque built by Shah Jahan, Sir Sayyid called for a new science of religious talk or theology ('*ilm al-kalam*). 'We need a new science of theology,' he urged, 'by which we should either refute the doctrines of modern science or show how they are in conformity with the articles of Islamic faith.'[12] For Sir Sayyid, modern science was blazing the new face of God for Muslims as well as non-Muslims. The only way forward for scholars of Islam was to show how the articles of Islamic faith conform to God's wisdom and power in this as in every age of humankind.[13]

III

Muhammad Iqbal had a similar outlook but a very different temperament from Sayyid Ahmad Khan. A Kashmiri, a Punjabi, an Indian, a Pakistani (by adoption), Iqbal combined competing identities, but above all Iqbal was a modern-day visionary poet, and it was the Qur'an that framed his vision.

Iqbal was born into a devout Muslim family in 1873. His ancestors were Hindus from Kashmir. Though Brahmins, they had converted to Islam during the reign of Shah Jahan (r. 1628–1658), the builder of the Taj Mahal. Iqbal's family later moved from the Kashmir valley to the plains of the Punjab. It was there that Iqbal received both a religious and secular education. He loved Arabic, for the great works of literature and philosophy that it opened to him, but above all for the resonance of the Qur'an. He wrote poetry from an early age. It took him into another realm, the realm of the imagination, dimming the reality of what confronted him and his fellow Muslims. By the turn of the new century the worldly fates of Muslims had become very sad. Mughal glory had been superseded by British rule.

In 1905 Iqbal went to England to learn from the new Mughals, the British Raj. There he earned his law degree. He also continued to study literature and it was at the behest of one of his English professors specializing in Persian literature that he later went to Germany. In Munich he earned his doctorate, before returning to India at the age of 35. Though he had to practice law to make a living, it was poetry that animated him. It gave meaning to his life, and earned him high renown. At first he wrote verse in Urdu, but then he switched to Persian, while still writing some lyrics in Urdu. In both languages he tried to merge the modern world with the Muslim aesthetic tradition, weaving new ideas into the many, many poems he composed.

In his poetry Iqbal exhorted people, particularly the young, to stand up and face life's challenges boldly. The central theme and main source of his message was the Qur'an. He considered the Qur'an to be much more than a book of religion or scripture. It was for him a source of foundational principles upon which to build a coherent system of life. This system of life was Islam. An Islam based on the permanent, absolute values given in the Qur'an, reasoned Iqbal, would bolster collective and individual, public and private identity. It would undergird perfect harmony, balance and stability in the public realm at the same time that it provided freedom of choice and equal opportunity for individuals in the private realm. Everyone could, and should, develop his or her life within the guidelines of the Qur'an. The Qur'anic way was the middle way. It eschewed rank individualism and collective tyranny. It ruled out a private subjective relationship with God that accented personal salvation, but equally it debarred theocracy, rule in the name of God, or dictatorship, rule through brute power. Tyranny, whether religious or secular, countermanded the free spirit of Islam announced and promoted in the Qur'an.

Because Iqbal was a poet-philosopher, his goal was to marry dialogue to dialectics in a way that neither the Greeks nor their modern successors had done. His beacon was Muhammad rather than Aristotle. In the Qur'an Iqbal found the true prototype of a dialogue between God and man. It was not one way but two way. It was continuous and freighted. It began with man's complaint. In 1909, after returning from Europe to India, Iqbal chanted *The Complaint* before a gathering of his fellow Muslims. His soft voice and gentle rhymes belied the stark message from his heart. Modern Muslims do have a complaint against God. It is a legitimate complaint framed by the trust of centuries, stretching back to the time of the Prophet. It is put at risk now, bemoans Iqbal, by the despair of present-day circumstances:

> *We [Muslims] blotted out the smear of falsehood from the pages of*
>   *history*
> *We freed mankind from the chains of slavery*
> *The floors of Your Ka'bah with our foreheads we swept,*
> *The Qur'an You sent us we clasped to our breast, [but now]*
> *Your blessings are showered on homes of unbelievers, strangers all.*
> *Only on the poor Muslim does Your wrath like lightning fall.*[14]

It was not Iqbal's intent to reject God, or belief in God, with this lament. But many of the religious people of his time saw it otherwise. They railed at him. They accused him of taking liberties in addressing God so frankly. His manner, they groused, was more that of a drunken Sufi, like Rumi, rather than that of a sober scholar, like Tabari.

Iqbal pondered these responses. He also conjectured what might be the response of God to his complaint. Four years later, in 1913, in his home city of Lahore, at the mosque built by the Mughal Emperor Shah Jahan, the same mosque where Sir Sayyid Ahmad Khan had spoken less than two decades earlier, Iqbal delivered God's answer to the complaint:

> *All you drink the wine of bodily indulgence,*
> *Leading lives of ease without strife.*
> *Dare you call yourselves Muslims?*
> *What kinship of the soul can there be*
> *Between your ancestors and you?*
> *As Muslims your forefathers were honoured and respected;*
> *But you gave up the Qur'an and now by the world are rejected.*

The human–divine dialogue did not come easily to Iqbal. It burned his soul. Raw and stark, it imitated the Sufis from the glorious past of Islam. Yet he challenged the present age to produce its own spiritual risk takers, those who would dare to intercede on behalf of others, seeking God's blessing and pursuing knowledge of His Will. He blazed the way. To this ancient dialogic form, familiar if not always acceptable to all Muslims, Iqbal brought a new content. His quest had been to bridge Islam and the modern world without embracing a colonial or purely occidental modernity. As he said in another poem, echoing one of his favourite Qur'anic themes, Abraham in the fire (Q 21:68–69):

> *I broke the spell of modern learning,*
> *I took away the bait and broke the trap.*
> *God knows with what indifference,*
> *Like Abraham, I sat in its fire!*[15]

In 1928, as the fire of nationalism swept through Indian Muslims, Iqbal tried to provide the answer to Abraham's dilemma. He provided the answer not in verse but in prose. He gave six lectures to Muslim students in Madras that were then published in a book titled *The Reconstruction of Religious Life in Islam*. In it Iqbal unfolds the Muslim past in the dialogic space of the European present. With the Qur'an as his litmus-test, he critiques his intellectual ancestors. 'While Greek philosophy very much broadened the outlook of Muslim thinkers, it on the whole obscured their vision of the Qur'an.' Yet the greatest of modern European thinkers, trying to wed science with progress, have also lost their way in the cosmos. 'Modern man, that is, modern European man,' observes Iqbal, 'has ceased to live soulfully, i.e., from within.'[16]

Both East and West need to attend to the soul. To reconstruct religious life in Islam one must first relocate, find and celebrate life from within, the experience of the Other as a dimension of everyday life. Iqbal used both the Qur'an in Arabic, *A Book of Signs*, and 'the Qur'an in Persian', Rumi's *Mathnawi*, to frame the arguments of *Reconstruction of Religious Life in Islam*. They are cited in order to address contemporary European thinkers, from Charles Darwin and Sigmund Freud to Bertrand Russell and Albert Einstein. 'With the reawakening of Islam,' writes Iqbal, 'it is necessary to examine, in an independent spirit, what Europe has thought and how far the conclusions reached by her can help us in the revision and, if necessary, reconstruction, of theological thought in Islam.' Because European social initiatives and technical achievements have benefited all humankind, one must apply a pragmatic test *even* to divine revelation. To the extent that the Qur'an confirms for modern man the eternal value of Gabriel's message to the Prophet Muhammad, it is because 'the general empirical attitude of the Qur'an engendered in its followers a feeling of reverence for the actual and ultimately made them the founders of modern science.'

Even as he was delivering these lectures in 1926, Iqbal seemed to recognize that he had let the jinn (or, as English speakers would say, the genie) out of the bottle. Though never citing Sir Sayyid Ahmad Khan by name, Iqbal was confirming that a new science of religion could be built on conformity with modern science rather than its rejection. As a result, however, the trust of God to humankind was no longer a book apart from other books; it was a book that stood tested, and confirmed, on the anvil of modern science, with its rules of evidence, its guidelines and its protocols. But how could it be otherwise? Did not science have to be the handmaiden of God, and were not its rules His rules? For the modern Muslim, as for their ancestors, the challenge was the same: never cease dialoguing with God. The question raised by modern science was the same question raised in every age: whose authority makes and shapes and confounds the world?

'Whose world is this – yours or mine?' was how Iqbal formulated the query in one of his most haunting poems published in 1935, just three years before his death. *The Wing of Gabriel* compressed meaning into sound, and made of the sound an echo that lingers. It was as though Iqbal the philosopher could only come to terms with the tragic separation of humanity from its divine source through verse:

> *Whose World is This – Yours or Mine?*
> *On the morning of eternity Satan dared to say 'No',*
> *But how would I know why?*
> *Is Satan Your confidant, or mine?*
>
> *Muhammad is Yours.*
> *Gabriel is Yours,*
> *The Qur'an is Yours –*

But this discourse,
This exposition in melodious tunes,
Is it Yours or is it mine?

Your world is illuminated
By the radiance of the star of Adam –
But whose loss was the fall of Adam, that creature of earth,
Was it Yours or was it mine?[17]

The key word of this poem is loss. The loss is occasioned by
Adam's fall, so graphically told in the Qur'an (Q 2:35–38):

And when We told the angels
to bow to Adam,
they bowed, except Iblis
– the one who despaired;
he refused, showing arrogance;
and he was a scoffer.

And We said, 'Adam,
dwell in the garden,
you and your wife,
and eat from it comfortably,
when and as you want.
But do not approach this particular tree,
lest you become wrongdoers.'

Then Satan made the two slip there,
and caused them to depart
the state they were in.
And We said, 'Descend in mutual antipathy,
yet you will have an abode
and belongings on earth for a while.'

Then Adam learned words from his Lord,
Who forgave him; for God is Forgiving, Merciful.

The Qur'anic accent on Adam's fate in the final couplet:

> *But whose loss was the fall of Adam, that creature of earth,*
> *Was it Yours or was it mine?*

spins the whole poem into a different realm of possible meaning. How does Adam's moral loss on earth, mirroring even as it anticipates the fall of Muslims from public power in India, compare to Adam's primordial ejection from heaven? After all, was not the fall of Adam from heaven also an epic moment of loss for the angelic realm? Did not paradise become less energized, its spectrum of creaturely response reduced, when Adam ceased to be part of the chorus echoing God's eternal praise?

It is a question as bold as it is rare. It is perhaps the major question of Muhammad Iqbal, the poet-philosopher, for his own generation, and for future generations, of believers: are not the fates of humankind and the divine intertwined? And behind that question of identity and destiny lurks a further question, the question that motivates Iqbal's own labour: what is the final worth of a poet-philosopher if not to voice concerns that, in the clunky prose of a theologian or the diatribes of a preacher, would seem banal at best, heretical at worst?

IV

The Qur'anic vision of Sir Sayyid and Iqbal could not contrast more deeply with any than it does with the dystopia of Osama bin Laden, the Saudi dissident and terrorist who remains Public Enemy No. 1 for the United States Government and for many Euro-American legatees of September 11 2001. Osama bin Laden has killed thousands in the name of religion. He has inspired tens of thousands of others to follow his path of hateful violence and wilful destruction. Yet he claims to be a Muslim. Indeed, the Qur'an for him ceases to be a Book of Signs. It is a book with one sign: kill the infidel in the name of Allah, pursue jihad as offensive holy war, no matter the cost.

Over three years after the coordinated attacks on the United

States that took almost 3,000 lives and launched the war on terror, leading to the American invasion first of Afghanistan and then Iraq, Osama bin Laden has remained at large. If he is physically elusive, he also escapes easy, psychological analysis. The key to understanding him is to grasp the disconnection he perceives between his adopted homeland, Saudi Arabia, and his spiritual benchmark, the Qur'an. The former has betrayed the latter. The infidel flourishes in the birthplace of Islam. The protectors of Islam have become its worst enemies; the Saudis are no longer believers but infidels.

The manifesto of his double war – against native infidels and their foreign allies, equally infidels – dates back to 1996. It was in his 1996 Declaration of War that he made an Islamic appeal to fight the 'Muslim' infidel.[18] The Saudis have become Muslim infidels because they have welcomed the 'Zionist-Crusaders' into the Land of the Two Holy Places (that is, Saudi Arabia in general but the area of Hijaz in particular, since that is where both Mecca and Medina are located). The basis for Osama bin Laden's Islamic opposition to the Saudis is framed by Qur'anic quotations. They dominate the structure, the tone and the argument of his 1996 Declaration of War. He begins by ascribing praise to God, and asking for both His help and His pardon. He also repeats the declaration of faith: 'There is no god but God, and Muhammad is God's messenger.' He echoes Q 39:23, and also Q 39:36–7, when he asserts: 'Whoever has been guided by God will not be misled, and whoever has been misled will not be guided.'

But the body of the Declaration rests not on a paraphrase or an allusion but on the direct citation of three passages (3:102; 4:1; 33:70–71) from the Qur'an:

> O believers, be conscious of your duty to God
> with the proper care due Him
> and do not die
> without having first surrendered to God.

> O people, be careful of your duty to your Lord,
> Who created you from a single being
> and created its mate of the same kind

and spread from these two, many men and women;
and be careful of your duty to God,
by whom you demand from one another your rights,
and be attentive to the ties of kinship.
Surely God is watching over you.

O believers!
be careful of your duty to God
and speak the right word;
He will make your actions sound
and forgive you your faults;
and who ever obeys God and his Apostle
will indeed achieve a mighty success.

None of these quotations would seem exceptional. They refer to 'duty to God'. They accent that duty in different circumstances, as creature, as family relative and as social being, but the duty is not otherwise specified. Yet in commentaries with which Bin Laden was familiar, the duty to God was very specific: proper duty to God was equated with jihad, or defensive war against those who attack Islam. For militant Muslims, this set of verses is not to be read except in conjunction with another Qur'anic verse (Q 22:78):

Strive in God's cause [with the proper care that] you ought to strive . . .

What links this verse to others that are cited above is the notion of 'proper care' or 'right' (*haqq*). To give this moral authority, Bin Laden then adds another verse from the Qur'an, linked to the Prophet Shu'aib:

He said, 'My people,
have you seen whether I am following
clarification from my Lord
who has provided me
a good provision
from the divine source itself?

I do not wish to violate
what I forbid to you.
I only wish for reform,
to the degree that I am able;
and I can only succeed through God,
in whom I repose my trust,
and to whom I turn.'

The Prophet Shu'aib was exhorting his people to oppose false gods and to seek redress for social injustice. Though he was a wealthy man, he earned his wealth by acceptable means, and since he was not doing something that he forbade others to do, he was urging his fellow citizens to reform their lives, reform them 'insofar as (one) is able', in this world through social justice and in the next world through acts of devotion. Bin Laden projects himself as a latter day Shu'aib, claiming his own wealth as legitimate but also yearning for social justice as the necessary expression of his privilege that faith demanded. The word for 'reform', *islah*, is itself one prized in modern Muslim movements. Though it occurs but eight times in the Qur'an, only here is it directly connected to a prophet.

A further Qur'anic reference (3:110) expands the collective appeal of Bin Laden's message:

You are the best of the nations
raised up for the benefit of men:
you enjoin what is right and forbid the wrong,
and you believe in Allah.

He then reinforces this partial verse with a tradition echoing the life of the Prophet Muhammad. 'God's blessing and salutations on His slave and messenger who said: "The people are close to an all encompassing punishment from God if they see the oppressor and fail to restrain him."'

As in earlier scriptural citations, it would be hard to see the militant edge of this cluster unless one recognized that Bin Laden's commentary refers the reader/listener back to the beginning of

Sura 3 where there is also a reference to the criterion between truth and falsehood (Q 3:4):

> As for those who repudiate the signs of God
> there is a severe torment for them;
> and God is Almighty, able to revenge.

Not everyone, reasons Bin Laden, has the same capacity to enjoin right and forbid wrong. It is incumbent, above all, on rulers to enjoin right, or command good, and also to recognize the signs of God. The Saudi rulers, implies Bin Laden, have not lived up to the scriptural mandate; they have forfeited their right to rule. Following this catena of scriptural references, Bin Laden condemns the Saudi leadership outright because they depend on American Crusaders. Without a trace of hyperbole, he asserts that 'the latest and the greatest of the aggressions incurred by the Muslims since the death of the Prophet – may God's blessing and peace be upon him – is the occupation of the land of the two Holy Places – the foundation of the house of Islam, the place of the revelation, the source of the message and the place of the noble Ka'bah, the Qiblah of all Muslims – by the armies of the American Crusaders and their allies.'

Later, he justifies his own labour as one that liberates not just the occupied land of the two Holy Places but also Jerusalem. 'Today we work from the Hindu Kush mountains to lift the iniquity that had been imposed on the *umma* (the Muslim community) by the Zionist-Crusader alliance, particularly after they have occupied the blessed land around Jerusalem, route of the journey of the Prophet – may God's blessing and peace be upon him – and the land of the two Holy Places. We ask God to bestow us with victory, He is our Patron and He is the Most Capable.'

Here the 'route of the journey of the Prophet' is an unmistakable allusion is to the Night Journey of the Prophet (17:1):

> Glory be to Him who took His servant by night
> from the sacred mosque to the farthest mosque,
> whose precincts We blessed,
> in order that We might show him some of Our signs.

Bin Laden moves beyond identifying himself with the Prophet Shu'aib. He not only takes the 'illegitimate' Saudis to task for inviting the Crusaders to the Two Holy Places. He also invokes the memory of Saladin. Saladin was a valiant holy warrior. In the 12th century he did what Bin Laden proposes to do in the 21st century: combat the Crusaders in the first Holy Land of Muslims, Jerusalem.

Throughout his declaration Bin Laden conflates the two objectives: to free the Two Holy Places and to reclaim the original Holy Land, Jerusalem. 'To push the enemy – the greatest *kufr* (unbelief) – out of the country is a prime duty,' he proclaims. 'No other duty after belief is more important than the duty of jihad. Utmost effort should be made to prepare and instigate the *umma* against the enemy, the American-Israeli alliance occupying the country of the two Holy Places and the route of the Apostle – may God's blessing and peace be upon him – to the Furthest Mosque.'

The focus on jihad is paramount. If there is more than one duty to be carried out, then the most important one should receive priority. Clearly after belief (*iman*) there is no more important duty than pushing the American enemy out of the Holy Land. For the people of knowledge, said a medieval Muslim scholar, 'to fight in defense of religion and belief is a collective duty; there is no other duty after belief than fighting the enemy who is corrupting the life and the religion. There is no precondition for this duty, and the enemy should be fought with one's best abilities.'

The scholar quoted here is Ibn Taymiyyah (1263–1328). He fought against the Mongols in the 13th century. Since the Mongols were nominal Muslims, Bin Laden is comparing the present-day status of those Arab Muslims living under Saudi rule to the earlier condition of Iraqis and other Muslims living under Mongol rule. Not only is jihad the necessary second pillar after faith, but jihad must be conducted against 'nominal' Muslims in the name of a higher principle of social justice and restoration of dignity. The declaration of jihad against Muslims as well as non-Muslims is a minority view, yet it does have precedent in the history of Qur'an interpretation. Bin Laden strides forth as the modern Saladin emboldened by the Qur'an commentary of Ibn Taymiyyah.[19]

Bin Laden uses other resources besides the Qur'an. There are many anecdotes and lessons from Traditions of the Prophet, as well as verses of poetry and commentaries that he invokes to justify his case against both the Saudis and their Zionist-Crusader allies, that is, Israel and the United States. Yet his embrace of a minority exegetical tradition of the Qur'an provides the backbone for his appeal. He does two things simultaneously. First, he selects only those Qur'anic verses that fit his message, and then cites them exclusively for his own purposes. He ignores both their original context and also the variety of historical differences among committed Muslims about how to apply their dicta. Second, he collapses the broad spectrum of Qur'anic teaching into a double requirement: first to believe and then to fight. There may be other duties but the first two – and by implication, the only two that matter in a time of crisis – are *iman*, then jihad, or defensive war on behalf of the *umma*.

Osama bin Laden follows the same interpretive strategy when he appeals to those who will be the foot soldiers in the jihad, or holy war, that he is invoking against Mongol Muslims, that is, the current Saudi rulers, and those who support them, the Zionist-Crusaders who have occupied the two Holy Places (Mecca and Medina). Claiming that the Saudis are apostates, he also charges them with failing to uphold both the *'ulama* and the righteous youth.

In the third and final part of his 1996 Declaration of War, he appeals directly to the righteous youth. 'I have a very important message to the youth of Islam,' he declares. '(They are) men of the brilliant future of the *umma* of Muhammad – may God's blessings and peace be upon him. Our youth are the best descendants of the best ancestors!' The phrase identifies the martyrs who volunteer for al-Qaida as equivalent not just to the companions of the Prophet but also to those who were exemplary in fighting for the creation and expansion of the Muslim community. Bin Laden reinforces their sacred role with verses from the Qur'an that seem to enshrine this loyalty as binding. Not only will they stand up to those who protect the infidel occupiers, but they will also understand that 'it is a duty now on every tribe in the Arab

Peninsula to fight, jihad, in the cause of Allah and to cleanse the land from those occupiers. Allah knows that their blood is permitted (to be spilled) and their wealth is a booty; their wealth is a booty to those who kill them. The Most Exalted said in the Verse of the Sword (*Ayat as-Sayf*, 9:5a):

> So when the sacred months have passed away,
> then slay the idolaters wherever you find them,
> and take them captives and besiege them,
> and lie in wait for them in every ambush.

Our youths knew that the humiliation suffered by the Muslims as a result of the occupation of their sanctuaries cannot be opposed and removed except by jihad.'

While there are many other verses that could be, and are cited on behalf of jihad, it is the Sword Verse from Sura 9 that becomes the shibboleth, the battle-cry, echoing other verses and etching their meaning in a single mandate. Probably no verse has occasioned more reflection as to its context and applicability. Since the chapter in which it occurs is among the last revealed to the Prophet Muhammad, militant interpreters want to make it the verse that trumps all others, mandating the battle against unbelievers as general and unending.

But the actual context begins with a crucial qualifier (9:3–4):

And an announcement from God and His messenger
to the people on the day of the Greater Pilgrimage
that God and His messenger are not liable to the idolaters;
therefore if you repent, it will be better for you.
And if you turn back, then know that you will not weaken God,
and announce painful punishment to those who disbelieve.
except those of the idolaters
with whom you made an agreement,
then they have not failed you in anything
and have not supported any one against you.
So fulfill your agreement with them to the end of their term;
surely God loves those who are careful in their duty

Taken together these two verses, qualify the implied all-out mandate of Q 9:5a, but even more extenuating is Q 9:5b, also omitted from Osama bin Laden's citation in the War Declaration:

> But if they repent and keep up prayer
> and give alms,
> then let them go free;
> for God is Most Forgiving, Most Merciful.

So while Q 9:5 may seem severe if excerpted in the form cited by Bin Laden, the full text of the Qur'an qualifies its 'clear' and 'singular' meaning. Bin Laden, however, is declaring war and urging terror. He is not interested in interpretive niceties. He wants to define jihad as second in importance only to belief. He wants to take Qur'anic passages as proof texts rather than moral directives. He wants to create a rigid polarity between Muslim youth, who alone are righteous, and enemy occupiers, who along with native collaborators become legitimate targets of attack 'by any means possible'.

Crucial and deliberate is the lack of any specificity about the means of waging jihad. It is assumed that because the atrocities of the aggressors are so evident and bloody, the means to oppose them must be comparable. It is all-out war, it is unending terror. There is no negotiation, no compromise, no modus vivendi with the infidel enemy.

What is the end result of Osama bin Laden's project? It is neither an Islamic state nor a restoration of the caliphate. Instead it promotes nothing but endless anarchy. Osama bin Laden is mislabelled as an Islamic fundamentalist. He is more the descendant of Rasputin and the Russian anarchists of the early 20th century than he is of Muhammad and Muslim warriors of the early seventh century. His Qur'an is not a signpost but a gravemarker.[20] While he is the best known Muslim name in modern media, he is the least representative of the broad engagement with modernity signalled by Sayyid Ahmad Khan and Muhammad Iqbal. The Qur'an is finally not univocal but plurivocal; its most enduring lesson is its openness to multiple interpretations and applications for the benefit of all God's children, whether within the Abrahamic fold – Jews, Christians and Muslims, or beyond it – Buddhists, Hindus and Sikhs.

3

Heroic Themes:
An Invitation to Muslim Worlds
John Renard

Yesterday the Republic of Indonesia's first warship and a Malaysian frigate, both named *Hang Tuah*, sailed within sight of each other through the Straits of Malaka. This evening an Egyptian raconteur entertained a packed coffeehouse with tales of Abu Zayd and Antar, and a bard in eastern Turkey charmed his listeners with the story of Köroghlu. Tomorrow a Central Asian couple will name their newborn son Rustam, or a daughter Manizha. Across the world, Muslim boys and girls bear the names of Muhammad and Aisha, 'Ali and Husayn, in memory of men and women associated with the beginnings of the religious tradition known as Islam. Ancient as their stories are, characters from a people's past have the power to distil a sense of deeply rooted identity. In many predominantly Muslim societies, a hybrid 'imaginary' has evolved, resulting in a surprisingly seamless blend of pre-Islamic local, regional, or national virtues in individual heroes and heroines, whether they originated locally or were 'imported' with the arrival of Islam. In their more developed forms, heroes exemplify what Muslims of a particular context consider essential to being a Muslim 'at home', and in some instances their stories also provide Muslims of a given region a sense of connection with the global community of believers. Whether heroic figures are of cultural or religious origin, they represent an essential theme in the 'habitus' of so many societies in which Islam has been, and continues to be, a formative force.

Heroic themes live on as an integral part of Islamicate cultures from North Africa to Southeast Asia, functioning as an entreé into the various societies and cultures in which Islam has played a dominant role. This chapter seeks to clarify how and why those themes have endured in Islamicate societies and will suggest several ways of understanding how the heroic image can high-light both religious unity and cultural diversity within that world. These are naturally complex matters, and any treatment as brief as this can only skim across the surface of a few prominent questions.

Three sets of global issues arise from a study of heroic themes. The first concerns the prevalence of such themes across the world and the place of Islamic heroic themes within that larger context. The other two concern how those themes are manifested within contexts explicitly modified by the Islamic religious tradition. One has to do with the various ways in which heroic narratives and images function within Islamicate societies. The other has to do with the twin phenomena of Islamization and indigenization. I will approach each of these sets of issues in turn.

Before I discuss those matters, however, several crucial terms need to be clarified. In *The Venture of Islam,* Marshall Hodgson addresses the need for a more precise terminology that would allow for a distinction between the religious tradition called 'Islam' (with its corresponding adjective, 'Islamic'), and the societies and cultures that have come under the strong influence of Islam but cannot be understood simply in terms of that religious associa-tion. So, for example, one can legitimately speak of 'Islamic Law' or 'Islamic Mystical Literature.' But because much of the litera-ture and art produced even in regions where Islam is the belief system of the majority is not uniformly 'religious' in the same way law and mystical literature are, Hodgson devised terms intended to reflect that complex relationship:

> There has been . . . a *culture,* centered on a lettered tradition, which has been historically distinctive of Islamdom the *society,* and which has been naturally shared in by both Muslims and non-Muslims who participate at all fully in the society of Islamdom. For this, I have used the adjective 'Islamicate'. I thus restrict the term 'Islam' to the *religion* of the Muslims, not using that term for the far more

general phenomena, the society of Islamdom and its Islamicate cultural traditions.[1]

I have on the whole adapted Hodgson's distinctions to present purposes, but will use the term 'religious tradition' where he uses 'religion'. The former suggests more of a living, organic process, and is less likely to be reified or regarded as a monolithic entity than the former term.

Treating a subject as far-ranging and intricate as this involves unravelling and disentangling numerous long threads. Since the beginnings and endings of those threads almost never come readily to hand, it becomes necessary simply to grasp them somewhere – true to the epic spirit – in *medias res* and follow where they lead. Throughout this chapter, the reader will encounter names of many as yet unfamiliar heroic figures, characters that invite and will reward a more intimate acquaintance.

Islam's Heroes in Global Perspective

Asked what Odysseus, Mother Teresa, John Henry the Steel Drivin' Man, Aeneas, Joan of Arc, Batman, Judith, and Nelson Mandela have in common, many would no doubt respond that they are all heroic figures. Yet the reasons for which people have conferred on them the mantle of heroism vary enormously. One general characteristic that links them, perhaps, is such exemplary virtues as resourcefulness, strength, fidelity, thirst for justice. But is exemplary virtue a sufficiently precise concept to define a class of persons across a wide range of cultural, ethnic and religious lines? Does one not need more specific attributes to delineate a category called 'heroic figures'? I have suggested elsewhere a larger typology of major heroic types, dividing them into folk, royal and religious types, and suggesting a wide range of sub-types.[2]

For the moment, however, I must keep my definition of the heroic rather general, employing only the following distinction between form and function. From a formal point of view, the hero or heroine is the protagonist: any character who plays a starring or strong supporting role in either major literary works or the visual arts, or both. The heroic figure must in addition function as a model, an ideal of exemplary behaviour as worked out in the context of adversity.

Every people and culture has its national treasures, or their equivalents; and what a people prizes most dearly is invariably an important clue to what that people regards as constitutive of the human ideal. If it were possible to gather into one image or person all of a people's national treasures, one might fully appreciate what that culture sees as the truly and essentially human. An old Arabic proverb says, 'Wisdom has alighted on three things: the brain of the Frank, the hand of the Chinese and the tongue of the Arab.' It suggests that the gift of wisdom has been granted to many peoples, that it is manifested in a characteristic form among each of them, and that eloquence and wit are a uniquely Arab treasure. One could say something similar of the image of the hero as human ideal: it is a virtually universal phenomenon and, at the same time, bears the unmistakable signature of every people and culture in which it is found. Another proverb might have said, 'The hero has a thousand faces: Rama, Buddha, the Confucian Scholar, Jesus, Moses, Muhammad . . .'

Study of Islamicate heroic themes highlights the striking extent to which major religious traditions and cultures have always inter-penetrated. A broad spectrum of Muslim attitudes toward non-Muslims is evidenced in the literature. Alexander's celebrity among Persians and Turks is a measure of the far-flung esteem, perhaps even *mystique*, that Hellenistic culture has enjoyed. A look at the array of visual materials reveals the stylistic and iconographic heritages of Byzantium, Central Asia, India, China. As for literary sources, Allessandro Bausani has made a preliminary analysis that indicates material from tribal Arabic stories, either pre-Islamic or contemporary with Islam (such as Antar); parts of Islamic tales (such as that of Hamza); Hellenistic and Middle Eastern (Alexander); Iranian legend (Bahram, Nushirwan), Hindu legend and myth (Indra and his heavenly attendants); Buddhist legends (Jataka stories); and local tales (Baluchi, Sindhi, Kurdish, etc.).[3] In short, the hero is capable of leading one on a journey with stopovers in every place human beings have called home. I will now propose some of the ways heroic themes have functioned across Islamdom, and several ways in which those themes can assist an analysis of relationships between Islam and its diverse cultural contexts.

Functions of Heroic Tales in Islamicate Societies

A study of the ways heroic themes function in Muslim cultures across the world provides an important key to appreciating the unity and diversity of Islamicate societies. Opinions vary among Muslims as to the continuing relevance of the classic heroic figures as models for contemporary societies. Just two examples from recent Arabic poetry offer an instructive hint as to the spectrum of views. The Egyptian Salah Abd as-Sabur's 'Dreams of an Ancient Knight' suggests that heroic imagery has by no means lost its appeal, even if it represents a rather distant and idealistic, perhaps even unrecoverable, mode. His is an ideal of romantic heroism. The poet talks of how the lover has, at least for now, left the hero behind. To his beloved he laments, 'I was once in bygone days / O my enchantress a steadfast warrior, a heroic knight *[fata, faris]* / Before my heart was trodden underfoot.' As hero he felt deeply, laughed like a brook, grieved, had compassion for the suffering, and would willingly have been set ablaze to offer them light. 'What befell the heroic knight?' he asks. 'His heart was plucked out and he took to flight dropping the reins.' To the beloved he offers 'the experience and skill bestowed on me by the world / In return for a single day of innocence / No it is only you who can make me again the ancient knight / Without any payment / Without any reckoning of profit and loss'.[4]

At the other end of the spectrum, Syrian-born Nizar Qabbani makes it clear that he believes the classic heroes have nothing more to say to him or his contemporaries. 'Bread, Hashish and Moonlight' decries the uncritical clinging of ordinary folks to the past and its legends. 'In my land, / In the land of the simple, / Where we slowly chew on our unending songs – / A form of consumption destroying the east – / Our east is chewing on its history, / Its lethargic dreams, / Its empty legends, / Our east that sees the sum of all heroism *[butula]* / In . . . Abu Zayd al-Hilali' (a major folk hero who represents a variation on the theme of the Bedouin Ideal). In his 'What Value Has the People Whose Tongue is Tied?' Qabbani complains how people of his time remain blind to the crucial problems. They 'Make heroes *[abtal]* out of dwarves, / Make the noble among us, vile, / Improvise heroism *[butula]*, / Sit lazy and listless in the mosques, / Composing verses and compiling proverbs, / And begging for victory over the foe / From His Almighty presence'.[5]

I will mention in the course of this chapter several other Muslim opinions as to the relative importance of the more traditional themes. For the moment, I will focus on some of the classic works' religious, social and psychological functions within Islamicate societies.

Two obvious religious functions are the renewal of devotion and religious education. Sacred figures from the greatest prophets to the local holy personage inspire and encourage when times are hard. One way to connect present with past is to associate a contemporary figure with a classical religious hero. This method is clearly evident in Iranian revolutionary posters that depict Ayatollah Khomeini as a new Moses who confronts a Pharaonic Shah with a staff-turned-dragon. Husayn's tragic journey to martyrdom, and Muhammad's triumphant odyssey into unseen realms and back, still move Muslim audiences across the world. Such heroic accounts supply a great deal of what many Muslims know about their faith tradition.[6]

A link between the specifically religious functions and the more general social functions mentioned below is the following instance of heroic themes as an exhortation to bravery. In addition to giving listeners a sense of connectedness to historical antecedents, heroic narratives, at least in Malaysia, also seem to have carried the power to bestir warriors on the eve of battle. Lode Brakel cites a fascinating text from the *Sejara Melayu (Malay Chronicles)* well worth quoting here. The setting is Malaka in 1511, the night before an expected Portuguese attack on the city. The two principal heroes mentioned are Hamza, an uncle of Muhammad, who arguably represents a variation on the folk heroic themes of the Champion and Comrade in Arms; and Muhammad al-Hanafiya, another but more distant relation of the Prophet Muhammad, and arguably a more explicitly 'religious' hero.

> It was night and all the captains and young men were on guard in the palace. And the young men said, 'Of what use is it for us to sit here in silence? It would be better for us to read some story of battle so that we might benefit from it.'
>
> 'You are right,' said Tun Muhammad the Camel. 'Tun Indra Sagara had better go and ask for the story of Muhammad Hanafiah, saying that perhaps we may derive advantage from it, as the Franks attack tomorrow.' Then Tun Indra Sagara went into the presence of Sultan Ahmad and submitted their remarks to his highness. And Sultan Ahmad gave him the romance of Amir Hamza, saying, 'Tell them, I'd give them the story of Muhammad Hanafiah but I fear they'll not be as brave as he: if they are like Amir Hamza it will do, so I give them the story of Hamza.' Tun Indra Sagara came out carrying the story of Hamza and told them all Sultan Ahmad had said, and they were silent not answering a word. Then Tun Isak said to Tun Indra Sagara, 'Tell his highness that he is mistaken. His highness must be like Muhammad Hanafiah and we like the captains of Baniar.' Tun Indra Sagara submitted Tun Isak's remark to Sultan Ahmad, who smiled and answered, 'He is right.' And he gave him the story of Muhammad Hanafiah too.[7]

Heroic themes provide a number of broader social functions, not the least of which is simple entertainment. Heroic stories bring people together. One result of that interaction is the strengthening of national pride.[8] A major social function is the capacity to inculcate a sense of honour and shame. In classical Arab tradition, for example, a sense of private honour was based on an awareness of one's natural goodness, independent of social consideration. That in turn was linked to *futuwwa* ('bravery in battle') and *muruwwa,* a value associated with protecting refugees and with vengeance, courage and generosity. The leader required most of all *'ird* ('dignity', 'good repute') and *hilm* ('intelligent forbearance'). The former consisted in ancestral nobility and illustriousness combined with natural praiseworthiness *(ash-sharaf, al-hasab* and *al-khaliqat al-mahmuda*). All of these the heroic narrative extols and reinforces. Heroes and heroines model a range of social virtues that preserve family honour as well. Blood vengeance restores balance, closes the circle of shame and restores honour. Single combat with its decisive duel in turn links the individual to the group. Honour and its opposite, shame *('ar/a'yar)*, were thus key concepts governing relations between individual and society. Heroines often modelled values of virginity, 'love of the eyes' and readiness to aid a prisoner. Shame for women typically involved false accusation of adultery, adultery and various forms of treachery.[9]

A related issue is the sense of tribal or racial identity. In the Antar story, for example, much is made of contact between blacks and whites. Important Arabian themes are intermarriage of human and jinn to explain the marvellous and single combat between an Arab and an Ethiopian, or between black and white serpents. Key themes in both the Sayf ibn Dhi Yazan and Antar stories include an assertion of the unity of warring Ethiopians and Arabians, as shown through a rediscovery of common ancestry. According to H. T. Norris, combat between black and white symbolizes either political conflict (in which case the Black may be identified with Abraha, the 6th-century Abyssinian invader of Arabia), or ethnic and religious accord (when the Black is identified with the Christian Abyssinian king, the Negus, who helped Muhammad in 615 by giving asylum to his community).[10]

Sayyid Hurreiz comments more specifically on this aspect of the psychological function of stories of Bani Hilal among the Muslim Ja'iliyyin people of the Sudan:

> Among the other narratives that perform psychological functions are the local variants of the romance of 'Abu Zeid the Hilalite'. Dealing with the earlier Afro-Arab or North-South relations, these narratives have great psychological significance for the Ja'iliyyin who belong to both ethnic groups. The audience identifies with the hero who is an Afro-Arab, or an Arab noted for his blackness. They implicitly realize the tensions underlying their identity and emerge from the tale triumphant and reassured of their social and

moral worth. After all, Abu Zeid is the leader and rescuer of his tribe.[11]

Finally, heroic narratives are said to provide a number of personal psychological benefits. Listening to a hero's tale can soothe and quiet anxiety. Firdawsi, author of the 11th-century Iranian 'national epic', asks his wife on the darkest of nights to help him find repose; she responds by telling him the story of Bizhan and Manizha, in which the beloved summons the hero Rustam to rescue her lover.[12] Iskandar (Alexander the Great) asks Aristotle to tell him stories from the *Shahnama* (that same Iranian epic) when he is discouraged, and the accounts move the king to tears.[13] One of king Hurmuz's last three wishes of his son Khusraw Parwiz is that Khusraw send the king a warrior of long memory to regale him with the exploits of kings and campaigns past.[14] Zal tells his young son Rustam that he should delay setting off to confront the rampaging Turanian King Afrasiyab and take some time to be inspired by the tales of heroes.[15]

Islamization and Indigenization

A major religio-cultural issue for students of Islamdom concerns the persistence of pre-Islamic ways and ideals after the coming of Islam, or the coexistence of Islamic and non-Islamic value systems. I would frame the issue this way: how can the theme of the hero facilitate a balanced approach to the study both of the Islamicate world as a whole, and of the unique cultural traditions that make up that world? Two large complementary dynamics come into focus – Islamization and indigenization. In the general sense, Islamization is the process by which the religious tradition of Islam becomes a major factor within a culture or ethnic group or region. Some understanding of that process can help clarify to what extent one can speak of Islamdom as a unity. Indigenization is the process by which a culture, ethnic group, or region puts its own stamp on Islam; it accounts at least in part for the diversity within Islamdom.

Scholars have long debated the question of the continuity or discontinuity one finds in the expression of cultural and religious values in the process of Islamization. The prime example is 7th-century Arabia. Ignaz Goldziher sees a major disjunction between Jahiliyya ('age of ignorance' as a characterization of the pre-Islamic world) and Islamic values.[16] Toshihiko Izutsu describes a somewhat less dramatic transformation of pre-Islamic virtues into the Qur'anic ingredients of a faith-informed value system.[17] M. M. Bravmann describes the transition still more explicitly as a continuum rather than a definitive break. Quoting the Arabic saying 'There is no religion *[din]* without "manly virtue" *[muruwwah]*', Bravmann says 'the virile ethics of the heathen period were appreciated even in the Islamic period, [but] in the course of time other qualities, of purely religious character, were added to them'.[18] In his study of fatalism in Persian epic literature, Helmer Ringgren makes a similar point in connection with the theme of 'destiny'. He infers that:

> [T]he attitude towards Destiny does not develop into indifference and complete resignation . . . . Even the fact that man complains of his fate shows that the fatalism of the epics is modified and mitigated by the belief in a God who acts righteously. But the latter belief, in its turn, has not been without traces of fatalistic ideas. There is a tension between fatalism in the real sense of the word and belief in a personal God as the Master of man's destiny, and this tension is never entirely removed.[19]

Islamization has also come to occupy the attention of scholars who study regions now solidly Islamized but originally far from the birthplace of Islam. Soewito Santoso, writing on early Indonesian and Malay literature, defines Islamization as 'the process of reforming any cultural product from another culture into something acceptable to Muslims and in accordance with the basic principles and notions of Islam'.[20] He also makes a useful distinction between 'Islamic' and 'Muslim', somewhat analogous to Hodgson's coining of 'Islamicate' as distinct from 'Islamic'. Santoso uses 'Islamic' to denote something 'in accordance with the basic principles and notions of Islam'. 'Islamic' thus explains the existence of a common element from Morocco to Malaysia, but it does not explain how those cultures differ. The term 'Muslim culture', on the other hand, can help explain how Indian Islamic culture differs from Spanish Islamic culture:

> As culture is the product of the minds of people, and as the adherents of Islam who bring forth this kind of culture are called 'Muslims', I feel that consequently it should be called 'Muslim culture'. And as the Muslims of India differ from the Muslims of Spain, the products of their minds are also different; they are either Indian or Spanish. So in fact the two cultural products are Indian and Spanish adjusted to basic Islamic principles or in other words *the cultures in both countries are in course of time Islamized by the Muslim culture-bearers of those countries.*[21]

In relation specifically to heroic themes, Islamization is the process by which an originally non-Islamic heroic figure (such as Hang Tuah, Köroghlu, Iskandar in Persia, Rustam or even Antar) gradually takes on a more or less distinctly Islamic religious cast. An Islamized hero thus participates in the legitimation of a religious tradition by conferring on it the kind of credibility it needs to take hold in new cultural circumstances.

Referring specifically to Malay and Indonesian heroic themes, Santoso notes two types of Islamization. One occurs through the insertion of Islamized stories, or of stories transplanted in their entirety from another Muslim literature, into indigenous works of non-Islamic origin. The *Sejara Melayu* exemplifies this type. Stories of Iskandar, a king who has already been Islamized before arriving in Southeast Asia, serve to Islamize in turn other stories of pre-Islamic origin in the *Sejara*. The second process involves the insertion either of phrases that extol the God of Islam as superior to other deities, or of meetings of the hero with famous Islamic figures who confer on the hero religious legitimacy.[22] The latter occurs in *Hikayat Hang Tuah* where, for example, the hero meets the mysterious and ubiquitous Khadir (Khizr). The prophet gives Hang Tuah a bottle of wondrous water that, when poured on his ears and lips, enables him to speak and understand foreign languages (Hang Tuah knows Siamese, Tamil, Turkish, Nigrama, among other tongues).[23]

The corollary to the process of Islamization is that of indigenization, whereby the receiving culture makes acceptable to itself stories from other cultures. By the term 'indigenization' I mean the process whereby an originally Islamic hero (such as 'Ali in Persia, or Muhammad in East Africa), or a hero previously Islamized en route to a farther destination (such as Hamza or Iskandar in India or Malaysia), begins to take on the features of a local character. An indigenized hero becomes part of the process in which evolving local or regional social and political structures cloak themselves in the antiquity, authority and universal claims of Islam. Just as Indonesia recast the Hindu Ramayana in its own moulds, so did it modify such Islamic characters as Hamza (Wong Agung Menak) into the likeness of the Javanese culture hero Panji.[24]

Islamization and indigenization go hand in glove. One can distinguish three major types of evidence of the twofold dynamic: first, changes in the use and popularity of certain literary genres; second, the adoption of certain heroes and the rejection of others; and finally, the impact of heroic themes and portrayal on social systems.

Islamization and the Introduction of New Genres

Bausani offers a comprehensive explanation of how Islam and indigenous literary types have interacted. His basic premise is that, through a process of demythologization, the Islamic tradition has braided together elements of both high and folkloric strands of 'epos' from across the world. The table below is a modified version of the chart by which he shows relationships among literary forms. As for content, Bausani suggests a much broader range of sources, recalling the global scope of human fascination with the hero discussed above. Bausani's model is not very specific as to precisely how the mechanism of demythologization works. It must suffice for present purposes to note that he regards the religious tradition as a kind of combination funnel and filter through which materials from the Islamic heartlands and hinterlands alike were blended and rendered palatable to Islamic sensibilities.[25]

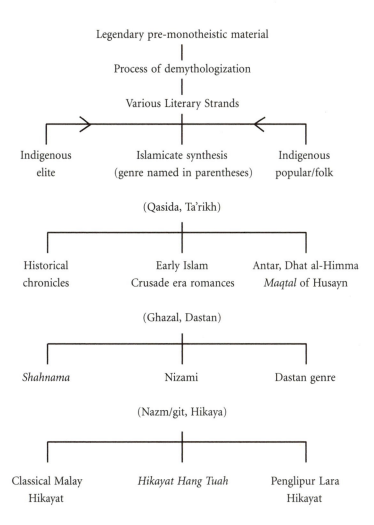

Legendary pre-monotheistic material

|

Process of demythologization

|

Various Literary Strands

Indigenous
elite

Islamicate synthesis
(genre named in parentheses)

Indigenous
popular/folk

(Qasida, Ta'rikh)

Historical
chronicles

Early Islam
Crusade era romances

Antar, Dhat al-Himma
Maqtal of Husayn

(Ghazal, Dastan)

Shahnama

Nizami

Dastan genre

(Nazm/git, Hikaya)

Classical Malay
Hikayat

Hikayat Hang Tuah

Penglipur Lara
Hikayat

Table: Genre and Islamization

Picking up on a major element in Bausani's analysis, Brakel has studied the origins of the Malay genre called *hikayat* (from the Arabic for 'narrative'). Several varieties of literature in other areas have gone by the same name. Brakel links the introduction of the genre to at least three changes in Malay society. First, Malay society became more integrated into 'Mainland Asian Muslim culture'. He theorizes that 'a stage had been reached where, not any longer satisfied with the study of the sacred texts Qur'an and hadith themselves, Malay Muslims felt the need to subordinate their recreational and magically inspired literature to Muslim values as well'. Second, an emerging 'cosmopolitan, international, post-feudal trading class' discovered that the new genre allowed them a much broader range of expression than either earlier Hindu royal cult-oriented literature or the sacral oral poetry of the Malay *penglipur-lara* ('dispeller of sadness') tales.

Third, though Malay culture had not welcomed a number of other significant Islamicate literary forms, the *hikayat* found a place because of the composite or 'hybrid' structure of the earliest to gain popularity there, the *Hikayat Muhammad Hanafiya.* Brakel finds a connection between that dual structure and 'certain features already present in Malay/Indonesian culture at the time'. He explains that the story of Muhammad Hanafiya may have achieved popularity initially because, while its second half is a genuine *hikaya,* the first is a *maqtal* or 'story of martyrdom'. It may therefore have gained initial popularity through recitation at commemorations of Husayn's martyrdom (Karbala, 680 CE). Brakel concludes that this work 'contains two features which . . . must have been familiar to Sumatran culture prior to its introduction: its pronounced religio-Muslim character . . . and its function as a magical tale recited at ritual occasions, like the *penglipur lara* texts'.[26]

William Hanaway makes some interesting observations about the development of the Persian popular romance in relation to the gradual dominance of Islam over ancient Iran's Zoroastrian religious ethos. Noting that both 'modes of thought' share the belief that good will ultimately overcome evil, Hanaway goes on to distinguish between the Islamic and Zoroastrian views of the role of the individual person in that struggle. He suggests that the characters of the Persian national epic, the *Shahnama*, seem 'more real and human' than those of the romances, because the poet Firdawsi's worldview still has the individual person acting as an ally of Ahura Mazda in the battle to preserve the world in its original, natural goodness. Even in the earliest of the romances, *Samak-i Ayyar*, Hanaway sees a 'strictly Islamic' setting and perspective. Samak himself remains closer to the heroes of the *Shahnama* than do those of the later romances, and the romance contains far less fantasy and divine intervention. Had the received text of the story derived from a later time, he contends, it would have featured a hero closer to a Hamza or an Iskandar, moving about in a world aflutter with *paris* (angel-like spirits) and subject to constant divine manipulation.

Hanaway suggests that, in the Islamic view, the human person no longer functions as God's co-worker but takes an infinitely subordinate role. Whereas the Zoroastrian hero could still choose not to engage in the battle against evil, the Islamic hero is simply swept up into the mêlée and can choose either to accept his lot in faith or to deny God's sovereignty. Hanaway writes:

> As the social and religious condition in Iran changed from the tenth century on, we see the popular heroes changing too. No longer is the hero of the romance a mighty warrior, defeating his enemies and gaining his ends by his own personal prowess. The hero slowly becomes a kind of strong, handsome innocent. He does not learn from experience or grow wiser with age, but maintains an eternal youth and freshness. His innocence is important, because he is the chosen one, the instrument of divine will by means of which evil is undone and injustice punished.[27]

The romantic hero's guidance comes from others wiser than himself, but even their wisdom never raises them to heroic status. Because his success is foreordained, the hero needs no wisdom of his own; nor does he have Rustam's fearlessness born of self-confidence. The Islamized hero virtually floats along in bubble of divine favour that no earthly force can puncture. Wielding only the divine names, in the direst straights the greatest name, the hero in his invulnerability no longer reflects actual human experience. The greater the divine protection, Hanaway argues, the more room in the story for the fantastic. Hence, the more pervasive the element of the miraculous in a romance, the greater the influence of an Islamic world view. Following a parallel logic, Hanaway explains the heroic deterioration of the *ayyar* (folk hero) character from the fierce fighting companion of the earlier main figures to a type picaresque or even buffoon. As the heroic portrayal declines realism, so does that of the once credible sidekick.[28]

Association of Certain Heroes with Islam

Iskandar serves as perhaps the best example of a hero whose literary journey across the world from west to east found him serving to Islamize as he himself became more Islamic and to legitimate the royal claims of any king who could trace his lineage back to Iskandar. J. J. Ras discusses the role of Iskandar in the *Sejara Melayu* and the *Hikayat Bandjar*. He concludes that the authors introduced Iskandar not because of the desire to associate the Malay or Bandjarese kings with Alexander's glorious deeds as such, but 'rather as a consequence of the need to give the old, essentially pagan, myth of their origin a "decent", quasi-Islamic, tinge, so as to legalize it and thus make it fit to be carried over into the new era, which was culturally dominated by the newly imported faith'.[29]

It is most instructive to see which heroic characters different Muslim scholars are willing to identify as Islamic. Ismail Hamid does not so much as mention Hang Tuah – a hero many consider to epitomize Malay national spirit – in his Malayan perspective on *Arabic and Islamic Literary Traditions*. In his sections on 'Malay Hikayats of Muslim Heroes and Pious Men', Hamid includes along with Muhammad such diverse figures as Hamza, Iskandar, Sayf ibn Dhi Yazan and King Jumjumah (allegedly a pious Muslim and former ruler of Egypt and Syria).[30] Kassim bin Ahmad, on the other hand, devotes an entire short study to the story of Hang Tuah, which he calls a *sastera ke-pahlawanan* or heroic epic. Although Ahmad never mentions Islam, he notes that Hang Tuah regarded the sultan as 'God's shadow on earth', a standard Islamic epithet for the leader. Ahmad proceeds to challenge the traditional view that Hang Tuah is the quintessential Malay (and by association, perhaps also Muslim?) hero.[31]

Another Malay study likewise challenges the received wisdom about Hang Tuah, but from a very different point of view. Hang Tuah represents not a good loyal Muslim but the antithesis of Islamic humanitarian heroism. In the view of Shaharuddin bin Maaruf, a major problem in his society is precisely the endurance of the old feudal values he sees extolled in the epic *Hikayat Hang Tuah,* as well as in such other national classics as *Sejara Melayu.* Maaruf criticizes the tendency of contemporary Malay elite society to cling to the uncritical attitude that perpetuates the exploitative and inhumane mores embodied in the ancient texts. Hang Tuah's amoral loyalty to authority and Hang Jebat's unbridled violence are equally incompatible with Islam. As evidence of moral decadence, Maaruf cites several examples of wrongheaded interpretation of the heroes of classic literature.

Maaruf sees two trends in the literary criticism of the Malay elite. 'Feudal romanticism' has five characteristics. First, it recommends passivity on the part of the masses; they must not presume to judge their leaders. Second, it applauds and finds much amusement in the debased morals of many alleged heroes, and claims that Hang Tuah was in tune with the needs of the people – whereas he actually cared only for his position in the court. Third, the romantic view glorifies all action done in service of the ruler, regardless of its ethical quality. The hero's apparently endless capacity for action, including all manner of bloodshed, is what makes him truly admirable. A character is heroic to the degree that he has allowed the voice of authority to drown out that of conscience. Finally, the romanticizers portray the feudal hero as the epitome of the Malay spirit, as quintessentially Malay, and thus do a great disservice to Malays. The hero is unfortunately touted as a model of the good nationalist, but in reality those feudal values stand in the way of authentic development.

'Feudal Conservatism' on the other hand, does criticize the blind loyalty of the ancient heroes. It prefers to see Hang Jebat as the true hero, in opposition to Hang Tuah, for Hang Jebat exercised independent judgement in rebelling against authority. The problem here, in Maaruf's opinion, is that

> The Malays are deceived into thinking that they have broken away from the feudal thinking, whereas in reality they have only substituted one feudal personality for another. Such a misleading innovation prevents the Malays from making a total break from their feudal past and to genuinely adopt the Islamic and modern humanitarian trend of thinking, more in keeping with contemporary challenges.[32]

To those who would criticize him for inappropriately applying modern criteria to medieval feudalism and its most popular personalities, Maaruf replies that Islam was already the Malay creed in the 15th and 16th centuries. He is merely applying an old, but still vital, set of criteria against which one must judge both past and present Malay social values as seriously deficient. As examples of true Islamic humanitarian heroism, Maaruf proposes the second caliph of Islam, 'Umar ibn al-Khattab (d. 644), Philippines patriot and revolutionary José Rizal (1861–1986), and Indonesia's nationalist general Sudirman (1915–1950).[33] In the same vein, the evolving processes of Arabization and Islamization in the Swahili folk traditions of East Africa have been explored by Joseph Mbele – including the significant role of female characters.[34]

Heroes, Social Systems and Islamization

Two of the many relevant social issues one could identify are the incorporation of heroic values into formal religio-social organizations, and the situation of women within the heroic milieu. Both matters are far too complex to discuss in detail here; but since they represent pervasive issues across the length and breadth of the Muslim world, they deserve some attention.

A code of heroic conduct that came to be known in Persia as *jawanmardi* and in Arabic as *futuwwa* plays an important role in heroic literature and themes. The latter connotes a pre-Islamic ideal of heroic conduct that then developed into the 'chivalry' often identified with the horseman, who was in turn associated with heroic virtue. In time the notion lost its connection with horsemanship and became an exclusively religious term that characterized the spiritual charter of religious brotherhoods.[35] The heroic type known as the *ayyar*, a subset of the folk hero, embodied above all the code of 'young manliness' (*jawanmardi*). The growth of organizations that identified themselves with the values of that code, at least in name, is a complex phenomenon. Suffice it here to observe the connection between a certain type of heroic value system, not necessarily religious in inspiration, and later orientations that continued to look to heroic models such as 'Ali, who are of decidedly religious significance.[36]

Various theories have been advanced as to the relative fortunes of women before and after the coming of Islam. On the whole, it is impossible to make convincing generalizations as to how Islamization affects the lot of female characters in either literature or art across the Muslim world. It does seem that in general heroines enjoy loftier place and esteem in courtly or elite literature than in popular genres; but here, too, one needs to take sweeping characterizations with a grain of saffron. In the popular *Iskandarnama*, for example, one finds a thoroughly flippant and demeaning tone used toward women. In Nizami, on the other hand, women are much more noble and are treated as real human beings. Nizami's emphasis on Shirin's quiet, patient wisdom is parallelled, perhaps, by the portrayal of heroines in the Arabic *sira* literature as strong and brave. In the Antar and Hilal sagas, major female characters are warriors and earth-mother types.[37]

Women in Kazakh Turkic epics possess idealized qualities like those of the hero, only slightly less advanced. For the most part, women are portrayed as intelligent and high-minded, though some epics do evidence a decidedly disapproving attitude. Even where the hero makes disparaging remarks about his wife, and about womankind in general, however, the principal female figure reasserts herself. Her wisdom and quick wit turn potential defeat into victory, and may even shame the hero into apologizing humbly. Some female characters model self-sacrifice, as in the case of the abducted wife and the mother who plead with the hero not to risk rescuing them from the enemy. Womanly beauty occasions some lyrical descriptions, but romance remains secondary to the theme of the hero's skill in battle.[38]

There is no question but that the male element dominates the heroic literature and art of Islamdom – as indeed of the occidental world – in that the men occupy centre stage far more often than the women. However, a number of heroines are featured in ways that most readers would find quite surprising. One strong theme that may not be quite so apparent at first is that the women invariably function as links to the outside world, to the lands and peoples beyond those of the principal heroes. Whereas the heroes tend to relate to the outside in the capacity of conqueror, and to see the outside as antagonist, it falls to the major heroines to form and/or to bring to light the more positive connections between inside and outside worlds. Heroes nearly always marry or pair up with women from national, ethnic or even religious communities other than their own. Though they may do so initially as a way of taking possession of the outside world, the heroines frequently offer the hero the challenge of breaking down the psychic and cultural barriers that prompt him to envision the world as parcelled out. Thanks to heroines, unification does not always happen through conquest. One could explore a number of other aspects of this expansive topic – including, for example, the relative presence or absence of visual depictions of women in illustrated manuscripts of heroic narratives of all sorts, from the more evidently 'secular' to the most explicitly 'religious'.

*   *   *

Heroic themes are integral to the cultural patrimonies of Muslim societies from Morocco to Malaysia. Remarkable individuals represent in every age a high level of exemplary commitment, motivation and achievement. In spite of their often glaring human failings, these characters embody qualities always admirable and sometimes within reach of imitation. Whatever their eventual breadth of popularity, heroes and heroines are typically born in local or regional contexts, fire the imagination of a 'people', and spread with the speed of the means of communication of the time. Exemplary figures who come to enjoy trans-regional and even global celebrity among Muslim societies often exemplify a blend of characteristics considered laudable in a figure's original pre-Islamic context with 'religious' virtues explicitly identified as 'Islamic'. What one finds at work here, in sum, is a most intriguing blend of cultural and religious 'imaginaries'. Muslims have continued to derive inspiration from stories of hybridized heroes and heroines. Even Saddam Hussein, an avowed secularist hardly legendary for his religious fervour, was wont to seek a sympathetic connection with his Shi'i subjects by hinting that he represented the values of the proto-martyr Husayn, who also rode a white charger and fought injustice.[39] In Afghanistan during the 1980s, freedom fighters known as *mujahideen* were not themselves lauded especially for their own spiritual achievements, but modelled prominently the most laudable features of pre-Islamic folk heroes. Nonetheless, during their struggle to rid their land of the Russian army, these *mujahideen* were likened to 'Ali – they too wielded the twin-tipped sword, Dhu'l-Faqar, that Muhammad had bequeathed to his son-in-law.[40]

Finally, all healthy 'imaginaries' need to be sifted and culled. Historical criticism offers the essential correctives of aesthetic distance and ethical perspective. 'Islamization' has been part of that process. But Islamic heroes, too, must change with the times in ways that reflect a consciousness that they share a world animated by other cultural and religious imaginaries. It is especially important to bear in mind the complexity and subtlety of the transformations through which ancient heroic traits and values have been 'Islamized' and made their way into contemporary imaginative discourse. Far from losing their inherent 'personal' dynamism and motivational force through their appropriation by Muslims, these perennial heroic models function as a vehicle for integrating the deepest aspirations of a people's culture (such as those of many Afghans) with the ethical mandates of the people's 'adopted' religious tradition. In this respect, one can hope for more research like that of anthropologist David B. Edwards in his *Heroes of the*

4

An Andalusian Modernity
in Narratives of Women

Hasna Lebbady

In 'The Politics of Recognition' Charles Taylor cites Saul Bellow's alleged statement to the effect that, 'When the Zulus produce a Tolstoy we will read him.'[1] The Zulus, whose oral literature and performance 'have been important features of South African society since the development of the earliest human communities on the subcontinent',[2] here are used to denominate one aspect of 'the other' against which Westerners have habitually contrasted themselves in order to maintain an image of the self as superior. The other culture which has often served the ends of such binary logic is that of the Andalusians, known in the West as the Moors and referred to by Diderot at one point as 'the hideous Moor'.[3] It is from the culture of these Andalusians that the tradition of Moroccan women's tales on which I base myself in this chapter emanates. The contributions of this culture to planetary civilization have been undervalued by Westerners and Muslims alike – fed by the tendency of both the Muslim world and the West to construct the self in opposition to 'the other'. This is inconducive to what Gayatri Spivak has termed 'planetarity'.[4] Yet the tendency has only been exacerbated since September 11, 2001, as the Islamophobia sweeping the West has fuelled extremism in the Muslim world.

Andalusian civilization as fostered by an Arab–Muslim regime that flourished on European soil enabled Jews, Christians and Muslims to coexist harmoniously, reminding us today that these traditions share rather more than oppositional ways of thinking suggest. A case in point is the paradigm of the social imaginary, symbolizing the process of coming to terms with both individual and cultural identity – which figures at the core of the women's tale that I unveil here. This figuration includes the major elements associated with the social imaginary by such contemporary Western theorists as Charles Taylor, who has linked those elements with the idea of 'multiple modernities' in order 'to differentiate European culture from that of cultures which preceded it or which belong to other modernities'.[5] Indeed, the image at the centre of the tale below can be said to draw upon the ethics, pluralism and world-liness associated with modern social imaginaries that facilitate democratic politics. Yet the tradition of this tale harkens back to the Middle Ages when al-Andalus was at its prime, and to an art-form which, like that of the Zulus, not only preceded the work of Tolstoy by many centuries but arguably rendered it possible.

The Culture of al-Andalus

The tradition of this tale goes back to the courts of al-Andalus, where the women who originally began crafting such narratives came into contact with some of the foremost scholars and poets of the time. Andalusian thinkers were concerned with harmonizing different ways of knowing. This is what Ibn Rushd (1126–1189) was able to accomplish, for instance, by synthesizing a theological view of the world with that of philosophy, pursuant to his trans-lation of the Greek philosophers whose different forms of knowl-edge he had no difficulty in assimilating. According to María Rosa Menocal, the 'series of commentaries he wrote on these philoso-phers and their work, the major thrust of which was a defense of the philosophical study of religion as opposed to that of the theolo-gians, was disseminated throughout Europe with astonishing rapidity'.[6] The ideas of this pioneer of what was to become European secular humanism were absorbed even by those Europeans who at first viewed them with suspicion and disdain.

Such absorption of Andalusian culture took many centuries, as the courtly traditions and literary salons that characterized al-Andalus were to develop in Europe only much later with the emergence of the bourgeoisie and an industrially advanced society.

It was then, according to Jürgen Habermas, that 'the humanisti-
cally cultivated courtier replaced the Christian knight'.[7]
Intellectuals like Ibn Rushd formed part of the highly literate and
erudite component of Andalusian culture that contributed exten-
sively to the elitist *adab* in classical Arabic works on the nature
of love as *Tawq al hamama* by Ibn Hazm (994–1064), and such
predecessors of the novel form as *Hay ibn yaqzan* by Ibn Tufayl
(c.1109–1185), as well as the poetry of Wallada (1011–1091), the
Muslim woman writer who presided over a literary salon in
11th-century Europe.[8]

Unlike Wallada's poetry, which has been preserved in writing,
the tradition of women's tales forms part of the more popular
component of their culture that contributed to the European
courtly love tradition which, according to Roger Boase, 'was rooted
in a popular and anonymous oral tradition'.[9] These women's tales
are closely associated with the other oral and popular tradition
characterizing their culture – its Andalusian music – that developed both *Muwashah* and *Zajal* poetry. These distinctively
Andalusian poetic forms harmonize between the one in elite classical Arabic – the *Muwashah* – and in dialect – the *Zajal*. Even
within the *Muwashah* there is a *Kharja*, the refrain or final part
of the poem, which is often expressed in the dialect. Refrains that
resemble the *Kharja* can be found in a number of the women's
tales that I have collected, which would have been narrated by
some of the same women involved in Andalusian music, who were
trained in both vocal and instrumental music.[10] It is one of these
narratives which, even while forming part of a pre-modern tradition of women's storytelling, depicts a representation conforming
closely to that of the most recent Western conceptualizations of
the social imaginary.

The tale in question is one that I compiled from the accounts
by numerous women in Tetouan, in the north of Morocco, still
in many ways an Andalusian city. Some features in this tale suggest
socio-political set-ups akin to those that existed in al-Andalus and
later in Tetouan. For the women who told it originally, storytelling was not only a source of entertainment but also a means
of remembering and articulating their concerns about the trauma

of exile and their position as women trying to come to terms with their new circumstances. The idea of exile became inextricably woven into the tale, which forms part of the oral tradition, but can be seen as 'a communal experience [where] writing participates in the constitution of a community'.[11] Thus, rather than the '[r]ivalry between wives and concubines [which] meant that poison was "the active agent" in many stories of harem life',[12] what becomes evident here is the collaboration in the storytelling among the women trying to adapt to their new circumstances in light of their heritage.

From al-Andalus to Morocco

Between the end of the 15th century and the beginning of the 17th successive waves of Andalusian immigrants came to Morocco from Spain, settling in such northern towns as Fez, Sale, Chefchaouen and Tetouan. The migrants brought a culture characterized by the Moorish architecture that distinguishes many of the buildings in those *medinas*, the Andalusian music that survives to this day, and the tales they told. These were later arrivals than the Andalusian émigrés whom Abdellah Laroui describes as having introduced 'court etiquette, formalism and diplomacy'[13] to the various Maghrebi courts of the 14th century. The later Andalusian immigrants were forced into exile; those who settled in Tetouan, which they rebuilt from scratch, began arriving between 1483 and 1485.[14] They came initially from Nasrid Granada, the only Muslim kingdom to preserve its autonomy after the rest of al-Andalus was conquered by the kingdom of Castile in the early 13th century. During the next two centuries, Granada developed its own culture and art form, known as *Mudejar* – the name designating the Muslims who remained in the parts of Spain conquered by the Catholics. Numerous features of that Nasrid and *Mudejar* culture can be found in Tetouan where, significantly, much of it has been preserved by women. As Miége, Benaboud and Erzini point out, the style of dress of the *Mudejar* women of Granada is still evident in the large hats, short coats and gaiters of the *jbala* women in the countryside around Tetouan, as are certain features of Nasrid jewellery that still form part of Tetouani jewellery.[15] Similarly, designs of Nasrid and *Mudejar* embroidery can still be found in some traditional Tetouani embroidery, the only one in North Africa where those designs have been preserved.[16] It is not surprising then that such Andalusian women, who preserved so many other aspects of their culture, are the ones who have also safeguarded the tradition of women's tales, including the name used to refer to them.[17]

The importance granted women in such Moroccan societies as that of Tetouan is partly due to the legacy of al-Andalus, where women had been protected by generous legislation,[18] permitting many of them to work not only as midwives and wet nurses but also as calligraphers and teachers,[19] as well as to become writers and poets. The original *Mudejar* immigrants in Tetouan were eventually joined by the *Moriscos* – Muslims who had been forcefully baptized by the Inquisition after Granada was conquered by the Catholic kings in 1492, but secretly preserved their faith. Eventually they were forcefully, at times brutally,[20] expelled from Granada, Castile and Aragon,[21] in two major waves, first in 1566–1567 and again in 1609–1610.[22] Often the only belongings these migrants could bring to their new homes in Morocco were their songs and tales,[23] which had managed to survive the havoc wrought by the Inquisition precisely because they were oral and hence invisible. Together, these different waves of immigrants constituted the Andalusian component of Tetouani society, which also became its bourgeoisie. Like the women in al-Andalus, these women also became calligraphers, teachers, midwives and doctors. Some were famous for the *jbeera* they made to heal broken bones,[24] others had substantial wealth at their disposal enabling them to wield political power and endow charitable and religious causes.[25]

Moreover, the importance of these women was not limited to those who have been recognized by historians, such as as-Sit al-Hurra (The Free Lady) who ruled Tetouan from 1525 to 1542,[26] but included less well-known women, including the servants and the *jawari*.[27] As in al-Andalus, to be *jawari* was not necessarily to be looked down upon.[28] In some respects, these women were advantaged in ways not available to upper-class women.[29] What becomes evident is that both led more rewarding and versatile lives than the image of the harem-bound Muslim woman suggests. Both the upper-class women who wrote poetry and the *jawari*, who were expert musicians and took part in poetic gatherings contributing their own improvised verses to those of the professional male poets, formed part of an enduring and rich literary tradition created by Muslim women. This is the tradition that appears to have evolved into the tales to whom no specific author – or date – can be ascribed but which contain a wealth of information about the women who told them and constitute 'systems of signification by which we make sense of the past'.[30] They present fascinating insights into the concerns of those Muslim women who have left us few written documents about themselves but who reveal the specifically Andalusian feature of their identity through narratives that, though in the process of dying out, are still told in households of Moroccan *medinas*, as is the case of 'The Female Camel'.

The Female Camel[31]

The protagonist in this tale is a princess, the only child of a sultan, who kept her hidden behind seven *hijabs* or curtains in her lavishly furnished room. Although he saw to it that she had everything she needed, the princess fell ill and began to pine away, losing her vitality by the day. Very upset, the sultan tried all within his means to find her a cure. He summoned the best doctors in the realm, one by one, but none could cure her.

In that same *medina* lived an old woman who had heard about the princess's malady. Deciding to try her luck with the sultan, she set out one fine day for his palace, at the gate of which she was asked about her business and treated with much amusement by the guards when she explained her mission. However, on perceiving how resolved she was they consulted with each other and eventually sent to inform the sultan – who was at first annoyed but then realized that since his other efforts had failed it would not hurt to try the old woman. She was led to the princess's quarters and left at the entrance by the servants. Asking permission to enter she was told, with the esteem due her age, 'Lift the *hijab* and enter, dear aunt spinster.' The sultan's daughter kept repeating the phrase until the woman had lifted all seven *hijab*s. Finally she found herself face to face with the princess, her pale demeanour in marked contrast with her sumptuous surroundings. The woman began enquiring about what might ail the princess; she found that the girl had never ventured outside her father's court. When asked if she would like to do so, the girl became alive with excitement, but observed that her father would never allow such a thing. The old woman mulled this over and assured the girl that she had devised a plan.

The sultan was surprised to see the old woman return after only a short consultation with his daughter, and more so to hear she knew what ailed his daughter and how it could be cured. He immediately wished to learn what she proposed. It was simple, claimed the old woman: what his daughter needed was to visit a saint's shrine. The woman knew the exact one and was ready to accompany her there. It seemed such an obvious solution that the sultan wondered why he had not thought of it himself; so they agreed upon a proper time for the visit.

On the appointed day the old woman came for the princess, who was in a state of great excitement as they set out, hardly able to believe that she was finally outside. The woman took her for a long walk in the country. When they became tired, they sat down to rest next to a river. They had not been sitting there very long, gazing into the river, when they noticed a rock lifting itself up and a female camel emerging from under it. The camel was laden with dirty dishes which it brought into the river and said, 'Get down my little dishes, get cleaned with all the fishes.' At this the dishes descended from the camel's back and proceeded to cleanse themselves thoroughly in the river. Once they were spotlessly clean she instructed them, 'Get back my little dishes, you've fulfilled all my wishes.' At this the dishes piled themselves neatly on its back and the camel exited through the same opening from whence it had emerged.

Thrilled by the spectacle, the princess could contain her curiosity no longer and wished to follow the camel. So they trailed it through the narrow passageway under the rock to soon find themselves in an enchanting garden. What fountains there were, what exquisite flowers of every colour! The further they proceeded into the garden the more dazzled they were with its beauty. Finally they sat down to contemplate the magnificent scene before them. At this point, they saw two pigeons come flying from a distance. One dived into a fountain of milk and emerged as a handsome white prince. The other dived into a fountain of tar and emerged as his black servant. The two young men came forward and began talking to the visitors. Having discerned the relationship between them, the prince asked the servant to take the old woman away and kill her. Then he and the princess sat in the garden where they conversed to their hearts' content. When night fell the prince spread for her a bed of roses and covered her with narcissus once she had fallen asleep.

When the princess awoke the next morning, she found herself in a wilderness where there was not a soul. The only trace that remained from the previous night was the bed of roses and narcissus which the prince had spread for her, so she got up and started walking. She had on her nothing apart from her fine clothes and jewellery, which it occurred to her she should conceal. After walking for some time, she came upon a shepherd herding his sheep and goats. She asked for the skin of one of his goats in exchange for one of her bracelets; only too pleased to oblige, the shepherd promptly slaughtered a goat and skinned it. She covered herself with goat-skin and proceeded on her difficult journey in the wilderness. As she walked the princess kept repeating:

> I have neither the shelter of my father's house,
> Nor nourishment for my love and a future spouse;
> I would rather that my beloved had left me with kisses
> Than spread my bed with roses and cover me with narcissus.

After many days of walking, she came upon the sights and sounds of a distant *medina*. On approaching it she could see that the people were preparing for a big event. She stood at the town gate for some time before summoning the courage to enquire what was happening; it turned out that preparations were under way for the wedding of their prince. So she offered to help in exchange for room and board. Mistaking the princess for a poor goat-skinned girl, they allowed her into the *medina* to assist with the work. She spent some time serving them, when one day she had the opportunity to witness the prince whose wedding was imminent – only to discover he was the same prince she had encountered in the enchanted garden.

At this point the princess began to despair, as it was the prospect of finding him that had kept her going. Her position in the *medina* became more precarious than ever after the wedding. In her plight, she went into the palace garden and wandered from one flower bush to the next. The first one she visited was the rose bush with which she pleaded, 'I'm weary of this life; pray strangle me with your bough', whence the rose bush replied, 'I'm a rose and you're a rose; I can't make such a vow.' So the princess proceeded to the jasmine bush, which responded in like fashion. She visited all the flower bushes before arriving at the prickly bush, which had no compunction about sending one of its rough boughs around her neck and strangling her.

The prince, who happened to be passing by shortly after, saw her dangling from the bush and recognized her. He was so upset at her death that he too asked the bush to strangle him, which it did. Then his bride, who came searching for him, confronted the tragic spectacle of their dangling bodies. She too asked the bush to strangle her, dying by their side. All three were buried the same day in neighbouring graves. Eventually, a beautiful rose bush sprang on the princess's grave, while on that of the prince emerged a sweet smelling jasmine. On the third grave, however, there grew only a prickly bush. A nightingale perched on a tree overlooking the graves was often heard by the people of the *medina*, its song repeating, 'The lover's with his desired/ but prickly bush's not required.'

A Narrative of Female Identity

The very title 'The Female Camel' foregrounds the gender dimension of this Muslim tale. The camel – a more precious beast of burden than the donkey or mule in the north of Morocco, since one can also eat its flesh and use its wool – is still more valuable when it is female as it also provides milk. What's more, the camel in this tale is not depicted as carrying burdens across the desert, but appears on a lush riverbank bearing its burden of dirty dishes (specific to women), implying that the tale itself is about matters of particular concern to women.

That the tale relates the process involved in becoming a woman is suggested by the different stages that the princess traverses, which are essentially three. The first is where she is hidden behind the seven *hijab*s. The second is the episode when she is led outside by the old woman and witnesses the spectacle involving the female camel on the river bank. The final stage is where the princess is forced to take on the disguise of a goat-skinned woman, which culminates in her suicide. What makes the tale an archetypal narrative of subject formation is the way the three stages can be read as corresponding to Lacan's real, imaginary and symbolic orders that the child traverses in the process of individuation.[32] Further, this process is cast within a paradigmatically Muslim public sphere, which is depicted in terms of a social imaginary that closely resembles what modern Western theorists propose, even as it remains distinctively Arab.

The Real or the World behind the *Hijab*

The seven *hijab*s behind which the princess is hidden at the start conform to the original and literal meaning of *hijab* which, according to Fatima Mernissi, is three-dimensional:

> The first dimension is visual: to hide something from sight . . .
> The second dimension is spatial: to separate, to make a border, to establish a threshold. And finally the third dimension is ethical: it belongs to the realm of the forbidden.[33]

All three dimensions of the *hijab* are apparent in the tale, where they are viewed from a specifically female perspective. On the visual dimension, the *hijab* is not merely what conceals the princess from sight, but also what keeps her from the rest of the world that is revealed to her only in the imaginary phase. The spatial dimension, which takes on particular importance in the symbolic, is at this stage reminiscent of the 'curtain behind which the caliphs and kings sat to avoid the gaze of members of their court'.[34] Such a *hijab* is what defines the princess as belonging to royalty rather than the common world. This becomes significant in a tale that depicts an escape from numerous *hijab*s to partake in the trials of common womanhood.

The third dimension of the *hijab* situates it within Sufi discourse, which people like the sultan used to sanction their confinement of women, including their own daughters. By making use of such religious discourse to confine his daughter, the sultan imposes a veil of subjectivity that limits her view of both the reality around her and of her own self (that is, on her social as well as personal identity). To this extent, her experience behind the *hijab* represents the real order, within which the child has no means of coming to terms with reality as it actually is, especially when the child has not yet acquired the language that would enable her to do so. Such confinement is what leads to the princess's malady, which is both a psychosis and a riddle.

Only the old woman can solve this riddle since she is the only one positioned to 'see' what lies behind the *hijab*s and to 'transgress' the boundaries they represent, thus enabling the princess ultimately to come to terms with the reality that is her self, as revealed within the public sphere in which she finds herself. Significantly, this can only be done once they leave the privacy represented by the sultan's court and its various *hijab*s. As Habermas points out, 'Only in the light of the public sphere did that which existed become revealed; did everything become visible at all.'[35] The old woman is also able to capture what Mernissi calls the 'ethical dimension' of the *hijab*, when she deploys against him the same religious discourse that the sultan uses to sanction his daughter's confinement. Her wisdom resides in the fact that she perceives the ambivalence of the discourse as legitimating those in power and the site where it can be contested. By assuring the sultan that his daughter needs to visit a saint's shrine, she plays on the Sufi reverence of saints whose intervention one may seek in all manner of problems. Hence the old woman takes on the role of the midwife who delivers the princess from the womblike world behind the *hijabs*, and of the analyst who uncovers what's ailing her by enabling her to express her wishes, the satisfaction of which facilitates her passage into the next stage of her development.

The Imaginary or the Order of the Female Camel

Once outside, the princess and the old woman are in a world that is diametrically opposed to that behind the *hijabs*. This world, where the princess can use the visual capacity constrained by the *hijab*, is characterized by open spaces and a river at whose bank they sit.[36] The watery medium suggests the threshold of other-worldliness; yet it does not include such supernatural beings as jinns, often associated with water. Nor does it include saints or their shrines, thus appearing to delineate its more worldly character, even though this is integral in Islamic discourse to the sacred sphere. This world is similar to the one which Bakhtin describes as freeing its occupants 'completely from all mysticism and piety. They are also completely deprived of the character of magic and prayer.'[37] The river here further suggests that 'fluid middle ground between embodied practices and explicit doctrines', which Dilip Gaonkar associates with the nature of the modern social imaginary.[38] Indeed, it is in this world that our protagonists can view the spectacle of the female camel – emblematic of their identity – emerging from under a rock with its burden of dirty dishes that it brings to wash in the river.

Dishwashing is not something that the princess would have had to do herself anymore than it is what camels normally do. But it is what would have been performed routinely by many of the women in the audience, who would have derived vicarious pleasure from having the task effortlessly done by the camel. What would have been even more enchanting about the camel's performance is that by taking the dishes to be washed outside, it blurs the distinction between the domestic and public worlds, as it does that between the common servant and the princess, thus stressing the common lot of women. The blurring of private and public spheres seems to anticipate the process Habermas associates with the modern development of civil society, which is characterized by the emergence in the public sphere of activities that were relegated to the household economy.[39] However, while dissolving the distinction between those worlds, this phase emphasizes the dimension of cyclical time. The emergence of the camel is a spectacle of special interest to the audience, its festive nature 'always essentially related to time, either to the recurrence of an event in the natural (cosmic) cycle, or to biological or historical timeliness'.[40] The association with cyclical time is further prompted by the act of dishwashing, which alludes to washing in ritual ablutions performed by women at specific phases in their lives, for example after menstruation or childbirth. Ablutions mark the end of one phase and the beginning of another, reinforcing an idea of time in which this whole episode is itself a phase.

The phase it represents becomes apparent when one considers that the river is what both the old woman and the princess are gazing into when the camel appears. Having enabled the princess to elude her confinement and acquire a vision of the world, isn't the old woman allowing her a perspective of another kind? Isn't the river the archetypal mirror into which the princess gazes to obtain an image of her own self? And is this not what she perceives in the form of the female camel that emerges to confront her? The phase suggested here conforms to Lacan's mirror stage, as the camel is both recognition and misrecognition – 'méconnaissance' – of the self, which is why it is imaginary.[41] In the tale the perceived image is even more illusory than the one suggested by Lacan, since it reflects not only the princess and the old woman but also all the women in the audience. This collective image they perceive, which constitutes the central trope of their identity, further suggests degradation in the status of the princess: 'that is, the lowering of all that is high, spiritual, ideal, and abstract, to the sphere of earth and body in their indissoluble unity'.[42] This is evident when one considers that the princess, like the camel, is a more dignified being in becoming burdened with the concerns of a common servant. It enables her to empathize with the comprehensive vision of womanhood she perceives, just as it enables the women in the audience to empathize with her. Hence, the tale conforms to Bakhtin's theory of narrative as an 'attempt to transform the relationship between performer and crowd in dialogic rituals so that spectators acquire the active role of participants in collective processes which are sometimes cathartic and which may symbolize or even create a community'.[43]

The dialogic relation between performer and crowd in this phase is reminiscent also of Taylor's contention that human identity is created dialogically.[44] By enabling such identification between the spectators and the protagonist – a public 'relation between strangers'[45] – this stage is akin to a social imaginary through whose 'collective agency a society is created, given coherence and identity, and also subjected to auto-alterations, both mundane and radical, within historical time'.[46] This is the phase that signals the protagonist's profound identification with all that is around her, notably with the community of women involved in the storytelling, who belong to 'a monumental temporality, without cleavage or escape, which has so little to do with linear time'.[47] The satisfaction she derives from the fact that she is at one with all that's around her, and forms an integral part of the community of women, explains why both the princess and the old woman are eager to trail the camel's footsteps and enter the next phase.

The Symbolic or the Order of the Cultivated Garden

When the princess and the old woman succeed in trailing the camel through the narrow passageway under the rock, they find themselves in an enchanted garden. This process recalls the Qur'anic *aya* which holds that only when the camel is capable of passing through the eye of the needle will it be possible for those who 'reject our Signs and treat them with arrogance ... to enter the Garden' (7:40). These two women are evidently not among those who disregard the signs. Their ability to perform the difficult task of following the camel through the needle's eye, as it were, confirms their ethical integrity and the genuineness of their faith. This moral emphasis serves to further associate their social imaginary with the modern version as conceived by Taylor and others, wherein the social imaginary encodes *normative* expectations.

That the garden in which they find themselves depends on the interpretation of signs suggests that it is *the* symbolic order. Unlike the world depicted in the previous phase, the one in which they now find themselves is not a natural space with a river, but a highly cultivated garden with fountains. The interpretation of signs is foregrounded by the arrival of the two pigeons that dive into fountains of milk and of tar, to emerge as a white prince and his black servant. The fountains represent more socially constructed types of mirrors than the river in the previous stage. Rather than just enabling the pigeons to obtain a view of their selves in reflection, these mirrors entirely reconstruct them into young men in accord with norms that conform to unfair dictates of power. It is their difference that is stressed as this is essential to signification. This order reveals itself to be 'the social contract [which,] far from being that of equal men, is based on an essentially sacrificial relationship of separation and articulation of differences which in this way produces communicable meaning'.[48]

Whereas the previous stage – representative of the women's social imaginary – stressed the sense of wholeness and feeling at one with nature, this stage – representative of the male symbolic – becomes characterized from the beginning by difference and separation. It consists of two fountains that produce two differently positioned social beings, where the powerlessness of the servant highlights the power of the prince. Both are revealed to be signifiers. The prince is 'le signifiant privilégié'[49] who takes control when he orders the death of the old woman and then seduces the princess. The old woman's death indicates the extent to which the symbolic is fraught with danger for women. Its significance is evident when one considers that she is the mother figure who must be excluded from the symbolic, which comes under the law of the father.[50] Within this male order, the notion of subjectivity is less communal than in that which previously united the women. By killing the old woman the prince separates the two women, depriving the princess of the communal sense of identity she had attained in the imaginary phase and facilitating her seduction. That she is now within the symbolic, or the order of language, is further confirmed by how she and the prince talk, and talk. This is what seduces her and transforms her, not only into a subject but into one subjected to that order. Within this order the princess becomes constructed into an image of femininity that, significantly, involves a loss of her original identity.

The idea of loss becomes apparent when she wakes to find that the enchanted garden has disappeared and she is alone in a wilderness where all that remains of the previous night is the bed of roses and narcissus. The symbolic significance of that bed would not have been lost on the adults in the audience, who would have grasped the fact that the princess had been deflowered. This becomes a good index of the extent to which 'sex is . . . a symbolic arrangement structured like language'.[51] It is at this stage that her identity is split, just as the world in which she finds herself becomes radically transformed from the beautifully cultivated garden into the wilderness. Here she feels obliged to adopt a mask, which marks her as a subject 'divided by the effects of language'.[52] Her entry into the symbolic constitutes her not so much as an entity with a unified sense of identity, but as a being split between two different versions of femininity: the idealized princess who is pure and virginal, and the goat-woman suggestive of animal lust and a more demonic version of femininity.

This division, however, is not what leads immediately to her death. She kills herself only much later, after travelling for some time and arriving at the 'other' *medina*. Only after she discovers the prince and he gets married does she decide to commit suicide. What we have is not just another version of the archetypal myth of the fall, but also an original Muslim version of the tradition of courtly love, which places women far more at the centre than the one that developed in Europe around the figure of the feudal knight. The erotic dimension is not missing as it is in some of the European versions where the knight idealizes a lady, often another man's wife, in a kind of Platonic relationship. The quest in this version is for legitimate sexual fulfilment, which prompts the protagonist to search for the prince and the prospect of a duly sanctioned relationship with him. What is especially interesting is that the courtly lover here – the equivalent of the Christian knight – is a Muslim woman.

This narrative, which is a real tragedy, is also a cautionary tale. The protagonist is a royal who has been degraded and drawn to a death that would have invoked the audience's pity and their terror, especially as she is propelled by forces essentially beyond her control and related to her being female. The women in the audience would have recognized similar possibilities of error in their own lesser selves, making the tragedy cathartic. Yet the tale does not end on a deathly note. After they all perish, the nightingale arrives to eulogize their love. By suggesting Ziryáb himself, the great musician who is said to have initiated Andalusian music and whose name meant blackbird, the nightingale serves to reinforce the link between Andalusian musicians and storytellers. The tale ends on a note of narrativity that continues after the death of all the main actors and is prompted by it, thus suggesting that it is a form of history.

The sense of history is further stressed by the temporal dimension that characterizes this phase, which is not the cyclical time of the imaginary phase but 'time as project, teleology, linear and prospective unfolding; time as departure, progression and arrival – in other words, the time of history'.[53] This notion of time recalls that during which the princess set out on her journey, a form of migration. A subtext is evident when one considers that by assuming the guise of a goat-woman the protagonist is shown to have been deprived of her 'origins' and taken on an 'acquired identity' that is less desirable. This looks very much like a Moriscan strategy where the original and ideal identity – associated with the true faith – must be repressed as a mode of survival due to circumstances that have forced on her a less desirable identity, which is why she dies.

It is her insertion into historical time that leads to her death, since such a temporality implies the idea of both a beginning and an end. It 'renders explicit a rupture, and expectation, or an anguish which other temporalities work to conceal. It might also be added that this linear time is that of language considered as the enunciation of sentences . . . and that this time rests on its own stumbling block, which is also the stumbling block of that enunciation – death'.[54] Her entrance into the temporal linearity of historical time and the '[a]wareness of being imbedded in secular serial time, with all its implications of continuity, yet of "forgetting" the experience of this continuity . . . engenders the need for a narrative of "identity"',[55] which is what the tale provides. By ending on the note of narrativity, it calls attention to itself and the 'imagined community' of women involved in its telling. Those are the women who, unlike the princess, were able to acquire the double vision that comes with reconciling the different identities imposed on them, thus letting them inhabit multiple women's time – both cyclical time and the linear time of history – and achieve 'the demassification of the problematic of *difference*'.[56]

Like present-day postcolonial and feminist theorists, the women involved in telling the tale were seeking 'to redefine the symbolic process through which the social imaginary – nation, culture or community – becomes the subject of discourse and the object of psychic identification'.[57] Although their position as women within the male symbolic was also fraught with danger, they could articulate themselves in ways not accessible to the princess – they could both express the kind of dilemma she faced and also survive it – thus keeping the spirit of the past alive through their ability to transform the symbolic to their own ends. By contributing to the tradition of this tale, which is neither a Zulu masterpiece nor one that can be attributed to a Tolstoy but contains elements of both their art forms, such artists remind us of the extent to which their culture synthesized the genius of the past and was also a forerunner of so much now considered to be exclusively Western.

Those Andalusians occupied the Iberian Peninsula for some 800 years during the Middle Ages, yet their extensive impact on European civilization has been greatly undermined, when not entirely overlooked by Europeans. Castoriadis, for instance, contends that the kind of autonomy which came about through 'society's process of self-instituting and self-understanding' happened only twice in human history, 'first in the Greek city-states and later in Western Europe at the end of the Middle Ages'.[58] This is typical of how European social and literary historians have tended to construct what Menocal calls 'The Myth of Westernness'[59] by, among other methods, skipping over the millennium when European culture was dominated by the Andalusians. Yet what they accomplished says much about pluralism not only among Muslims, Jews and Christians but also among modes of knowing, including theology, science and philosophy. The religious domain did not exclude matters such as sexuality that Westerners consigned to a separate space. Islam provided for sexual fulfilment for women as well as for men; Christianity had to be segregated from a secular domain where such fulfilment could be achieved.

Within the Andalusian context there was no discrepancy between being a theologian and writing a masterpiece on erotic love; a case in point was the *Tawq al hamama,* known in English as *The Ring of the Dove*, by Ibn Hazm. Similarly, the women involved in 'The Female Camel', greatly endowed with the spirit of such Andalusians, could present us with the poignant image of a Muslim woman caught in the tragic dilemma of not knowing how to reconcile the women's social imaginary with the demands of a predominantly male social contract, which they rendered with a dramatic vitality not easily surpassed by an art form whose modernity is simply a matter of its literacy or conformity to the norms of print culture.

The accomplishments of such Andalusians remain under-appreciated not only by Westerners but also by Arabs and Muslims themselves, who have tended to neglect the popular side (to which 'The Female Camel' belongs) as well as the more canonical works. Thus even Ibn Rushd's genius in harmonizing artistic, philosophical and religious discourses fails to receive its due. As for the popular and oral Andalusian tradition, for which the vernacular form of Arabic was used from the outset, this has hardly been considered for a position in the canon. Yet it is this tradition that actually contributed to the use of the vernacular in serious European literature, like that of Dante.[60] Ironically, the process that occurred in

5

Civil Sounds: The Aga Khan
Music Initiative in Central Asia

Theodore Levin and Fairouz R. Nishanova

On a crisp autumn night in 2004, a sold-out London Coliseum, home of the English National Opera, reverberated with the thrum of Central Asian lutes, jangling of tambourines and plangent timbres of powerful voices that initiated the elegant concert hall's largely neophyte audience into a musical world all but unknown in the West. The 2,364-seat Coliseum, one of London's largest and best-equipped theatres, may seem like an unlikely venue for a performance of traditional folk and classical music from the 'stans' – Afghanistan, Kazakhstan, Kyrgyzstan, Tajikistan and Uzbekistan, as well as Azerbaijan, Central Asia's neighbour to the west, across the Caspian Sea. Yet the choice of the Coliseum was part of a deliberate and mutually advantageous strategy on the part of the event's co-producers, the English National Opera and the Aga Khan Music Initiative in Central Asia. For the Opera, presenting a carefully curated programme of voice-centric music from beyond the West held the promise of broadening the company's audience base. For the Music Initiative, the Coliseum concert offered an opportunity not only to acquaint listeners in Britain with the rich and diverse traditions of Central Asia, but also, by presenting some of the region's finest musicians in a prestigious European performance venue, to promote respect for the musicians and traditions they represent within Central Asia itself. This 'mirroring' strategy was used to great effect in the 1950s and 1960s by the pioneering Indian music specialist and orientalist Alain Danielou to promote interest in Indian classical music on the subcontinent. These days, it serves a key role in the long-term programme of the Aga Khan Music Initiative to help local musicians in Central Asia address one of the principal artistic challenges of our time: how to nourish global connections while retaining a link to art rooted in a sense of place and tradition.

Music may seem an unlikely domain for an international development organisation whose aim is to 'realise the social conscience of Islam through institutional action', as the Aga Khan Development Network (AKDN) describes its mandate. But the rich musical heritage of Central Asia, a region where the impact of Islam as a spiritual and cultural force has been sustained over thirteen centuries of dramatic political, social and demographic change, indeed offers fertile ground for institutional action through a specialised form of cultural advocacy, or 'cultural development' work. Music and the training of young musicians have long served social groups in Central Asia as a means of preserving and transmitting beliefs, practices and moral values that contribute to the construction of social identities on levels ranging from local to regional and national and in so doing, assuring and re-affirming links between past and present. These links, however, are anything but straightforward. Present-day political boundaries that define the nations of Central Asia are largely incongruent with cultural boundaries shaped by centuries of migration, rivalry and intermingling among the region's social groups. As a consequence, the efforts of post-Soviet Central Asian nations to provide their citizenry with a coherent cultural history often resemble a kind of historicism and for many residents of the region, the relationship between cultural identity and citizenship remains vexed. By contrast, it is local cultural heritage – the traditions of a particular city, province, autonomous region, or even of a clan or family lineage – that typically resonates most strongly with Central Asians.

This chapter describes how the AKDN, through the Aga Khan Music Initiative in Central Asia, has used the rubric of 'development' to help musicians, music educators and grassroots cultural strategists to recast Central Asian musical traditions in contemporary forms and contexts rooted in local cultural heritage. Such recasting has used a variety of approaches: encouraging innovation within traditional performance styles, revitalising musical genres and musical instruments that have fallen into a state of desuetude, rethinking music education and building networks that integrate music and musicians from Central Asia into the global music marketplace. More broadly, the Music Initiative's mission focuses on the role that revitalisation of cultural heritage can play in the contemporary development of states that embrace a dynamic cultural and intellectual pluralism. In all of its interventions, a principal issue for the Music Initiative is how to facilitate the reimagination of traditional musical culture within a cosmopolitan and pluralistic Central Asian modernity shaped by multiple social, economic and cultural forces. At the same time, Central Asian modernity – cultural or otherwise – cannot be seen as somehow autonomous from other modernities, post-Soviet or Western. Rather, these alternative modernities overlap in the expression of musical traditions and identities, even as indigenous voices strive to be heard amid the clamour of hegemonial ones that often purport to be exclusively modern.

The Rupture of Tradition

Central Asia is commonly understood to encompass the territory of six nations: Afghanistan, Kazakhstan, Kyrgyzstan, Tajikistan, Turkmenistan and Uzbekistan. All except Afghanistan became part of the Soviet Union in the years following the Bolshevik Revolution of 1917, and through the 1920s and 1930s, underwent radical social transformations that ruptured many aspects of traditional culture. In the formative decades of the Soviet Union, the incompatibility of tradition and modernity was taken as axiomatic by political and cultural leaders and expressed in the form of a national cultural development strategy that mandated a 'battle against the past' as a necessary precondition for the establishment of socialist culture. In Central Asia as well as other regions of the USSR whose indigenous populations were predominantly non-Slavic, culture policies contributed to this battle in four principal ways: by combating the legacy of feudalism, enforcing a policy of atheism, reifying officially sanctioned national identities and nurturing cultural evolution among peoples who, in the Eurocentric Marxist-Leninist view, lagged behind European Russia's high level of cultural development. 'Nationalist in form, Socialist in content' was the slogan that set the course for artistic work in the fifteen Soviet republics and dozens of subordinate political entities – autonomous republics, autonomous regions, provinces, territories – where Soviet cultural strategists forged distinct ethnolinguistic identities in literature, art and music.

In Central Asia, where music has traditionally served not only as a marker of social identity but as a means of preserving spiritual practices and beliefs as well as transmitting history, philosophy and ethics, the effect of Soviet interventions in musical life was felt particularly strongly. Beginning in the early 1930s, Soviet cultural strategists launched a large-scale movement to modernise indigenous Central Asian music according to the conventions of European classical music. At the same time, Soviet nationalities policies divided Central Asia into a number of distinct nationalities based on an ethnolinguistic consciousness that was fundamentally alien to indigenous concepts of group identity. Music, like language, literature, folklore, plastic arts, film and theatre, became a vessel for realising the practical goals of nationalities policies. Stalin had defined a nation as 'a historically evolved, stable community of language, territory, economic life and psychological make-up (national consciousness) manifested in a community of culture,' and it was this definition that Soviet nationalities were meant to satisfy. Stalin's definition had no place for the fluid and imagined boundaries, hybridity and contested identities, de-territorialisation and re-territorialisation that figure so prominently in the culture theories of postmodern social science.

From the many fragmented strands of group identity that existed among Central Asian peoples, the Soviet government created five distinct nationalities, each with its own prescribed ethnic identity, territorial boundaries, language and cultural history: Uzbek, Tajik, Turkmen, Kazakh and Kyrgyz. In addition, a few ethnic minorities, such as the Qaraqalpaks, Uighurs and Dungans, were given various degrees of autonomy ranging from an autonomous territorial area (Qaraqalpak Autonomous Soviet Socialist Republic, comprising one-third of the area of Uzbekistan), to the authorisation of separate schools and cultural establishments.

Soviet culture and nationalities policies resulted in the loss, rupture or transformation of much of Central Asia's traditional heritage. Orally transmitted classical repertories that had for centuries flourished under the patronage of the Central Asian nobility were subject to particularly strong condemnation because of their association with the cultural elite and with Islamic spirituality. To supersede the small ensembles that performed this traditional classical court music, the Soviet Ministries of Culture created folk orchestras and consorts of Europeanised instruments that used Western-style notation. Ministries of Culture in many countries subsequently adopted the Soviet model of professionalised folklore as a solution to the untidy problem of representing 'national' artistic traditions both to outsiders and to their own populace.

The folk orchestra movement did not disappear with the break-up of the Soviet Union in 1991. On the contrary, it has remained strong, even as leaders in the fields of education, culture and the arts in the newly independent nations of Central Asia express support for the preservation and revitalisation of older forms of indigenous traditional culture. The reason for this anomaly is twofold. First, Soviet models of cultural development have not been broadly challenged by a comprehensive vision for the support of traditional culture on its own terms. Second, the financial resources that would give impetus to such an alternative vision have not materialised. With the exception of Kazakhstan, government patronage of the arts has been minuscule compared to funding levels during the Soviet era. Meanwhile, international NGOs active in Central Asia have provided only modest funding for arts and culture, often in the form of one-time, short-term grants that have led to unrealistic expectations of achieving long-term sustainability and in the end, proved counterproductive. The Aga Khan Music Initiative has helped fill that void and has used the prerogatives of patronage to shift Central Asia's growing interest in cultural heritage away from the Soviet legacy of folk orchestras and Europeanised instruments towards forms of traditional music that are at once rooted in older performance styles and receptive to innovation.

The Aga Khan Music Initiative in Central Asia

In 2000, His Highness the Aga Khan, founder and chairman of the Aga Khan Development Network (AKDN), created the Music Initiative as an integral facet of the Network – which brings together a number of development agencies, institutions and programmes that focus on health, education, culture, rural development, institution-building and the promotion of economic development, primarily in the poorest parts of Asia and Africa. The Music Initiative is one of the newest programmes of the Aga Khan Trust for Culture, the lead agency within the AKDN dedicated to the identification, study and enhancement of the cultural assets and heritage of countries in which Muslims have a significant presence. The schematic chart below illustrates the organisation of the Aga Khan Development Network and highlights the major role of culture as an element of the AKDN's overall development strategy. Programmes focusing on culture and education are grouped together within the Aga Khan Trust for Culture. They include, in addition to the Music Initiative, the Aga Khan Historic Cities Programme, the Aga Khan Award for Architecture, the Aga Khan Museums Unit, the Aga Khan Program for Islamic Architecture at Harvard University and the Massachusetts Institute of Technology and ArchNet.org, an online resource focusing on architecture, urban design, urban development and related issues in the Muslim world.

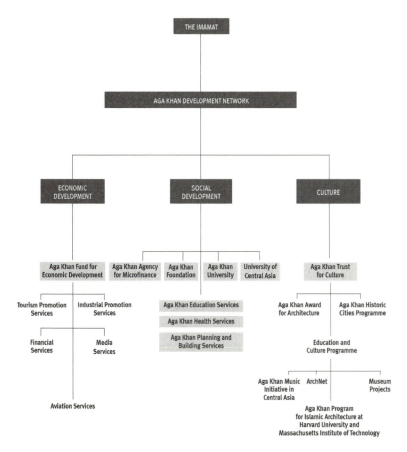

Institutions of the Aga Khan Development Network

Musical Tradition and Cultural Pluralism

The Music Initiative's programmes and development goals represent an understanding of musical tradition antipodal to that of Soviet cultural strategists, who viewed the forces of tradition and modernity as incompatible and irreconcilable opposites. A more enlightened view of tradition arises from the premise that culture evolves through a combination of continuity and change and that traditional arts can thrive in pluralist, post-traditional societies. In the arts, living traditions are invariably receptive to innovation, while modernism devoid of reference to tradition, if such is even possible, can become a profoundly alienating force in society. The defining feature of tradition in the context of pluralist modernity is that an individual's embrace of transmitted practices or beliefs ought to represent a choice, not a necessity beholden to lineage, caste, religion, ethnicity or other inherited social markers. More specifically, in the domain of art, tradition as a system of transmitted formal and stylistic constraints ought to become simply one among many possible sources for creativity and imagination.

Nothing in the creative process of working within transmitted artistic styles and forms renders the products of such work inherently anti-cosmopolitan or anti-pluralist. For traditional musicians, for example, musical creativity may assume the form not of the personal artistic statement or 'rugged individualism' venerated in Western modernism and postmodernism, but of outstanding craft, refined technique or luminous spirituality. These qualities, no less than formal or stylistic innovation, may elevate, edify and inspire listeners and contribute to the cultivation of social tolerance, empathy and inclusiveness. Moreover, innovation may be understood from multiple perspectives and, in the experience of the Music Initiative, has played a central role in the revitalisation of traditional music. Indeed, 'innovation in tradition' through a reconsideration of musical form, technique and performance style is a core concept in the Music Initiative's efforts to stimulate the revitalisation of intangible cultural heritage.

Revitalising Musical Tradition

The Aga Khan Music Initiative pursues its goals by investing in three principal programme areas: Supporting Tradition-Bearers, Documentation and Dissemination and International Music Touring. Each of these programmes is described below.

Supporting Tradition-Bearers

'Supporting Tradition-Bearers' addresses the Music Initiative's core mission: helping assure the transmission of musical skills, knowledge and experience from one generation to the next and raising the prestige of traditional music and musicians in Central Asia. The launch of 'Supporting Tradition-Bearers' came at a critical moment for Central Asian music when, demoralised by economic hardship, governmental neglect and lack of interest and recognition from the public, many traditional musicians had abandoned their careers as performers and teachers. The Music Initiative identified musicians – *ustâds* or masters – committed to the survival of their cultural heritage who were not only consummate performers and talented educators, but also demonstrated innovation and entrepreneurship in their approach to sustaining musical traditions. Formally inaugurated in 2003, the Tradition-Bearers programme presently funds projects in Afghanistan, Kazakhstan, Kyrgyzstan and Tajikistan. Small grants have been awarded as well to projects in Uzbekistan. Master-musicians work both in self-initiated music centres and schools and within guild-like networks that encourage collegiality and communication among independent master teachers. These organisations accomplish their mission by developing new materials and methodologies for teaching traditional music, involving students in ethnographic documentation of local traditions, establishing workshops for building high-quality musical instruments and building appreciation of authentic traditional music among audiences in Central Asia. The map overleaf illustrates the geographic distribution of the centres.

Pedagogic methods of the centres extend along a continuum that ranges from intensive training of an elite group of advanced performers to cultivating future audiences by teaching the elementary grammar of traditional music. Differences in the age range of students, the focus of the curriculum and the educational goals of each centre reflect the different ways in which they have implemented the Music Initiative's mission to preserve and reanimate traditional music and assure its transmission to the next generation of performers and audiences. To date, some 2,500 students and master musicians have directly benefited from the Tradition-Bearers Programme through support of *ustâd-shâgird* centres and teacher training seminars. The Programme's considerable visibility

| Music Initiative | Supporting Tradition-Bearers Programme |

Aga Khan Music Initiative
Tradition-Bearers Programme
Ustâd-Shâgird Schools, Central Asia

Kazakhstan
Pavlodar
Astana
Aktobe
Taldy-Kurgan
Qyzylorda
Almaty
Taraz

Kyrgyzstan
Bishkek
Issyq-Kul
Talas
Naryn
Jalalabad
Osh

Tajikistan
Kanibadam
Khojend
Khorog
Isfara
Istaravshan
Pendjikent
Dushanbe

Afghanistan
Kabul
Herat

■ Existing centres, 2003-2006
● Expansion, 2007

in Central Asia stems not from its size, which is modest, but from the effective model it offers of how to preserve and further develop intangible cultural heritage in the conditions of a free cultural marketplace.

Sustaining traditions by supporting tradition-bearers involves far more than aiding individual musicians. The vitality of any musical tradition is closely linked to the broader social and economic context in which it exists. Talented performers need to feel appreciated and connected to a community of listeners among whom the profession of musician is imbued with some hope of economic viability. Reanimating musical traditions that have suffered rupture, repression or censorship requires a comprehensive approach to cultural advocacy. Issues that ought to be addressed both locally and globally include:

- Training and pedagogy: assuring the quality of teachers and curricular materials and providing democratic access to educational opportunities for students.
- Taste and aesthetics: encouraging appreciation for a tradition's highest achievements.
- Mediation and commerce: developing distribution networks for audio and video recordings.
- Cultural self-identity and hybridity: advocating for music rooted in a sense of place while helping musicians develop worldwide connections with other musical traditions.

Each of the Tradition-Bearers programmes works towards these goals in ways that reflect its particular educational mission, as well as its demographic and social context. Brief descriptions of the Tradition-Bearers centres are provided below.

1. Afghanistan

Ustâd-Shâgird *Music Training Programme in Kabul and Herat*

Launched in late 2003, the *Ustâd-Shâgird* Music Training Scheme is the most recent addition to the Tradition-Bearers Programme. Its activities demonstrate the priority that the Music Initiative has given to forging links between intangible and tangible cultural heritage. In Kabul, the main focus of activities is the spiritual and physical revival of Kucheh Kharabat, the musician's quarter in Kabul's old city that long served as a centre for the teaching and performance of Kabuli art music. Depleted in the late 1970s as well as during the Coalition Period, when musicians fled Afghanistan (mostly for Peshawar and Quetta), Kucheh Kharabat was physically destroyed during the rule of the Taliban.

Today, many master musicians are returning to Afghanistan; six of them have been engaged by the Music Initiative and are now based at its centre in the Kabul premises of the Aga Khan

Trust for Culture, itself actively involved in a wide range of conservation activities. In 2006, another group of *ustâds* began teaching students in Herat, the principal city of western Afghanistan. Each *ustâd* has a minimum of ten students to whom he provides two-hour group instruction four times a week. All students are selected on the basis of merit. While the initial group of students was all-male, efforts are being made to recruit female students. Music-making by and for women is an old tradition in Afghanistan, while the inclusion of female musicians in a predominantly male music school represents an innovation that is just beginning to gain traction.

2. Kazakhstan

Kökil Music College in Almaty

In Almaty, Abdulhamit Raimbergenov, founder and director of Kökil Music College, is working to expand his innovative approach to teaching Kazakh traditional music to children through the *Murager* (Heritage) Programme that he conceived and developed. Students participating in the programme are not specially selected for musical talent and most do not intend to become professional musicians. Instead, Raimbergenov's goal is to build educated audiences for the next generation of traditional musicians under the assumption that their music will not survive unless it is performed within a social milieu that supports it. Initially sceptical Ministries of Education and Culture officially recognised and declared support for the programme in 2004 and earmarked funds to develop *Murager* as an experimental programme for secondary schools nationwide. 'Parents and teachers are demanding more classes', said Abdulhamit Raimbergenov recently. 'The average number of students in a class is twenty-five to thirty, but the more students in a class, the better the results seem to be'. Future development of *Murager* will include an elite training section for musically talented students who hope to become professional performers.

Turan Centre in Qyzylorda

Renowned epic performer and scholar Almas Almatov founded the Turan Centre in 1998 as an outgrowth of his work in the Department of Traditional Epic Singing at Qyzylorda University. Almatov's work has focused on collecting, archiving and transmitting onward the epic traditions of central Kazakhstan to the next generation of elite performers. To date, Almatov has gathered material from some 300 epic performers. Almatov's students are trained both as performers of epic poetry and as researchers. Research activities include conserving and digitising archival recordings, performing sound restoration work and electronically transcribing epic texts from handwritten notebooks kept by performers. Almatov's future plans include the publication of critical editions of epic texts and the production of recordings of epic singers for local listeners and for students at universities throughout Kazakhstan.

3. Kyrgyzstan

Centre Ustat-Shakirt in Bishkek, Kochkor, Issyq-Qul and Jalalabad

Ustat-Shakirt is unique among the Tradition-Bearer programmes in that its core teachers and students are geographically dispersed rather than concentrated in a single community. Following a traditional model, students travel to their teacher's domicile and become members of his household, living, practising and helping with chores. At present, the centre's roster includes five teachers and thirty students who are studying *komuz* (three-stringed lute), *qyl-qiyak* (bowl fiddle) and wind instruments (*choor, chopo choor, sybyzgy*). Students, many of them from families of modest means, receive a stipend of 200 *som* (five dollars) per month. The Centre has also equipped a musical instrument workshop where master luthiers build instruments and train apprentices in the crafting of high-quality traditional instruments.

Teachers affiliated with the Centre Ustat-Shakirt have been particularly active in the Music Initiative's Touring Programme.

Abduvali Abdurashidov (foreground, seated), director of the Academy of Maqam in Dushanbe, Tajikistan, with the Academy's eight graduate students.

Afghan *rubab* player Homayun Sakhi is frequently featured in the Music Initiative's International Touring Programme.

Young students at the Music Initiative-sponsored Centre Ustat-Shakirt in Bishkek, Kyrgyzstan.

Soheba Davlatshoeva, leader of the Badakhshan Ensemble, featured on Vol. 5 of *Music of Central Asia,* a 10-volume CD-DVD anthology of Central Asian musical traditions.

The pride and artistic stimulation that result from presenting their traditions to an international audience are reflected in the enthusiasm with which these teachers have embraced their pedagogic work. The Music Initiative regularly invites advanced students to participate in concert tours and such participation provides an added incentive to excel.

4. Tajikistan

Academy of Maqâm in Dushanbe

The Academy of Maqâm was founded in 2003 by Abduvali Abdurashidov, a leading music scholar and celebrated performer of Tajik-Uzbek classical music (*Shashmaqâm*). The Academy offers comprehensive training to highly qualified students in historical, theoretical and practical elements of *Shashmaqâm*. Currently, eight students are enrolled in an intensive, four-year course of study and another six completed a portion of this programme and remain professionally involved in performing and teaching Tajik classical music. Students who qualify for graduation will earn a diploma validated by Tajikistan's Ministry of Education. The Academy's curriculum includes fifteen different subjects ranging from vocal technique, performance on musical instruments and music theory to the history of world religions, analysis of classical poetry and Persian language. The Academy occupies a detached house and courtyard in a quiet, central neighbourhood of Dushanbe, where students meet for classes, rehearsals, computer work and impromptu performances on the traditional grape arbour-covered *takhta* (carpet- and cushion-covered platform) in the courtyard. Students in the Academy are active participants in the Music Initiative's Touring Programme and their recording of *Maqâm-i Râst*, one of the six song cycles that comprise the *Shashmaqâm*, is featured in the first group of CD-DVD releases through the Music Initiative's Documentation and Dissemination Programme. In autumn 2006, it was nominated for a Grammy Award in the category 'Best Traditional World Music Album'. The Academy's achievements have also attracted the attention of the President of

Tajikistan, who frequently asks them to perform at state occasions and to accompany him on visits to other countries to represent Tajikistan's cultural heritage.

The Khunar Centre in Northern Tajikistan

With its grant from the Music Initiative, the Khunar Centre sponsors *ustâd-shâgird* programmes in five cities of northern Tajikistan: Khojand, Isfara, Istaravshan and Penjikent. In contrast to the Academy of Maqâm, whose focus is on advanced students, the Khunar Centre accepts children from eleven to sixteen years of age. In 2005, over one hundred youngsters auditioned with the hope of becoming one of sixty-five accepted students. In addition to offering lessons with its thirty teachers, Khunar Centre sponsors frequent concerts, prepares cassettes and CDs for its students and publishes music method books. An opportunity to teach young people has had a significant impact on the social life of communities and teachers, many of whom are pensioners without sufficient income. Future projects for the Khunar Centre include creating a musical instrument workshop to train luthiers and expanding the *ustâd-shâgird* programme to other towns in northern Tajikistan. 'The government can't take care of old people who are living on pensions', said the Khunar Centre's director, Sultonali Khudoberdiev, 'but we're taking care of them. And this is reflected in cities where we work, where a lot of listeners are interested in our programmes.'

Evaluating Results

What indicators most accurately measure the success of a programme whose aim is to assure the transmission of tradition? The ultimate indicator, of course, will be available only to future generations. In the short term, evaluation relies upon a combination of qualitative and quantitative indicators that, *mutatis mutandis*, are used by development specialists to evaluate a variety of social interventions. In the case of the Tradition-Bearers Programme, qualitative indicators focus on the critical evaluation of music itself, while quantitative indicators best measure a musical activity's social resonance.

Quantitative Indicators

At the end of its fourth year of operation, the Music Initiative's internal evaluation procedures provide strong evidence of the following results:

- The number of well-qualified applicants to Tradition-Bearer centres has increased and the admission process is becoming increasingly selective.
- Students in the *ustâd-shâgird* programmes are competing successfully in regional, national and international music competitions.
- The *ustâd-shâgird* model of oral pedagogy is being adopted for broader use by education and culture ministries and by NGOs that sponsor music education programmes. European educational institutions have also demonstrated interest in the *ustâd-shâgird* model.
- Music Initiative-sponsored centres are amassing intellectual property in the form of pedagogical publications, videos and recordings.
- Young musicians involved in other musical idioms such as Western classical, pop and rock music are being attracted to the study and performance of traditional music.
- The number of general education schools offering training programmes in traditional music is expanding.
- Local broadcast and print media are paying more attention to traditional music and musicians.
- Local audiences for traditional music are growing larger and more enthusiastic.
- International and local commercial activities that arise from traditional music, e.g., concerts, recordings, festivals, are expanding.

Specific indicators vary in different communities and depend on local social and economic conditions as well as on the musical focus of the various schools and centres. Notwithstanding these differences, however, general patterns are readily apparent. The most significant of these are described below.

1. Applicants: critical mass and quality

A universal evaluation tool for educational institutions is the size and strength of their applicant pool. By this standard, the Tradition-Bearers Programme has been very successful. Growing interest in musical heritage and tradition is reflected in an increased demand for lessons. At present, Music Initiative-sponsored schools and centres cannot accommodate all applicants. The number of students in each centre is limited by physical space and by the availability of qualified instructors and funds to pay them.

2. Motivation and results

Students enrolled in the *ustâd-shâgird* programmes typically are highly motivated and their musical achievements have been recognised locally, nationally and internationally. In spring 2005, a group of debutante students in the AKMICA Bishkek-based Centre was awarded first place in a musical competition in Naryn Region and won a trip to Istanbul to perform in an international festival of young musicians, where they were awarded first prize. Students from the Khunar Centre have won several first prizes in local and national music competitions. In November 2005, five advanced students from the Academy of Maqâm received medals from the president of Tajikistan for outstanding contributions to the arts; in October 2005, the director of the Academy, Abduvali Abdurashidov, and Aqnazar Alovatov, member of the Ensemble Badakhshan, were decorated as *Commandeur* and *Officier de l'Ordre des Arts et des Lettres* by French President Jacques Chirac. The order is bestowed upon recipients in recognition of outstanding achievement in the arts and literature. As mentioned above, the CD recording of performances by students in the Academy of Maqâm was nominated for a Grammy Award in the 'Best Traditional Music Album' category.

3. Publications and curriculum materials

All centres have ambitious plans for publication projects to support their educational mission and facilitating these initiatives is a priority for the Music Initiative. The publications include manuals for teachers, critical editions of important musical repertories, method books for students and a textbook that illuminates historical and cultural connections among Central Asia's diverse musical styles and genres.

Qualitative Indicators

Is a musical performance fresh and compelling or merely perfunctory? Who is a master and who is an epigone? How successfully do musicians balance respect for tradition with imaginative innovation? These and other critical assessments of talent, craft and artistic potential represent core criteria for the evaluation of students in the Tradition-Bearers Programme from a qualitative perspective. The programme's four-year results are encouraging. Student performances at a recent gathering of schools and centres ranged from good to outstanding. Among the best, a 23-year-old *dutar* virtuoso at the Academy of Maqâm who has already performed as a soloist on concert stages in Europe and South Asia, shows sure signs of becoming the most musically inventive and technically sophisticated *dutar* player of his generation, while a *qyl-qiyak* player in Kyrgyzstan performs at the highest professional level with exceptional self-assurance. Students who are not the most talented in their cohort nonetheless display a solid command of technical skills, a broad knowledge of traditional repertory and an interest in creating new pieces that expand the repertory of their instrument.

Another useful qualitative indicator concerns the social prestige and respect that surrounds traditional musicians in their own communities. Evidence indicates that respect for master musicians in the Tradition-Bearers Programme has increased as a result of the programme's interventions – an increase that may be partially attributed to a perception by local communities that their traditional music and musicians are valued by listeners in the West.

International Music Touring Programme

The Music Initiative's Music Touring Programme was created to celebrate Central Asian musical traditions in regions where they are little known and integrate leading exponents of these traditions into the global network of music presenting institutions. Since its inception in 2002, the Touring Programme has produced numerous well-attended concerts in Europe, the United States, Africa and selected countries in Asia. Before the Music Initiative began its work, concerts of music from Central Asia were rare in Europe and North America. Typically restricted to small venues frequented by audiences whose focus was specifically 'world music', the choice of musicians tended to be haphazard and the quality of the concerts uneven. The Music Initiative is striving to professionalise the presentation of Central Asian music by organising worldwide concert tours and music workshops with a focus on the educational and cultural contextualisation of performance. Concert venues are chosen with the aim of reaching new audiences of diverse profiles and age groups and performances are adapted for international audiences through the use of innovative visual techniques.

The results of this work have had a deep impact on the artists involved and have resonated strongly among concert and festival presenters. The programme's next challenge is to adapt international touring mechanisms to the music market in Central Asia and to create a credible and self-sustaining regional touring programme.

Documentation and Dissemination Programme

The principal activity of the Music Initiative's Documentation and Dissemination Programme is collaboration with the Smithsonian Institution's Center for Folklife and Cultural Heritage for the production of *Music of Central Asia,* a ten-volume CD and DVD anthology of Central Asian musical traditions. The aim of the series, released worldwide by Smithsonian Folkways Recordings, is to present leading exponents of Central Asia's rich and diverse musical heritage to listeners outside the region. *Music of Central Asia* documents the work of musicians who represent both a mastery of their own tradition and a contemporary spirit of innovation expressed through new approaches to performance style, repertory and technique. An example of such a traditionalist innovator is the Kyrgyz musician Nurlanbek Nyshanov, leader of Ensemble Tengir-Too, which is featured on volume one of *Music of Central Asia (Tengir-Too: Mountain Music from Kyrgyzstan)*.

Nurlanbek Nyshanov's life in music was shaped both by his childhood in Naryn, a mountainous region in northern Kyrgyzstan, and by his experience as a student in the music education system created in Central Asia during the Soviet era. A graduate of Kyrgyzstan's State Institute of Arts (now the National Conservatory), Nyshanov draws on his compositional skills to craft for small ensembles striking arrangements of repertoires typically performed by solo players and singers. Unlike Soviet-era folk orchestras and consorts, however, Tengir-Too performs on traditional Kyrgyz instruments and works within the boundaries of conventional Kyrgyz musical forms, textures and genres. The group has attracted an enthusiastic following in the West and in Kyrgyzstan's competitive freemarket music economy is making steady progress at sustaining a livelihood from concert performances at home.

Music in Central Asian Modernity

The music teachers and performers who collaborate with the Aga Khan Music Initiative represent only one part of Central Asia's eclectic musical soundscape. Other patrons – most notably, state ministries of culture – as well as the commercial market for both live and mediated entertainment support diverse musical endeavours, both local and transnational. In Central Asia, long a byway of trans-Eurasian trade and commerce, global connections are nothing new, and these days forging global connections is arguably the easier part of creating art that is both cosmopolitan and rooted. Dramatic decreases in the cost of digital audio and video technology, coupled with the rapid spread of Internet access, have enabled musicians living practically anywhere to represent themselves to a worldwide audience. With an inexpensive digital camcorder or even a cell phone, a music ensemble can upload digital sound or images onto any subscription-free, user-friendly audio- and video-sharing website, thus gaining instant visibility – or audibility – around the world. More challenging is the other part of the equation: retaining a link to art rooted in a local sense of place and tradition. For what do 'sense of place' and 'tradition' mean in the art and music of the 21st century?

For every person who is settled or emplaced in a stable community, territory and tradition there is another person who is displaced: a refugee, émigré, migrant, guestworker or homeless person. And everywhere the displaced gravitate to cities. Throughout Central Eurasia, urban populations burst with newcomers searching for safety, stability and even a tenuous connection to the juggernaut of globalisation. For these people, music that links them through cultural memory to traditional lands and communities can be bittersweet. The music that speaks to them and for them expresses the anxiety and, often, the anger of displacement. In Azerbaijan, a young refugee boy from the war-ravaged Caucasian territory of Nagorno-Karabagh performs the virtuosic classical music known as *mugham*, the local form of the vast art music tradition that spans the core Muslim world from North Africa through the Middle East to Central Asia. The text he is singing, however, is not the traditional mystical allegory about love and paradise, but an elegy to loss and displacement:

> Hey, friends, our houses are burned and only the ashes remain,
> My heart yearns for the ashes, even the ashes of our burned grave.
> We have no right to speak of 'our Mountains'
> Unless we free them from our enemies.
> What makes me cry right now is my being made
> A stranger in my own land.

Meanwhile, in the urban soundscape of Almaty, Bishkek, Tashkent, Baku and other cities in the region, the music that dominates the radio and that comprises the sonic background of restaurants, stores and many private homes is largely pop music sung in English and recorded in Los Angeles, London or New York by musicians who have never laid eyes on Central Asia and probably never will. A recent visit to the music section of the main department store in Bishkek, the capital of Kyrgyzstan, turned up hundreds of new CDs representing music mostly from Russia and the West, but in the entire collection, a saleswoman could locate only three recordings of traditional Kyrgyz music.

Notwithstanding the personal musical taste and preferences of international NGO strategists, the music section of Bishkek's department store represents a face of globalised musical modernity to which the denizens of any culturally pluralist society surely ought to have access. To deny citizens of Kyrgyzstan the opportunity to purchase music produced in Los Angeles and sung in English would constitute a form of cultural imperialism as distasteful as the Soviet Union's erstwhile 'battle against the past'. In culturally pluralist societies, musical taste and fashion cannot be legislated on the basis of nationality, nor the meaningfulness of cultural symbols, including music, limited to the citizens of one or another state.

The challenge to governments that want the artistic achievements of their nation to be represented to the world community is in some sense paradoxical: to be entrepreneurial in seeding artistic creativity, but at the same time, to stay out of the way. The most effective strategies for cultural development come down to identifying, supporting, protecting and promoting talented new voices and educating young audiences so that they come to feel comfortably rooted in their own cultural traditions. As Anthony Appiah points out in *Cosmopolitanism: Ethics in a World of Strangers* (2006):

> The connection people feel to cultural objects that are symbolically theirs, because they were produced from within a world of meaning created by their ancestors – the connection to art through identity

– is powerful. It should be acknowledged. The cosmopolitan, though, wants to remind us of other connections. One connection – the one neglected in talk of cultural patrimony – is the connection not *through* identity but *despite* difference. We can respond to art that is not ours; indeed, we can fully respond to 'our' art only if we move beyond thinking of it as ours and start to respond to it as art. (pp. 134–35)

The achievement of European artistic modernity has been to free art from national fetishisation. Central Asian artistic modernity still largely awaits that freedom.

In the end, it is open and candid conversations between diverse artistic voices that create a thriving arts environment. Crossing conventional boundaries of style, genre and sensibility releases creative energy. And as illustrated by musicians affiliated with the Aga Khan Music Initiative, such musical crossings can just as felicitously occur in so-called traditional music as in any other musical domain. The musicians who participated in the concert at the London Coliseum and the two-week European tour that followed it came away inspired. Their late-night jam sessions and conversations not only helped stimulate new artistic visions but inspired the musicians to delve more deeply into their own traditions. Building respect for both old cultural knowledge and new is key. Creating a dynamic interchange between the two, stimulating experimentation, nourishing visionary talent and encouraging cross-cultural exchange – all of these will invigorate the arts and make them a vital part of Central Asian modernity. As expressions of cultural identity, soundscapes – in all their aesthetic and performative pluralism – remind us that alternative modernities are at the same time both distinctive and overlapping.

6

Forbidden Modernities:
Islam in Public

Nilüfer Göle

Islam has acquired new forms of visibility in the last two decades, as it makes its way in the public avenues of both Muslim and European societies. Social issues that were thought of as being limited to Muslim-majority countries have become agenda-setting challenges in European immigrant settings. Islamic headscarves in public schools and universities have become a divisive issue both in France and Turkey, provoking a larger debate on secularism. The visibility of religious difference unsettles the secular imaginaries that underpin the formations of the public sphere and gender equality. Studies on contemporary Islamic movements focus on the political and ideological aspects, placing emphasis on actions that relate to the exercise of state power. Yet it is the public sphere that must be understood as the site where Islam and modernity enter into dialogue (and conflict), altering both religious and secular imaginaries.

Two different phases of contemporary Islamism can be distinguished.[1] The first, beginning in the late 1970s and reaching its peak with the Iranian Islamic revolution in 1979, was characterized by mass mobilizations, militancy, a quest for collective Islamic identity, and the exercise of politico-religious power. In the second phase, the revolutionary fervour had declined, the ideological chorus gave way to a multiplicity of voices, and a process of distancing and individuation from collective militancy led to an 'exit from religious revolution'.[2] In this phase, after the assertion of a collective and exacerbated form of difference, Muslim identity is in the process of 'normalization'. Actors blend into modern urban spaces, use global communication networks, engage in public debates, follow consumption patterns, learn market rules, enter into secular time, get acquainted with values of individuation, professionalism and consumerism, and reflect upon their new practices. Hence we observe a transformation of these movements from a radical political stance to a more social and cultural orientation, accompanied by a loss of mass mobilization capacity, leading some researchers to pronounce the end of Islamism and the 'failure of political Islam'.[3] But a more cultural orientation does not mean a less political one. Indeed, instead of disappearing as a reference, Islam has penetrated further into the social fibre and imaginary, thereby raising new political questions, of concern not only to Muslims but also the foundational principles of collective life at large.

An analytical concern at the level of ideologies (such as Islamism), or of political formations (such as the state), cannot explain this process of interpenetration and dialogical relation. The public visibility of Islam and the specific gender, corporeal and spatial practices underpinning it trigger new ways of imagining a collective self and common space that are distinct from the Western liberal self and 'progressive' politics. Exploring these Islamic makings of the self and the micro practices associated with it will lead us to understand fresh social imaginaries and transformations of the public sphere.

Non-Western Publics

Although the idea of the public is Western in its origins and its basic features are understood as universal access, individualism, equality and openness, it circulates and moves into contexts other than the West. The ways in which these concepts, ideas and institutions travel and are adopted in non-Western contexts depend on local agencies and cultural fields. The experience of colonization in India, for example, or voluntary modernization in Turkey, has shaped the ways in which the public sphere is imagined and institutionalized. Studying the adoption of modern concepts at the level of language, their entry, translations and transformations

– namely, the historical semantics – can reveal the diversity of meanings and trajectories, and hint at the particular conjunctions between the universal definitions of the public sphere and home-grown practices and idioms.[4] The articulations and tensions between two different cultural codes, modern and indigenous, intervene in distinguishing and defining public and private spheres, interior and exterior spaces, licit and illicit practices. Sometimes they are simply juxtaposed in mutual indifference, sometimes they compete with each other, and sometimes they engage in a dialogue that produces interpenetrations and displacements.

The conception of exterior space, civility in the European sense of order and discipline, can therefore take on a different meaning and form in non-Western contexts. To indicate the differences between a Brahminical notion of cleanliness and purity and a Western notion of hygiene, Sudipta Kaviraj describes how the exteriors of houses in India are abandoned to an intrinsic disorderliness, while the interiors are kept impressively clean.[5] The interior, intimate, gendered space is similarly valorised and highly disciplined in Muslim societies, leading to different envisioning and institutionalization of modern public and city life. Although the cultural programme of modernity has a great capacity to influence and circulate, the encounter between the two cultural codes leads not to a simple logic of emulation or rejection, but to improvisations in social practices and cultural meanings. Studying the public sphere as a social imaginary may offer new clues to map out these improvisations in a non-Western context.

The social imaginary is, as Cornelius Castoriadis tells us, 'the creation of significations and the creation of the images and figures that support these significations'.[6] There is an 'essential historicity of significations: apparently similar "institutions" can be radically other, since immersed in another society, they are caught up in other significations'.[7] Institutions are not to be conceived as external to social imaginaries and social practices. There is no institution without signification, but the signification is not legitimate without shared practices. Although European modernity has constituted the crucial starting point and continual reference point, it is continuously and creatively appropriated and altered. These distinct cultural foundations and institutional formations should be analyzed, as Shmuel N. Eisenstadt and Wolfgang Schluchter remind us, 'not only in terms of their approximation to the West but also in their own terms'.[8] An analysis of the public sphere as a social imaginary can illuminate the circulation of a universal code of modernity, as well as the particular significations and practices. Approaching the public sphere as a social imaginary in Castoriadis's sense emphasizes its dynamic aspect, as an ongoing process, a creation of significations and practices rather than an 'imagined' and 'pre-established' frame. Furthermore, it defies the thesis of time-lag and 'deficiency of modernity'[9] for non-Western countries, giving intellectual credibility to societal practices in historical contexts other than the West.

The public sphere in a non-Western context is neither identical with its counterparts in the West, nor totally different. It manifests asymmetrical differences as it is continuously altered by a field of cultural meanings and social practices. Modern social imaginaries, as Charles Taylor reminds us, are social in the sense that they are widely and commonly shared.[10] Unlike theories and ideologies, they are not in the hands of a few. Social imaginaries are embedded in the habitus of a population, or carried in implicit understandings that underlie and make possible common practices. Even in cases where the public sphere is introduced by colonizing agents or adopted by modernizing elites, it cannot be understood as an alien structure or as an imposed idea from above. As a social imaginary, the public sphere works in a social field and penetrates and blends into cultural significations.

In the Turkish context of voluntary modernization, the public sphere is institutionalized and imagined as a site for the implementation of a secular and progressive way of life. An authoritarian modernism – rather than bourgeois, individualist liberalism – underpins this public sphere. Religious signs and practices have been silenced as the modern public sphere has set itself against a Muslim social imaginary and segregated social organization; modern codes of conduct have entered public spaces ranging from the Parliament and educational institutions to the street and public transport. In a Muslim context, women's participation in public life, corporeal visibility and social mixing with men all count as modern. The modern gendered subject has been constituted through female role models and repetitive performances, including language styles, dress codes, modes of habitation and modes of address.

Here we see the social imaginary of the public sphere at work. While it adheres to some of the basic universal principles of the Western public sphere, these principles are selectively highlighted, coupled and translated into social practices that are creatively altered as well. The central stakes of the modern subject are worked out in tension with Muslim definitions of self; hence the access of women to public life and gender equality acquire a more salient signification in the public imaginary. Moreover, in non-Western contexts, the public sphere provides a stage for the didactic performance of the modern subject in which the non-verbal, corporeal and implicit aspects of social imaginaries are consciously and explicitly worked out. Because the public sphere provides a stage for performance, rather than an abstract frame for textual and discursive practices, the visible aspect of the creation of significations and the making of social imaginaries is vital. Social imaginaries are carried by images. The body, as a sensorial and emotional register, links the implicit non-verbal practices and learned dispositions (habitus) into public visibility and conscious meaning. Public visibility refers to the techniques of working from inside out, transforming implicit practices into observable and audible ones. This chapter argues for the centrality of gender and related bodily regimens and spaces in the making of the public sphere.

The ways in which Islam emerges into the public sphere defy modernist aspirations for a civilized (read Westernized) and emancipated self, yet follow a similar pattern in regard to gender, body and space. The covered woman deputy walking into the Turkish Parliament, and walking out the same day, serves as an icon, an image that crystallizes the tensions emanating from two different cultural programmes in the making of the self and the public, a visibility that by the same token reveals the ways in which Parliament as a secular public sphere is imagined, constructed and instituted in the Turkish Republican context. Therefore, a two-layered reading is required. One concerns the modern self-presentation and its migration into the Turkish context of modernity. The second concerns the counterattack of Islamic practices as a competing form of pious self-making and social imaginary. And with this second reading, through an examination of the ways in which Islam is problematized in the public sphere, we become aware of the unspoken, implicit borders and the stigmatizing, exclusionary power structure of the secular public sphere.

The Headscarf in Parliament: A 'Blow-up'

For the first time in its republican history, Turkey witnessed the election of a 'covered' Muslim woman, an Istanbul deputy from the pro-Islamic Party (Fazilet Partisi) during the general election of April 1999. But it was Merve Kavakçi's physical presentation in Parliament, not her election, that provoked a public dispute. On the very day of its opening on 2 May 1999, Kavakçi, a 31-year-old woman wearing a white headscarf with fashionable frameless eyeglasses and a long-skirted, modern two-piece suit, walked (over)confidently into the meeting hall of the National Assembly for the opening session. The men and women deputies stood up and protested against her presence with such vehemence – especially twelve women from the Republican Party, now called the Democratic Left Party [DSP]) – shouting 'Merve out, ayatollahs to Iran', 'Turkey is secular, will remain secular', that she was obliged to leave without taking the oath of office.[11] Kavakçi's Islamic covering challenged the unwritten laws of the Parliament and enraged the deputies as well as (secular) public opinion.[12] The most well-known secular women's association organized meetings and condemned the headscarf in Parliament as an 'ideological uniform of Islamic fundamentalism', challenging republican state power and secular reforms.[13] She was treated as an 'agent provocateur' in the Turkish press, which accused her of having close links with the Palestinian group Hamas and working for foreign powers such as Iran and Libya. It was discovered that Kavakçi had become a US citizen shortly after becoming a parliamentary candidate. As she had not officially disclosed that she was holding another passport, authorities were able to use this legal pretext to strip Kavakçi of her Turkish citizenship.[14]

This story cannot be narrated merely as a political incident. At a micro level, instantaneous social reality and the tensions that generate history can be condensed and concealed. The trivial can be revealed as meaningful. In Georg Simmel's words, in these 'momentary images', snapshots, fragments of social reality, we are able to glimpse the meaning of the whole.[15] We can unpack the nature of the social discord between the secular and religious practices compressed in this political incident if we first take it as it is – that is, frame it as a picture or snapshot. Visualizing the story and the players will bring into focus the corporeal, gendered and spatial aspects of the social cleavages. Secondly, we need to defamiliarize our gaze. The picture is taken from the present day. It is widely and commonly shared. Its accessibility makes its understanding even more difficult, because it appears as 'ordinary' and 'natural' to the common eye, duplicating the given terms of public controversy. This *trompe l'oeil* poses a challenge to sociology. A sign must be interpreted using 'thick description' and placed in historical perspective, if we want to reveal all its possible meanings.[16] We need to go back and forth between micro and macro levels of analysis, between empirical practices and theoretical readings.[17] In his film *Blow-up* (1966), Michelangelo Antonioni tells the story of a photographer who by chance takes a picture that appears at first incoherent and incomprehensible. Then he enlarges a detail of photograph, which leads him to read the whole picture differently.[18] Let us enlarge – 'blow-up' – the picture taken of the veiled deputy in the public sphere.

Merve Kavakçi's portrait is both representative and distinctive in relation to other Muslim women in the Islamic movement. The trajectory of the Muslim female deputy follows a social dynamic similar to that of female students who have sought the right to attend university classes wearing headscarves since the beginning of the 1980s.[19] Access to higher education, daily experience of urban life, and use of political idiom and action expose new female Muslim actors to modernity; this exposure is problematic for both secular and religious actors. The case of Merve Kavakçi, though not an exception, serves as an example that carries the process of interaction with a programme of modernity to its very limits; and it thereby blurs oppositional boundaries. Kavakçi had access to higher education, became a computer engineer, trained at the University of Texas and lived in the United States, had two children, divorced her Jordanian-American husband, returned to Turkey and became a member of the pro-Islamic party. She had access, therefore, to powerful symbols of modernity and was simultaneously engaged in Islamic politics. Living in the United States, speaking English fluently, using new technologies, fashioning a public image (light-coloured headscarf and frameless eye-glasses) – these are all cultural symbols of distinction in a non-Western context of modernity. Islamists are not insensitive to acquiring such cultural capital. Indeed, though they are in a political struggle with secularists, they often mirror them and search for public representatives who speak foreign languages and belong to the professional and intellectual elite. Even Kavakçi's choice of a two-piece suit rather than an overcoat is a duplication of the republican woman's dress code. With all her elite credentials, Kavakçi could have been used to bolster Islamic pride – if only she were not so 'foreign'.[20]

Her trajectory is not only a sign of distinction; it also distinguishes her from other Muslim women and brings her socially closer to the Western-oriented, secular elites of Turkey. It's a closeness that creates more enmity than sympathy. The appropriation of social signs of modernity, such as language, comportment, politics, public exposure and being in contact with secular groups, without giving up the Islamic difference (marked by the headscarf) – this is the source of trouble. It is the 'small difference' and the small distance between her and the secular women that ignites political passion. Only when there is this feeling of a stranger's intrusion into one's own domain, places and privileges is there an issue of rejection or recognition of difference. The figure of the stranger, in a Simmelian perspective, represents the ambivalent relation of proximity and distance, identity and difference, through which a group reproduces social life and hierarchically structures social space.[21] This is why the small difference is crucial in understanding the rejection of those that are closest.

In Turkey, one of the arguments widely used against the head-scarf is that it has been appropriated as a political symbol, so the desire to wear it is not a disinterested one. Many will say they are not against their grandmother's headscarf, that on the contrary they remember it with affection and respect. This is certainly true to the extent that grandmothers sat in their corners at home and didn't step into modernity, or doffed their headscarves as they walked outdoors. Such behaviour is in conformity with the scenario of national progress and the emancipation of women, key elements of the modern social imaginary in a non-Western context. But today the play has changed, and so have the actors. The Muslim headscarf is deliberately appropriated, not passively carried and handed down from generation to generation. It is claimed by a new generation of women who have had access to higher educa-tion, despite their modest social origins (many come from the periphery of big cities or from small towns). Instead of assimi-lating to the secular regime of women's emancipation, they press for their embodied difference ('Islamic dress') and their public visibility (in schools, in Parliament), and stir-up modern social imaginaries. They project ambivalence in being 'Muslim' and 'modern' without wanting to give up one for the other. They are outside a regime of imitation, critical of both subservient tradi-tions and assimilative modernity. The ambiguity of signs disturbs both the traditional Muslim and secular modernist social groups. And this goes further than a question of abstract identity. It takes place in the public sphere and involves face-to-face relations. Difference is marked on the body; it is an embodied difference, visible to others. Islamic visibility (and not solely the identity) creates such a malaise because it has a corporeal, ocular and spatial dimension. These dimensions are only intensified in the case of Merve Kavakçi.

She is both local and 'foreign' (in a literal sense too, since she became a US citizen). Her education, individualistic posture and political language belong to the modern world; she is a woman who follows an Islamic dress code, yet does not adopt the traditional dress, behaviour and representations. Professional and political ambitions, as well as divorce, are all indicators of a non-traditional life and personality. Further, that she did not collapse into tears under heavy pressure and criticism, and does not speak the collective language of those who were persecuted, interposes a psychological distance between her and the traditional Muslim community. The latter uses widely the idiom of suffering and victimization, and through common emotional practices, such as crying and lamenting, reproduces a repertoire of cultural signs, a sense of social belonging, and a collective social movement. Kavakçi's individualist and composed self-presentation creates trouble in an Islamic social imaginary. Secular women, too, were no less suspicious of her 'cold-blooded attitude'; it was taken as one more strike against her, revealing militant discipline and premeditated behaviour at the service of a political conspiracy. Kavakçi cannot be situated in terms of geographical location, communitarian belonging or cultural coding; as she crosses the boundaries, circulates among different locations and places them in 'disjunctive' relation to one another, new social imaginaries are shaped.[22]

Kavakçi's fearlessness in the face of intimidation and her insensitivity to established relations of domination between Muslim and secularist women are perceived as arrogant; yet her carriage and discourse change the codes of interaction. Her political language is that of constitutional rights, which resonates more in a US-style democracy than in Turkey, where the constitution tends to provide more trouble than rights. Her language makes reference to an ultramodern space, whereas her covered body suggests Muslim privacy and modesty. The ambiguous signs carried by Kavakçi's presence create confusion and disturbance among Muslims, but also among secularists (including the journalists from CNN to whom her American-inflected language was more familiar). The fact that she comes from 'elsewhere' and makes reference to another mental space disturbs – and also helps to transgress – the social rules of conduct and interaction. As Goffman writes, the rupture of the framework is used by those from below, trying to discredit and disturb an adversary.[23] Such surprising crossovers bring into question the fixity of categories and boundaries.

The social dispute generated by the public visibility of Islam is carried by corporeal performances and self-presentations, not by textualized subjectivities and discursive practices. The public sphere is not simply a pre-established arena; it is constituted and negotiated through performance. In addition to constituting the public sphere, these micro practices enact a way of being public. We have a 'performative reflexivity', as Victor Turner sees it, 'a condition in which a sociocultural group, or its most perceptive members acting representatively, turn, bend or reflect back upon themselves, upon the relations, actions, symbols, meanings and codes, roles, statuses, social structures, ethical and legal rules, and other sociocultural components which make up their public "selves"'.[24] The dress code exemplifies this performative reflexivity. The practice of veiling restores a link with past traditions; it signifies the immutability of religion and non-secular time. Through repetition, rehearsal and performance, the practice of veiling is reproduced again and again, acquiring legitimacy and authority and contributing to the making of the modest pious self. But the veiling is not derived directly from prevailing cultural habits and pre-established conventions. On the contrary, it bears a new form, the outcome of a selective and reflexive attitude that amplifies and dramatizes the performative signs of 'difference'. It is transgressive with respect to Muslim traditions as well as to modern self-presentations. The new covering suggests a more rather than less potent Islam, which accounts for secular counterattacks against the headscarf for being not an 'innocent' religious convention but a potent political symbol.

Let us turn our gaze back to secularist counterattacks, a detour to the linkage between women and the making of the public sphere that will introduce a historical perspective without which we cannot explain the destabilizing force of Islam in secular social imaginaries. One has to remember that secularist women have entered into modernity through 'emancipation' from religion, which was symbolized by taking off the veil. They have experimented with modernity as a tangible entity inscribed on their bodies, clothes and ways of life – and not exclusively as an abstract and distant category of citizenship. They are products of a historical, emotional, corporeal fracture with Muslim identity, a fracture with the past that made it possible for them to have access to modernity.

Public Site as Visual Secularism

The grand narratives of modernity typically describe the elements of modernity in non-Western contexts as insufficient. However, when the concepts of Western modernity travel into different contexts, they often acquire not only different meanings but also an unexpected intensity. Secularism is an example. Because of its locus in Western historical development, secularism is expected to be a marginal element in other contexts, notably Muslim ones. Yet in the Turkish case, we observe not only its role in nation-state-building and its penetration into civil and military elite ideology but also its emergence in civil society and in women's associations. Secularism works as a social imaginary.

It is possible to speak of an excess of secularism, when it becomes a fetish of modernity. Modern social imaginaries cross boundaries and circulate but take on a different twist and a modified accent in non-Western contexts – a sense of 'extra'. We can read 'extra' both as external to the West, and as additional and un-ordinary. The evolutionary concept of historical change can hardly imagine that there can be a surplus or excess of modernity in some domains of social life in non-Western settings. Modernity functions as a fetish. Its manifestations are overemphasized, as are the performances of belonging to modernity. The excess of secularism in some Muslim contexts of modernity is such an example. The public sphere becomes a site for modern and secular performances. In contrast with the formation of the public sphere in the West, characterized initially as a bourgeois sphere that excluded the working classes and women, in Muslim contexts of modernity, women function as a pivotal sign/site in the making and representing of the public sphere.[25]

In a Muslim context, women's visibility and the social mixing of men and women attest to the existence of a public sphere.

Women as public citizens and women's rights are more salient than citizenship and civil rights in the Turkish secular imaginary. The removal of the veil, the establishment of compulsory coeducation for girls and boys, civil rights for women that include eligibility to vote and to hold office, and the abolition of Islamic family law, guarantee the public visibility and citizenship of women. Women's participation in public life as citizens and as civil servants, their visibility in urban spaces and their socialization with men, all define a secular way of life and indicate a radical shift from the social organization and gender roles framed by traditional Islam. Women are symbols of the social whole: home and outside, interior and exterior, private and public. They stand in for the making of the modern individual, for the modern ways of being private and public. Women's corporeal and civic visibility, as well as the formation of heterosocial spaces, underpins the stakes of modernity in a Muslim society.

Secularism is enacted as a modern social imaginary through gendered, corporeal and spatial performances. In that respect, some common spaces are transformed as they gain additional symbolic value and become public sites of visual modernity and gendered secular performances. In addition to Parliament, schools and the workplace, spaces such as beaches, opera and concert halls, coffeehouses, fashion shows, public gardens and public transportation, all become sites for modern self-presentations. They are instituted and imagined as public spaces through these daily micro practices in which men and women rehearse and improvise in public their new self-presentations, dress codes, bodily postures, aesthetic and cultural taste, and leisure activities.

The implicit dimensions of modern social imaginaries, namely the aspects that are embodied in the habitus of a population, in the modes of address, living, habitation and taste, all become explicit features of performative modernity in a non-Western context. Even as the public sphere denotes a space for the making of the new modern self, it excludes others, namely those who do not conform to this 'new life' and habitus – Muslims, for example. Acts of performance are not socially neutral; they are situated in and produced by social relations of domination and exclusion.

Again, over-politicized definitions of identity and arguments of conspiracy exclude the possibility of finding semblance and familiarity; they reinforce demonic definitions of the adversary. In Merve Kavakçi's case, she is not recognized as a woman, an individual, a Muslim, a deputy and a citizen, but rejected and stigmatized as a militant, an Islamist and an outsider.

A social bond with the stigmatized and excluded is the essential problem of democracy.[26.] In the case of Islam in the public sphere, there is a double movement that causes uneasiness: Islamists seek to enter into spaces of modernity, yet they display their distinctiveness. There is a problem of recognition to the extent that Islamists start sharing the same spaces of modernity, such as Parliament, university classes, television programmes, beaches, opera halls and coffeehouses, and yet fashion a counter-secular self. In contrast with being a Muslim, being an Islamist entails a reflexive performance; it involves collectively constructing, assembling and restaging the symbolic materials to signify difference. The symbols of Muslim habitus are reworked, selectively processed and staged in public. Performative acts of religious difference in secular public space defy the limits of recognition and of social bonds, and unsettle modern social imaginaries.

Choreographies of Ambivalence

The Islamic critique of Western modernity can be interpreted as a new stage in the process of the indigenization of modernity in non-Western contexts. The Islamic subject is formed both through liberation from traditional definitions and roles of Muslim identity and through resistance to a cultural programme of modernity and liberalism. Alain Touraine claims that the subject owes her existence to a social conflict or collective action that criticizes the established order, expected roles and logic of power.[27] Thus the Muslim subject is created by a collective action that is critical of the subjugation of Muslim identity by both community (religious and otherwise) and modernity. The search for difference and authenticity expresses a critical resistance to the assimilative strategies and homogenizing practices of modernity. Especially in non-Western contexts, the reflexive nature of modernity, the critical capacity to surpass its limits, is weak.[28] Criticism of modernity is engendered when modernity becomes an indigenous, everyday practice.

Indigenously defined modernity is not only thought of as a discursive regime that shapes subjectivity but also as constituted and negotiated through performances. The Habermasian model of the bourgeois public sphere as worked out by 'rational-critical debate' fails to always provide a frame for the performative basis of indigenously defined modernity, particularly when this relates to gender and other embodied identities. Performance of difference through corporeal and spatial practices requires a new reading of non-verbal communication, embodied information and sensorial interaction.

Where issues of religion and gender are at stake, the vocabulary of gaze and spatial conventions acquires a greater salience. When Muslim women cross the borders between inside and out, multiple senses – sight, smell, touch and hearing – feature in concerns over redefining borders, preserving decency and separating genders. A public Islam needs to redefine and recreate the borders of the interior, intimate, illicit gendered space (*mahrem*).[29] The notion of modesty (*edep*) underpins the Muslim self and its relation to private and public spaces. Veiling points up the importance of the ocular (avoiding the gaze, casting down one's eyes), and the segregation of spaces regulates gender sociability. These acts, counter-aesthetics, body postures and modes of address are public performances; they seek to gain authority and legitimacy through their repetitions and rehearsals. They are not alien to Muslim memory and culture; they are rooted in the religious habitus. But they are not simple conventions that have always been there and that are unconsciously handed down from generation to generation. The habitus provides, in Pierre Bourdieu's account, a source of improvisations; it allows for a process of continual correction and adjustment.[30] However, Islamist public visibilities are not implicitly embodied in a Muslim habitus; they often mark a break with traditions, through the exacerbation of difference. This makes the habitus (secular and religious) explicit and conscious. Grandmother's veiling is 'natural'; the new veiling is less 'innocent'. Secularists are not wrong to read it as a symbol. Although not rendered discursively, a non-verbal embodied communication in the veil conveys information; it disobeys traditional and secular ways of imagining self-emancipation and becoming public.

Islamic public visibility presents a critique of a secular version of the public sphere. The work of Richard Sennett has shown that the initial development of the public sphere in the West was inseparable from ways in which people experienced their bodies; the body was linked to urban space by religious rituals.[31] According to Sennett, the dematerialization of the public sphere and its separation from the body is the secular version of the public sphere. The divorce of urban experience from religious understanding inhibits the creation of intense civic bonds and 'civic compassion' in a multicultural city.[32] Drawing on this analysis, I suggest that Islamic public display retrieves a phenomenon that has been repressed by secularism. This public display attempts to reconstruct the social link between subjectivity and public space through the reintroduction of religious self-fashioning, performances and rituals. Women are the principal actors in this process as they display the boundaries between private and public, licit and illicit, body and imaginary. Islamism reinforces the boundaries in social relations through regulating bodily practices in public spaces; this regulation, in turn, serves as a public display of Islamic subjectivity. The Muslim body becomes, for actors of Islamism, a site of resistance to secular modernity. It is a site where both difference and prohibition are linked to the formation of a new subject (neither traditional Muslim nor secular modern) and a new sociability. She incorporates the limits, the boundaries and the interdictions that render her a 'forbidden modern'. Self-limitation and self-disciplining go together with becoming modern. Ambivalence, which is a feeling that is normally alien to both the religious and the modern, undergirds the contemporary Muslim psyche. In *Another Modernity: A Different Rationality*, Scott Lash draws on Kant's 'reflective judgement' to define ambivalence as a third space, the margin between the same and the other, where difference is more primordial than either presence or absence, and instead exists as a space of ambivalence and undecidability.[33]

Castoriadis insists on the complementary nature of social representations; without this complementarity, society would not be possible. For example, the relation between serf and lord – and feudal society itself – is made possible through the institutions and representations that bind them.[34] However, Islamic social imaginaries and practices are worked out through ambivalence rather than complementarity. Surprising crossovers between Muslim and modern and between secular and religious practices take place, unsettling the fixity of positions and oppositional categories. Turkish experience provides us with a privileged terrain for this choreography of ambivalence. Voluntary modernization means a processed and displaced form of Western modernity as well as the absence of a colonial Other against which to direct Islamic oppositional discourse. Mutually inclusive categories create not binary oppositions, counter discourses or emulations, but multifaceted, intertwining modern performances. This ambivalence operates basically through crossing over, losing one's positionality, and circulating in different spaces, categories and mental mappings. Rather than resulting in peaceful juxtapositions, hybridities and augmentations, it is worked out in double negations (neither Muslim nor modern) and ambiguities (forbidden and modern), resulting in fragmented subjectivities and transcultural performances.

I have sought in this chapter to illustrate ways in which Islam is carried by new Muslim figures into secular publics, thereby unsettling the prevailing modern imaginaries. Gender equality, privatisation of religion and women's liberation are all secular values that underpin social imaginaries. The headscarf and other forms of the presence of Islam in public challenge easy oppositions of privatized religion and secular public sphere, gender equality and religious difference, freedom and faith. I do not refer here to compulsory veiling imposed by state power or communal norms, but to the voluntary adoption of dress (covering) and conduct (modesty) by Muslim women. Women who choose to adopt the headscarf and assert their presence in public life offer an unspoken critique of the modern secular values of women's emancipation and citizenship. When adopted as a form of self-definition and religious agency, this poses new questions for our grasp of elemental ideas of modernity, self, gender emancipation and private/public distinctions.

In a context such as that of Turkey, the public sphere is imagined and institutionalized as a site for Westernized self and nation; the exclusion of Islam as an organizing principle underpins secularism. Rather than measuring the gap between Turkish secularism and its Western counterparts – and qualifying it as a deficient and perverted form of Western secularism – I have highlighted its distinctive features and creative adaptations. Does public Islam in this setting signify the failure of a modern imaginary in a non-Western context, or a new step in the indigenization of modernity that involves a conflictual appropriation? Readings of Islamic practices as a deficiency of secularism, or as a failure of modernity, ignore the fact that public Islam questions hegemonial definitions of self and modernity. 'Multiple modernities' draw our attention to the different forms that imaginaries such as secularism take in shaping contexts outside the West – and often within it too. For Charles Taylor, it means that 'we finally get over seeing modernity as a single process of which Europe is the paradigm'.[35] We certainly need to attend to different trajectories and creative adaptations. But opening our readings of modernity to non-Western contexts implies also a critical rethinking of Western secular premises of modernity.

7

Revivalism and the Enclave Society
Bryan S. Turner

Introduction: Global Mobility

Modern sociology has encouraged us to believe that social boundaries are disappearing and that the social world is a system of global flows and networks. This view of modern societies is associated with, for example, the work of John Urry, who has criticized mainstream sociology for its alleged focus on nation-states, and has advocated a new 'mobile sociology'.[1] He is clearly correct to draw our attention to the importance of global flows and networks as key features of the modern world. These global scenes are, of course, closely connected with what Arjun Appadurai has called a world of global 'scapes' or new sites of contest and cultural creation.[2] These emerging global sites provide various opportunities for 'grassroots globalisation' or 'globalisation from below', where social actors can develop counter-globalisation strategies.[3] Such political and cultural opportunities for action against the negative features of the global economy are also associated with the idea of 'new imaginaries', that is, collective cultural methods of formulating a vision of alternative societies and practices.[4]

Against these conceptualisations of global politics, I want to propose a somewhat more pessimistic argument. As the economy becomes increasingly global, especially in terms of the flow of finance and commodities, the polity in many respects becomes more rigid in attempting to defend the foundations of sovereignty. There is, therefore, often a profound contradiction between the economic requirements of flexibility and fluidity and the state's objective of defending its territorial sovereignty. In particular, with the growth of a global 'war on terror' after 9/11, states rather than becoming more porous have defended their borders with greater determination. Reasserting state sovereignty is now part of a more general securitisation of society – a new development in the growth of 'governmentality'.[5]

From a historical perspective, it is useful to remind ourselves that the flow of people has become more rather than less restrictive. For example, the invention of the passport as a method of surveillance and regulation is, as John Torpey[6] has argued, a product of 20th-century statehood; in a similar fashion, Saskia Sassen[7] in *Guests and Aliens* has shown how the free-flow of workers in Europe that had been traditional during harvest time was stopped by the transformation of such guests into political aliens. While there may be an increasing global flow of goods and people, there is emerging a parallel 'immobility regime' exercising surveillance and control over citizens and aliens. If sociology is to be criticised, it is not because it has neglected globalisation; it is because it has overlooked the rise of global security systems, in particular to protect residential populations against the perceived risk of mobile populations – illegal migrants, the underclass, the criminal community, and the flotsam and jetsam of global labour markets. President Bush's decision in 2006 to complete the wall separating Mexico and the United States is simply one dramatic illustration of the development.

There is consequently a central paradox of labour migration. The labour markets of the advanced economies depend on high levels of migration, because they have ageing populations and because their own labour force is not sufficiently mobile geographically, and is reluctant to take on unskilled or low-paid work. Markets need migrant labour, but democratic governments, responding in part to electoral pressures and media campaigns against foreigners, minorities and migration, cannot be seen to be too lenient toward the urban consequences of high levels of migration. After 9/11, there has been a tendency to conflate three different categories of persons: migrants, refugees and asylum seekers. Conservative or right-wing parties have successfully mobilised electorates against liberal policies favouring labour mobility and porous frontiers. While migrants contribute significantly to economic growth, they are often thought to be parasitic on the host society. They do not fit easily into a welfare model of contributory rights.

Governments in general have been reluctant to give citizenship status to migrants without stringent criteria of membership; naturalisation is often a slow and complex process. Furthermore, dual citizenship is often regarded as an anomaly. There is an increasing level of social criticism against quasi-citizenship, dual citizenship and flexible arrangements, because these forms of citizenship are thought to undermine the hegemonic model of traditional political membership. In the United States, this type of criticism has come from sociologists like Nathan Glazer who have supported such policies as affirmative action.

How does religion fit into this sociological argument? The globalisation of the migrant labour market has been one cause of the globalisation of world religions, especially Islam, and the creation of new diasporic religious identities. Many diasporic Muslim youth, once outside their original homelands, have abandoned the traditional religion of their parents and have embraced various forms of renewal and revivalism. These religious changes often involve a greater emphasis on personal piety and stricter religious adherence to the reformed standards of modern Islam. Social and geographical mobility have produced a redefinition of Islam as a modern, transnational identity in a context where citizenship identity is often denied or delayed[8]. These changes have been reinforced by the growth of literacy, the expansion of higher education, and the introduction of women into the formal labour market. In general this amounts to a 'pietisation' of religious practices,[9] indeed to a new urban imaginary of anti-secular spirituality.

The long-term political solution to social conflict within the context of sovereign nation-states has been the creation of a common legal and political framework, namely citizenship. Arguments in favour of flexible or global citizenship are problematic unless they can resolve the relationship between rights and duties, namely the nature of social contributions. While human rights offer some protection to minority groups and migrant workers through such instruments as the International Covenant on Economic, Social and Cultural Rights (1966) and conventions of the International Labour Organization (ILO), ultimately human rights (including freedom of religious expression) require the support of states that promote active citizenship. The framework of citizenship is an important mechanism of democratic education and protection of rights. The paradox is that citizenship is in one sense an exclusionary institution; but the erosion of citizenship is also a threat to the liberal view of multiculturalism and cosmopolitanism. Can liberalism and religious revivalism be reconciled?

The Laws of Peoples

Given the growth of various forms of religious revivalism, there are important political questions about how plural societies can adapt, about the role of urban cosmopolitanism, and about the possibility of a normative commitment to cultural pluralism. What policies might support a commitment to ensuring civil harmony in societies that are necessarily more complex and heterogeneous because of international migration and involvement in the global economy? The classic liberal solution has been presented by John Rawls. In his *The Laws of Peoples*[10] he argues that a 'decent liberal society' will require 'an overlapping consensus' in which social order must be rooted in a reasonable political conception of right, and where justice is affirmed by an overlapping consensus of comprehensive doctrines. In attempting to offer the classical liberal defence of freedom of speech and conscience, Rawls struggles with the problem that some religious fundamentalists or political groups may not accept the liberal version of a plural society. Rawls provides no real practical solution to this problem. In historical terms, liberalism solved religious conflict by making religion a matter of private belief, separating church and state, excluding compulsory religious instruction from schools, and making 'hate speech' a criminal offence. Many religious groups that fall outside the framework of liberal Protestantism have not or cannot accept this Westphalian framework.[11]

Rawls's solutions are thus essentially legal and political: rule of law, norms of compromise, reasonableness, criminalisation of racism and protection of individual rights. From a sociological perspective, 'an overlapping consensus of comprehensive doctrines' presupposes the existence of overlapping social groups. However, inter-group reciprocity and cooperation often appear to be in decline in modern societies. The prospects for civil harmony as a result often look bleak. In addition, the actual debate about cultural cooperation and consensus has been bedevilled by the problem of cultural relativism. Recent political philosophy has sought to develop notions of cosmopolitanism that may counter this slide towards cultural particularism.[12] While liberal multiculturalists have embraced 'recognition theory' as an ethical platform for inter-cultural cooperation and mutual respect, such a position does not pay sufficient attention to the existence of widespread disagreement, mutual criticism and distrust. What happens in multicultural societies where 'men of good will' simply disagree about basic issues to such a degree that no overlapping consensus is possible? One response is to seek out elements in other cultures where the prospects for recognition and agreement are promising; this keeps open the possibility of dialogue even where there are large areas of disagreement. If there is to be a dialogue between Western secular liberals and religious leaders outside the West, we need some common ground. We need to find a religious imaginary in which dialogue is possible and where there is less emphasis on mutually exclusive notions of religious truth. Ibn al-'Arabi (1165–1240)'s commentary on the diversity of religions may be such a starting point.

The Rise of Identity Politics

These issues around religious conflict and the crisis of liberal multiculturalism are an aspect of the rise of identity politics, and to understand this form of politics we need to pay attention to some key features of social change in the rise of post-industrial society. The notion of 'industrial society' became important in the sociological debates in the early part of the 19th century in the work of French sociologists Auguste Comte and Claude H. Saint-Simon. Their view of industrial society was essentially optimistic. It spelt the end of the hierarchical and military societies of feudal Europe, and it would give rise to new social classes – namely, the urban working class and the industrial bourgeoisie. The French Revolution and the Industrial Revolution spelt the end of land-owning aristocracies and rural peasantry. The new classes were urban, and they brought a new dynamism to society. Comte and Saint-Simon also thought that these revolutions signalled the end of the hegemony of the Catholic Church; a new religion would sweep through the developed world in the shape of humanism. Industrial society could now be planned in terms of rational models under the guidance of a science of society that they called 'social physics' or 'positivism' or 'sociology'.

The principal assumption behind the theory of industrialisation, such as the sociology of Karl Marx, was that modern industrial society would be essentially secular, a system in which public institutions were relatively free from religious control, religion would be a matter of private conscience, the state would be separated from religion, and religious leaders (ministers and priests in Western societies) would not be civil servants. Here again there were important differences among northern European societies, where secularization was a dominant feature of industrialism, the United States, where religion played an important role in civil society in the absence of a welfare state, and communist societies, where formal religions were driven underground by a political system that was dogmatically committed to secularisation.

The central issue in the sociology of industrial society was the ever-present threat of social disruption from the clash of social classes either through relatively peaceful means (industrial disputes such as strikes and lockouts) or more violent confrontations (general strikes, industrial espionage or armed conflict). There are many explanations given for the failure of class confrontation to disrupt or dissolve capitalism, such as the existence of a dominant ideology.[13] Other explanations involve the institutionalisation of industrial conflict through legislation, the growth of citizenship and the rising prosperity of the working class.[14]

By the 1970s it was more common for sociologists to talk about 'post-industrial society', as in Daniel Bell's *The Coming of Post-Industrial Society*[15] and J. F. Lyotard's *The Postmodern Condition*.[16] Post-industrialism meant the dominance of the service sector over the manufacturing industry, the rise of a new middle class (of managers), the centrality of the university and research centres to industrial production, the rise of leisure, consumerism and hire purchase, and the computerisation of knowledge. Class as a primary feature of identity disappears as gender and ethnicity become increasingly important. Religious identity reappears as a major issue, yet in post-industrial or postmodern society these religious identities themselves become commercialised as an aspect of lifestyle. Youth movements often embrace religious lifestyles, but these are often post-institutional, post-denominational and hence syncretic and hybrid. Traditional religious leaders have to compete with the Internet for audiences, and traditional forms of text-based authority have to compete with or employ new methods of communication.

Many sociologists have identified global movements that lead towards the 'desecularisation' of the world.[17] These religious revivals are often associated with fundamentalism (especially in evangelical Christianity and Islamic revivalism) but they can also involve the global spread of popular religions or new forms of hybrid spirituality. Sociologists have referred to modern societies as 'spiritual marketplaces' in which religious groups compete for a 'market share' alongside other movements selling spiritual lifestyles.

If industrial society was a class society, then post-industrial society has been characterised by ethnic identity and identity politics, multiculturalism, the politics of ethnic difference and post-national social movements. What are the conditions of successful multiculturalism with the rise of a conflictual framework of identity politics? An examination of multiculturalism in North America, northern Europe (especially Sweden), Australia and New Zealand suggests that they have been relatively successful multicultural societies. Similar claims could be made for Singapore and Malaysia. Insofar as they have been relatively successful multicultural societies, the conditions of success appear to include:

- significant and sustained economic growth without which migrant communities become an underclass; safety-net welfare arrangements;
- effective income taxation and some redistribution of wealth through a progressive tax system to minimise income inequality;
- the absence of an ethnic underclass which can become the target of racial politics;
- state neutrality to protect minorities against a dominant ethnic group;
- an open 'marriage market' permitting frequent and successful intermarriage between social groups and some corresponding degree of formal gender equality;
- the entry of women into the formal labour market as a consequence of an egalitarian, largely secular, education system;
- a state educational system that in principle offers children common cultural experiences and a shared understanding of membership; enforceable legislation to criminalise ethnic stereotyping, hate speech and racial bigotry;
- a compensating nationalist ideology and provision of language training in a common public language;
- relatively generous criteria of naturalisation based on residence and easy access to citizenship;
- the rule of law, providing formal guarantees of procedural fairness ('justice'), often enshrined in a bill of rights.

This liberal model of successful multiculturalism is based on the idea that migrants can achieve social mobility (at least in the second generation), that their culture receives some public endorsement from governments, that there is a national ideology of inclusion, and that the rule of law guarantees some degree of legal security.

The conditions that undermine multiculturalism are numerous and pressing, but they include as a minimum situations where a government is seen to take sides in ethnic conflict, and appears to promote the interests of one group over another. Communal hostilities are then fuelled in situations where the rule of law is overtly flaunted by states. Ethnic conflict creates conditions for the development of civil strife, and civil strife can lead ultimately to civil conflict, escalating ultimately to ethnic violence and 'news wars'[18]. Chronic civil distrust is sustained by the lack of intermarriage, and the prohibition on intermarriage is typically sustained by fundamentalist religious prescriptions on eligible marriage partners. Finally, there are important economic circumstances that contribute to conflict, especially high levels of unemployment, low wages and exploitative working conditions. These socio-economic conditions make it difficult for young people to benefit from secular citizenship, and these circumstances in turn make militant or militaristic alternatives look attractive. These forms of social and cultural alienation are the breeding ground of terrorism.

The Crisis of Liberal Tolerance

Civil society, the rule of law and the enjoyment of rights are important to provide a minimal security for our condition of vulnerability. There must be some level of social order and trust if citizens are to be protected from the vagaries of life. Human vulnerability and the precarious nature of social existence have been severely strained over the last two decades by a rising tide of terrorism, communal violence, civil strife and warfare. Cosmopolitanism, democracy and multiculturalism have become standard policy responses to the strains created by social and cultural diversity. However, this political debate has often taken place at a rather general level in terms of the rule of law and the Westphalian 'privatisation of religion'.[19] Rawls argues that the achievement of any form of reasonable pluralism in a liberal democracy requires tolerance between religious groups, in which no one group imposes its hegemonic beliefs on any other group.

These very general assertions about the separation of religion and politics, the secularisation of the public sphere and political tolerance tell us very little about how people in religiously diverse societies, within which there may be significant religious revivalism, actually go about the task of managing their everyday lives. To express this in the language of ethno-methodology, how do people do 'being religious'? What are the daily practices by which we can recognise the 'good Muslim' or the 'good Jew' as a social personality?

In societies that are being transformed by global labour migration and the emergence of large diasporic communities, people in their everyday lives find that they may be forced increasingly to interact with, eat next to or talk with strangers – that is, people with very different religious commitments, customs and lifestyles. How do ordinary people manage the complexity of everyday life in terms of selecting friends, choosing restaurants or sending their children to school? How does the global transformation of religious identities work out at the everyday level of managing situations which may be perceived as embarrassing, contaminating or even dangerous? To take a mundane example from contemporary Singapore, the Singaporean government supports racial harmony through such events as 'Racial Harmony Month', but this official project can be somewhat undermined by the informal compartmentalization of daily life around racial groups or CMIO (Chinese, Malay, Indian and Others). At a daily level, tensions often emerge around customary practices.[20] While Chinese middle-class housewives like to keep dogs as pets, increasingly devout Muslim neighbours embracing customary Muslim/Malay norms regard dogs as religiously polluting. How does one behave towards neighbours when faced with the threat of religious pollution? There are, of course, studies of similar situations in the West. Kathryn Spellman in *Religion and Nation: Iranian Local and Transnational Networks in Britain*[21] explored the domestic lives of Iranian women in London in terms of how they manage 'private' religious identities within a diaspora that exists in a secular capital city. But there is relatively little comparative work on religious diversity and growing pressures on the public adoption of religious identities. How does the private, domestic world interact and interconnect with broad changes in global religious identities, especially where the emerging religious cultures have such significant consequences? Islamic fundamentalism, Christian evangelism, Hindu revivalism and

Jewish ultra-orthodoxy are, in socially and religiously diverse societies, posing the question: how do I behave as a 'good Muslim' (or 'good Christian' and so forth)? Traditional standards of religious behaviour are being both redefined and intensified by such processes, and these changes make the achievement of liberal tolerance, cosmopolitan virtue and multiculturalism deeply problematic.

There is evidence of a worldwide growth of religious fundamentalism,[22] and there are consequently important political questions about how plural societies can survive, the role of urban cosmopolitanism, and the possibility of a normative commitment to pluralism.[23] What policies might support a commitment to ensuring civil harmony in societies that are necessarily more complex and heterogeneous because of international migration and involvement in the global economy? What policies might be relevant in societies with religious groups that are being transformed by fundamentalism, conservative orthodoxy and revivalism? Rawls argues, as we have seen, that a decent liberal society will require an overlapping consensus of beliefs if it is to avoid social disharmony. In particular, he suggests that '[b]ecause, philosophical or moral unity is neither possible nor necessary for social unity, if social stability is not merely a *modus vivendi*, it must be rooted in a reasonable political conception of right and justice affirmed by an overlapping consensus of comprehensive doctrines'.[24]

Rawls is acutely aware that his liberal model is problematic in the face of determined exclusionary 'comprehensive doctrines', such as those emerging from the belief systems of evangelical movements or fundamentalism. He admits that 'differences between citizens arising from their comprehensive doctrines' may turn out to be 'irreconcilable'.[25] His solution is to propose a criterion of 'reasonableness' or reciprocity in which citizens offer one another fair terms of cooperation for political justice', according to which they will accept each other even at the cost of their own interests. He defines this criterion of reciprocity by appeal to a classical notion of Greek political philosophy, namely 'civic friendship'.[26] Because 'friendship' has in modern English lost its political, if not its ethical, significance, Rawls's argument might be lost on a modern audience. In classical Greece, friendship (*philotes/philia*) designated a set of obligations on the part of the head of a household (*oiko-despotes*) towards strangers, involving mutual respect. In the *Nichomachean Ethics*, Aristotle claimed that friendship was a universal emotion forming the basis of the *polis*, because the citizen was always the fellow-citizen of the *civis*.[27]

Rawl's ideas are valuable and it is certainly difficult to see how any civil society could function without the rule of law, tolerance and mutual respect. Civil society needs the social solidarity that is associated with fellow feeling. While these ideas are praiseworthy, are they realistic and does the mere promise of reciprocity solve the problem of mutually exclusive belief systems? On the basis of changes in the nature of everyday norms and customs in religiously plural societies, Rawls's criteria for 'a realistic utopia', that is for 'reasonably just constitutional democratic societies', look decidedly unpromising.[28] Even allowing for the plausibility of realistic utopian principles, these criteria of functional democracies are seriously challenged by contemporary religious movements. The principal weakness of Rawls's argument is sociological – that is, a consensus of overlapping comprehensive doctrines can only provide the basis for a workable consensus if there are indeed overlapping social bonds. A multicultural society with diverse comprehensive doctrines – the product of diverse fundamentalist religions – can only function without conflict if there are overlapping social groups. The existence of overlapping social groups is only possible where there are high rates of intermarriage, state schools catering to ethnically distinct communities, sports teams that recruit from various ethnic groups, neighbourhoods that are not zoned by separate housing arrangements, restaurants serving a variety cuisines, and government policies that promote multicultural participation across the society. In view of the growth of rituals of intimacy with the new piety, such overlapping social bonds are not easily sustained because the implication of fundamentalisation is the creation of a social mosaic of separate and sequestered communities. Fundamentalisation means social sequestration.

If we consider the most basic and traditional sociological perspectives on the social group, we would have to conclude that the dynamics of group life tend in plural societies to work against Rawlsian reciprocity.[29] Sustaining group loyalty through revivalism and exclusionary religious norms is important for maintaining group cohesion. But they are not compatible with the idea of cosmopolitan societies emerging with social pluralism. In particular, marital homogamy ('like marries like') has long been recognised by sociologists as a fundamental feature of courtship and marriage. The trend towards marital homogamy in Southeast Asia has increased with religious norms prescribing marriage between partners of the same faith as a religious duty. A series of *fatwas* from the Indonesian Council of Ulemas (MUI) in July 2005 proclaimed that inter-faith marriages were against shari'a law, and condemned ecumenical activities between different faiths. These pronouncements are not automatically underwritten by the state but they significantly impact on daily practice. For example, Indonesians of Chinese descent and Indonesians whose religion falls outside the official list of recognised religions have difficulty getting their marriages registered; very few officials will participate in weddings of couples from different religions. In Malaysia PAS (Parti Islam Se-Malaysia) has advocated the creation of a strong Islamic state that would enforce customary *hudud* penalties on women, requiring severe limitations on their rights to divorce, and permitting men to have numerous wives.[30]

The emphasis on conversion and the dangers of apostasy make the achievement of social harmony within cultural diversity highly problematic. Several cases have recently appeared in the international media. Most spectacular was the attempt in March 2006 by some Afghan *'ulama* to put to death an Afghan convert to Christianity, Abdul Rahman. The apostasy rule is controversial and has been challenged by contemporary Muslim scholars. It allegedly goes back to the foundations of Islam, when tribal leaders joined in a social contract with the Prophet that was the basis of the Constitution of Medina, creating the original Muslim *umma*. When the Prophet died, some of these tribes attempted to leave the community, resulting in the *Ridda* or Apostasy Wars. Hence, the apostasy rule that any Muslim leaving the *umma* and who maligns or abuses the community shall be punished. This rule has been and is open to different interpretations. For example, it has been criticised by some Muslims, including the former Indonesian president who pointed out in the *Washington Post* that the teaching of the Qur'an states 'Let there be no compulsion in religion'.[31] Nevertheless there is considerable customary pressure not to quit the community.

Revivalism and an emphasis on strong religious identities mean in practice that women, or more specifically mothers, are very important in the construction of religious identities because women are responsible for domestic arrangements such as managing the children's religious education, making choices about food and diet, and organising private space. Group cohesion is enhanced by in-marriage, by ensuring the effective transmission of culture across generations, and punishing all attempts to exit the group. Group cohesion requires the domestic and public regulation of women, and hence patriarchal religious norms are typically invoked when social groups are under threat, or perceived as such. In Indonesia's Aceh province, newly enforced religious rules prevent local women from serving alcohol to Western visitors; Syarifah Binti Jauhari was sentenced to ten months in jail for breaking this rule in May 2006. Similarly, attempts to impose rules against pornography in Indonesia seek to prevent women having bare arms in public spaces.[32] Since the fall of Suharto in 1998 Muslim militant groups or vigilantes are now common in cities in Indonesia enforcing restrictive sexual norms, typically against single women in public.

Rituals of Intimacy

These group norms are more likely to be invoked when a community is a minority, or where the majority feels it is under threat by an economically dominant minority. These everyday norms that are important for defining religious differences, sustaining group identities and maintaining the continuity of the group may be called 'rituals of intimacy'. This phrase attempts to express ideas about social contexts and the expressions of self from the works of Erving Goffman, notably *The Presentation of Self in Everyday life.*[33] These everyday rituals are part of the drama of representing the religious self in contexts that may be ambiguous, contradictory or dangerous. These rituals are guides to good action (can I serve alcohol to strangers and maintain my identity as a 'good woman' ?). Such rituals or codes of conduct provide a series of answers to questions about how to behave towards strangers who are not co-religionists, and how to maintain religious purity in secular societies. Norms regulating correct behaviour have, of course, been present in all traditional religious systems. In traditional Muslim cultures, there are well-established customary guides to correct action. These behavioural guides were often fashioned in traditional societies along social class lines; what applied to court administrators would not apply to peasants.[34]

What then is new in the contemporary situation? One can argue that Islamic norms were originally constructed for the guidance of behaviour in societies that were wholly or predominantly Muslim. With the growth of the worldwide Muslim diaspora, there is a new perceived need to define correct behaviour and expunge 'foreign elements', whether these are Western or indigenous folk components. For example, Al-Kaysi's *Morals and Manners in Islam*[35] warns of the need to Islamize customary behaviour and ensure that children are brought up according to correct norms. The second issue is that with fundamentalism there is, as it were, an inflationary pressure to increase the scope and depth of these norms. As Muslim imams compete for lay followers, there is a tendency to increase the strictness of norms that are seen to be required by the shari'a. One interesting example is that while *halal* food with its prohibition of pork is well known, in an inflationary religious setting these norms come to include the idea of *halal* water. The pornography bill before the Indonesian Parliament will inflate the range of activities and circumstances that can be defined as pornographic, from kissing in the street to revealing 'sensual' body parts. Thirdly, the growth of the Internet has greatly increased the sense of a global *umma*, and the importance of strict adherence to norms.[36] Finally, there are a series of contingent circumstances that have enhanced the perceived need to defend Islamic practice. In particular after 9/11, the notions of a 'clash of civilizations' and the 'war on terror' have converged to enhance the norms of group identity.[37]

These rituals of intimacy define what Pierre Bourdieu has called the 'habitus'.[38] These daily practices include preferences for food and dress, the selection of intimate friends, the organization of courtship and marriage. How do women in different social classes manage the everyday life of immediate intimate contacts? How do they sustain separate and pure religious practices? Where do they get advice about proper conduct? Are these rituals changing over time to become more exclusive? Bourdieu's notion of habitus has become popular in contemporary sociology to describe the dispositions of individuals that define their taste. The concept is useful in defining the religious dispositions of individuals and how their taste for a range of religious services and commodities (such as *halal* food) is shaped. However, this modern usage often obscures the fact that the notion of habitus is actually derived from the tradition of so-called 'virtue ethics' in the philosophical tradition of Aristotle. In this tradition, habitus contributes to the shaping of ethical practices that in turn create particular types of character. The religious habitus is designed to create a particular character, namely the good Muslim or the good Christian.

The rituals of intimacy are in effect rituals of exclusion. If a ritual or norm defines a person as my friend or peer or co-religionist, it automatically defines some other person or group as not my friend, peer or co-believer. Intimacy is an exclusionary practice that creates a circle of intimates and outsiders. The stronger the code of intimacy, the more intense the web of exclusion. My hypothesis is that these rituals are partly a creation of modern times (through religious inflation), where religious identities are becoming more critical and challenging. At the same time these rituals quarantine the everyday world, making future inter-group conflicts more likely, and reducing the conditions for Rawlsian reciprocity.

These micro-practices of the everyday world make the achievement of social harmony far more problematic insofar as this micro-world diverges significantly from the liberal framework of a tolerant, integrated or multicultural society. The liberal world of secular multiculturalism is under attack.[39] Of course, this view of heterogeneity in modern times is constantly challenged by the historical imagination. Is ethnic complexity a consequence of modernity, or were such issues always present in, for example, pre-colonial Southeast Asia or in Islamic Spain or in the Ottoman Empire? Within a historical perspective, the Ottoman Empire provides an interesting example of the tolerance of other communities, especially so-called 'people of the book', namely Jews and Christians.

The argument about the growing disjunction between the state and the public realm, on the one hand, and the everyday world, on the other, can be rendered more valuable from an analytical perspective by drawing a distinction between popular religion – official or institutional – and spirituality. The dichotomy between the great and the little tradition or between official and popular religion has been a fundamental idea of both anthropology and sociology.[40] Indeed, this distinction was fundamental to the whole legacy of Kantian philosophy that shaped the sociology of religion of Durkheim and Weber.[41] The presence of popular forms of religion has in part articulated this cultural gap between the everyday world of peasants and the official culture of the literate, urban classes. The development of modern fundamentalism can be seen as yet another attempt to control, to cleanse or to eradicate popular religion by inculcating norms that essentially rationalise everyday life in the name of a stricter, more ethical code.

This development is close to the original meaning of jihad as an ethical struggle to purify religious practice. In modern Islam there is a widespread 'peaceful jihad' involving a negotiation of identity against a background of secular modernity.[42] There is good reason, therefore, to regard fundamentalism as a global version of Weber's Protestant ethic that brings everyday behaviour under the control of discipline, which attacks magical or mystical practices, and which enforces literacy through the study of sacred texts and discourses.[43] Fundamentalism is simply the modern version of an attack on popular religion that has been under way, for example in Islam, since at least the rise of Wahhabism in the

late 18th century under the leadership of Muhammad Abd al-
Wahhab (d.1791). But the difference is that these fundamentalist
reforms are genuinely global, and they are no longer confined to
specific regions or religious groups.

We can, however, argue that the globalisation of religion takes
three forms.[44] There is, as we have seen, a global fundamentalism
that is based typically on some notion of institutionalised religion
(whether it is a church, a mosque, a temple or a monastery) and
an orthodox set of beliefs that are imposed authoritatively. Secondly,
there is the continuity of various forms of popular or traditional
religion that is practiced predominantly by the poorly educated
who seek healing and comfort from such traditional religious
practices. Examples of these traditional practices are numerous –
one can point, for instance, to the importance of healing and
sacrifice in contemporary Morocco,[45] which have been explored
in North Africa since the beginning of anthropological research.[46]
Finally, there is also the spread of syncretic, urban, commercialised
religiosity. These religious developments are no longer local popular
cults, but burgeoning global popular religions carried by the
Internet, movies, rock music, popular TV shows and 'pulp fiction'.[47]
These forms of popular spirituality are transmitted by films such
as *Hidden Tiger, Crouching Dragon* and *House of Flying Daggers*.
They represent part of the new 'techno-mysticism' that is displayed
with spectacular effects in modern cinema culture. To these films,
one can add the popularity of such publications as *The Da Vinci
Code*. These have been called 'new religious movements'[48] or
'spiritual market places'.[49] Such forms of religion tend to be highly
individualistic, they are unorthodox in the sense that they follow
no official creed, they tend to be syncretic, and they have little or
no connection with institutions such as churches, mosques or
temples. They are post-institutional and they can be called
'postmodern religions'. If global fundamentalism involves
modernization, the global post-institutional religions could be said
to involve 'postmodernisation'.

In order to describe these new developments, some sociologists
have usefully called them new forms of spirituality in contrast to
religion and religiosity. Globalisation thus involves the spread of

spirituality, on the one hand, and fundamentalist religion, on the other. Spiritualities typically offer, not so much guidance in the everyday world, but subjective, personalised meaning often combined with therapeutic or healing services, or the promise of personal enhancement through, for example, meditation.[50] My hypothesis is that fundamentalist norms of rationalization appeal most to social groups that are upwardly mobile, such as lower middle-class, newly educated couples. Spirituality is more closely associated with middle-class singles who have been most significantly influenced by Western consumer values.

Religion, folk religiosity and spirituality can be seen to be in a state of mutual conflict and antagonism. The spiritual individualism of the upwardly mobile, cosmopolitan, middle-class habitus is incompatible with the rationalised norms of fundamentalism. We can assume that this explains the intellectual hostility of fundamentalist religious leaders to the consumerist individualism of the new spirituality. Although there is conflict and competition between these expressions of religion in post-industrial society, all three forms are also involved to some degree in the processes of religious commodification. In modern Israel, there are special shops for the sale of ultra-orthodox religious objects. There is a worldwide market for Muslim cassettes of preachers and recitations from the Qur'an, just as there is a global market for Sufi music and dance. There is another global market for the sale of traditional Buddhist amulets. While there is much criticism in religious circles of Western capitalism or the dominance of Hollywood in global popular culture, religion has itself become one dimension of a new commercial culture in which religious groups promote specific lifestyles.

Cosmopolitanism versus Enclave Society

Much of this chapter has been about understanding the implications of *da'wah* or Islamic outreach, but we can draw some general sociological lessons from these specific Muslim examples for a more general theory of what I want to call an 'enclave society'. Such a society is certainly a version of the 'social imaginary' of multiculturalism; yet it falls far short of an ideal cosmopolitan society. It is neither a melting pot nor a mosaic, but rather a collection of ethno-religious communities with little interaction or overlap. The danger is that the emphasis on cultural difference may well contribute to 'enclavement'.

Walls, like the Great Wall of China, are traditional methods of enclavement. There are walls being built in Baghdad, the Palestinian West Bank, in Padua, Botswana and the Czech Republic. The Berlin Wall was symbolic of the division of the world into East and West, and when it fell in November 1989 there was a general democratic euphoria; but these emotions were short lived. Walls enclave subject groups that are seen to be threatening, socially, culturally and genetically. In modern Padua, a steel barrier is being erected to separate the honest citizens of respectable society from the criminal neighbourhoods dominated by drug dealers, most of whom are Tunisian. Walls keep out illegal migrants in Melilla in Morocco and in San Diego they staunch the flow of illegal migrants from Mexico. Similar structures in Botswana attempt to keep out workers from Zimbabwe. In Baghdad, walls are emerging to create a safety zone and to separate Sunni and Shi'a communities.[51]

There are also religious enclaves arising from the rituals of intimacy that are, in turn, the outcome of pietisation. The call to return to a primary identity represents the creation of a spiritual enclave. This notion was a major argument in the Chicago research on fundamentalism in *Strong Religion*,[52] because the spiritual enclave is a wall against modernity and its seductive consumer culture. This 'wall of virtue' separates the morally upright from the corrupt outside world, dividing the world into an inside and outside. This enclave allows the believer to follow dress, dietary and sexual codes without secular interference. These enclaves are especially prevalent in piety movements in modern Islam, such as in Indonesia's Laskar Jihad.[53]

The idea of an enclave society suggests that, in order to survive, the society needs a strong interventionist state that can support the rule of law and prevent enclaves from descending into ethnic conflict. What is the relationship between state and society when civil society is an ensemble of separate enclaves? Although the revival of political theory in recent years has depended on the argument that the state cannot be reduced to society, but acts instead as an autonomous historical force, the Israeli state perhaps proves the opposite state-in-society theory that has been championed by Joel Migdal in his *State in Society*.[54] Migdal's argument is that states vary in effectiveness depending on their ties to society. States are not unitary actors, but are composed of clusters of institutions and groups with conflicting interests, and as a result state policies reflect the pressures from this broad social context. Finally, state and society can under some circumstances stand in a mutually corrosive relationship to each other. In modern Israeli politics, Shas as a political party does not make a significant impact on social cohesiveness;[55] but, following Migdal, a case could be made that Shas, along with other enclaves, actually damages the functions of the state. Shas recruits primarily from new migrant communities from North Africa and has flourished in a political environment where sectional interests are rewarded from state funding for religious education and other welfare benefits. One lesson from the recent crisis in Lebanon may well be that Hizbollah, rather than acting as a valuable element of civil society, replaces the state and reinforces sectional interest. The general lesson of any enclave society is that these enclaves preclude any effective policy response to ethnic stratification and do not create social capital.

Conclusion: Towards an Islamic Imaginary

Multiculturalism and tolerance of others can be sustained only where there exist some overlapping associational supports for social harmony and where there is sufficient social bonding to counteract political tensions arising from cultural (in this case religious) complexity. These conditions for social harmony are various: economic, cultural and educational, and political and juridical. Recent sociological criticism of multicultural policies claims that governments that have emphasized difference and identity politics have, perhaps consciously, obscured the importance of economic equality. What has been referred to as 'critical multiculturalism' requires mutual recognition and redistribution of national economic resources to create some equality of objective condition between host and migrant societies.[56] However, greater economic equality will never in itself be sufficient. In this respect, the multicultural record of social democratic societies which enjoy considerable economic or at least income equality, such as Denmark and Sweden, is not entirely encouraging. There must be direct governmental confrontation with racism and racist ideologies alongside the creation of effective social policies.

In fact, the principal foundation for tolerance and successful multiculturalism in Rawlsian democracies must be the presence of overlapping social and cultural ties that create social bonds between diverse groups. A critical issue in cultural recognition and the forging of consensus is the question of gender; this is reflected in rates of interfaith marriage. In this chapter, I have drawn attention to the low level of interfaith marriages in many societies experiencing religious revivalism. Marriages between different communities can be taken as a measure of the coherence of civil society as a whole, whereas marriages within communities are likely to solidify existing ethnic and cultural divisions. Because various religious groups favour such arrangements, it is unlikely that secular policies by governments to change such traditions can be successful. Issues surrounding gender (such as legal equality, absence of polygamous marriages, female education, freedom to reject the veil and seclusion and the prohibition of cliterectomy) remain the most significant aspects of the debate about multiculturalism and social tolerance. This conflict is not just about Islam, but about all faith-based communities such as ultra-orthodox Jewry.

Rawls's liberal philosophy of civil peace is an attractive framework for multiculturalism. In this discussion, I have explored the limitations in his approach with respect to fundamentalism, piety and what I have called 'rituals of intimacy'. A second problem with Rawls is the unabashed focus on 'Western' philosophy. If we are to obtain overlapping consensus among comprehensive doctrines, then we ought to take other, non-Western philosophies more seriously.

In response to Rawls, we may note that religious diversity is hardly a modern question. The matter of 'other religions' has been a vital aspect of theological debate in the three major prophetic, monotheistic religions since their foundation. In fact, we can argue that the issue of religious diversity becomes an acute problem primarily in monotheistic religious cultures. Cosmopolitanism is often associated with Western traditions, especially for example with the Stoics. In order to stimulate dialogue between different religious traditions, it will be important to seek out versions of cosmopolitanism that are not primarily or exclusively Western in origin. In Islam, the issue was famously addressed by Muhammad ibn al-'Arabi, also known as *Muhyi al-Din* (the Revivifier of Religion) or *al-Shayk al-Akbar* (the Greatest Master). Ibn al-'Arabi is particularly pertinent to the modern debate about diversity, partly because his contribution has been recognised by contemporary political philosophers. Born in Murcia in south-eastern Spain in 1165, he died in Damascus in 1240. Ibn al-'Arabi has been defined as a Sufi teacher who embraced the idea of the 'Unity of Religions'.[57] This oversimplified interpretation has been questioned by recent scholarship.[58] His philosophy has enjoyed something of a revival in the West, where his neoplatonism was explored by political philosophers like Leo Strauss. Because Ibn al-'Arabi was particularly concerned about the issue of religious diversity, the importance of his writing on the diversity of religions has been recognised by social scientists in recent analyses of the problems of multi-culturalism.[59] Ibn al-'Arabi's philosophical and theological account of religious differences is directly relevant to the search for a theory of religious pluralism.

Following Qur'anic teachings that recognise the existence of multiple prophets in different lands and traditions, Ibn al-'Arabi affirmed their validity. These different religious revelations were all reflections of a divine presence and deserved respect. Parens argues that Ibn al-'Arabi provides an alternative to both Kantian Enlightenment universalism, on the one hand, and postmodern cultural relativism, on the other. He rejected the ambition of revealed religion to aspire to universal rule, recognising that diverse communities are best served by their own diverse laws and customs. He realised, however, that from the point of view of political

8

Modern Citizenship,
Multiple Identities
Eva Schubert

The main hope of harmony in our world lies in the plurality of our identities, which cut across each other and work against sharp divisions around one single hardened line of vehement division that allegedly cannot be resisted.

Amartya Sen[1]

Citizenship is a political idea. It is linked to concepts of social and political rights, and the status of individuals vis-à-vis the state. In a world where mass migration, displacement and political disenchantment are rife, it is an idea that may seem to have shrinking relevance. In what follows, I will briefly trace the history and evolution of the concept of citizenship and examine its vital function in modern democratic states, most notably its application to political ideals and diverse publics. It is necessary to understand citizenship in its historical and theoretical context in order to identify the ways in which it is manipulated as a tool of exclusion. These civilisational narratives have been magnified and given new meaning in the wake of September 11, pitting a Western secular model against supposedly oppositional 'Others', most notably Muslims. The traditional idea of the secular public square will be critically analyzed with reference to its history, promise and relevance for globalised national populations that no longer share roughly similar cultural and religious traditions – or the Western historical experience from which that civic model is derived. Finally, I will explore an updated vision of the relationship between religious reasoning and civic action. This understanding is vital to a social imaginary that incorporates the widely varied range of communities, associations and individuals that inhabit the public sphere. Unless citizenship is redrawn outside its traditional boundaries, it will become obsolete.

The proper scope of citizenship and its primary purpose are a subject of some dispute. Recent events in the world which seem to link religious beliefs to political actions – sometimes of a terrifying and incomprehensible nature – have only served to reinforce a well-documented Western insistence on the separation of Church and State, not only as institutions but also as ideas. While I have no intention of attacking the institutional separation, I will argue that its meaning has increasingly been framed by a dogmatic secularism, which is quite a different matter. This distinctly modern claim has serious consequences for many actors in civil society.

The problems of this assumption will be the central theme of my chapter, and they affect a range of groups that vary in religious persuasion or lack thereof. The focus here will be on Muslims in France and Turkey, because their public presence and claims have generated such animated debates on national identity, civic values and religious freedoms in recent years. Both countries face a perceived challenge from Muslim communities cast as alien for various reasons. The French experience is similar to those of other European countries in the struggle to assert an essentialised national identity. The Turkish case is unique in that it combines a majority-Muslim population and history with a secularist vision of the state and modernity. The experiences of religious groups in these contexts reveal both the limitations of modern democratic culture and the ideological nexus between secularism and modernity.

The meaning of modernity itself has inspired much scholarly comment. For our purposes it is necessary to distinguish the vernacular use of 'modern' as merely contemporary from a larger philosophical meaning. This has been variously described, but usually invokes an individualistic, technocentric, secularizing model of society. Frederick Cooper gives a useful overview of the notion of modernity as an analytic category. He identifies four positions around this idea – three of them centred on 'the West' and one seeking to transcend it. The first position defines modernity as a project rooted in the history of Western Europe but universal in its scope and in the range of those aspiring to it. The second position derides modernity as a Western imperial construct which has a damagingly homogenizing intention. The third option defends modernity as a European achievement which cannot be mastered by others. Finally, there are multiple modernities, recognising that non-Western cultural forms do not necessarily reflect resurgent traditions, but rather distinctive approaches to progress.[2]

Cooper suggests that instead of applying scholarly rigour to developing more precise definitions of modernity, we should consider ways in which the concept is actually used in different places for various agendas. It should be clear that modernity is not merely the experience of the contemporary; it is a concept used to shape experiences in ways that privilege some values over others. Alongside claims of national identity, the 'requirements' of modernity are often invoked to justify a particular vision of the democratic state which frequently excludes Muslims, among many, many others. If recent historical scholarship has not attracted enough attention to make these exclusive claims dubious, the tensions in our increasingly diverse societies should give us pause. Xenophobia and monopolistic claims on ownership of tolerance, liberty and modernity seem to have sharpened.

Religious radicalism throughout the world seems more prevalent today than ever, and makes temperate discussion of religion and citizenship difficult. I will not be arguing for any kind of institutional religious authority in state policy. Versions of theocracy, old and new, have demonstrated the abuses that result from any coupling of governance with absolutes, religious or otherwise. Throughout this chapter I will argue that religious loyalty can furnish an inclusive sense of community identity and a model of moral reasoning that transcends immediate, subjective political issues. Both of these factors are essential features of a democracy that functions in its fullest sense, not merely as a system of voting, but as a vibrant social model which offers the opportunity for the realization of plural conceptions of the good. To put it another way, religious identity is capable of supplying both the motivation and the tools required for a robust, engaged sense of citizenship, with all its attendant rights and responsibilities. I am not asserting that only religion can provide these tools, but rather that its capacity to do so in a modern society has been overlooked. Without a concept of citizenship strong enough to sustain and welcome groups that fall outside traditional Western assumptions about legitimate and rational sources of civic activity, we risk largely denuding the concept of relevance for its modern public. This would render citizenship quite meaningless, divesting modern democracies of one of their richest sources of legitimacy and direction – the social capital of a robust civil society.

Citizenship in the Modern World

Despite the conflict of loyalties inherent in the tension between local and global senses of community and obligation, the practice of citizenship has been wedded to national contexts. Of course, the evolution of nationhood came long after the small city-state model of Greek political thought. Nonetheless, as Will Kymlicka observes, Western political theorists persist in building upon an idealized version of the Greek polis, conceived of as an entity with linguistic, historical and cultural homogeneity.[3] The problems that this assumption creates in modern democracies, where populations are often divided by very different loyalties and visions of the social good, will be examined more fully at a later point.

A comment by the famed 4th-century Athenian orator Pericles reveals the participatory aspirations of Greek citizenship: 'we do not say that a man who takes no interest in politics minds his own business; we say he has no business here at all.'[4] Since ancient times then, the citizen has been one who has an active interest in the collective good, motivating him to partake in public activities and debates. It is obvious that these qualities are superfluous in a context where the individual is not in a position to have any effect on the formation of policy or the shape of power. In other words, citizenship cannot properly be the possession of an individual merely because he is the subject of a state or sovereign.

The status of citizenship seeks to provide an equalizing level of claims and obligations within specified limits, so that particular social or economic groups do not bear a grossly inordinate share of obligations while others enjoy untrammelled privileges over them.[5] To be more specific, Michael Walzer explains that the status of citizenship establishes a set of relationships that make domination impossible. A citizen may, for example, have a higher status than his fellows in the judicial realm by virtue of holding the office of judge; but he is not thereby given more privileges in other areas, as by being taxed less or being free to break particular laws.[6]

Modern citizenship does not specify property ownership, gender, or age as qualifications, though the full exercise of its rights may be unequal for reasons varying from personal inclination or ability, to impediments of an economic or legal nature. Feminist critics, notably Ruth Lister, have observed that the universalist claims of citizenship are frequently complicated by issues of gender (and disabled) access to the full exercise of citizenship activities.[7] This is not to say that the goals of fully participatory citizenship are unrealistic. Rather, they should be considered with conscious reflection on their empirical limitations, for that is the only way we can make the ideal more realizable.

So far this account of citizenship has recounted a list of passive rights and responsibilities, such as could be provided in the service of a benevolent ruler. This might be thought of as a 'thin' description, which can be augmented by one's particular commitments. Those with a commitment to a conservative political orientation tend to emphasize patriotism, loyalty and civic engagement as the focus of civic virtue. Those with more liberal political commitments tend to direct more attention to the exercise of individual freedom and the protection of human rights as the core values of citizenship. In fact, neither set of objectives is possible independent of the other.

Civic engagement and loyalty can be nurtured only in a state that permits an active civil society and provides opportunities for the realization of diverse ambitions and goods. Conversely, the protection of human rights and individual liberty can be ensured only by active engagement with civil society and a posture of vigilance toward the state.[8] These goods require a 'thick' version of citizenship, which envisions a vital and active role for the individual in society. Attempts to export 'freedom' through democracy – so popular in US foreign policy – have shown that simply instituting a system of government and the ballot box are not enough to make power accountable and effective. For democracy to function as more than a token political arrangement, it requires a social setting in which individuals envision themselves in a particular relation to the state and to each other, as active citizens.

A primary responsibility of the citizen is the exercise of informed judgement and commitment to the collective good in monitoring the state's actions against a common standard of conduct, a kind of transcendent ethical code – transcendent because not purely personal or otherwise centred on narrow segmentary interests.[9] Active citizens then, exercise moral agency and reasonable detachment in judging their state and society. Indeed, it is the consciousness of larger ethical principles that frequently expands the boundaries of citizen concern from national to cosmopolitan causes, from attention to domestic policy alone with its immediate personal relevance – to foreign policy and actions. Doing so in the face of majority opinion – and sometimes against the tenor of the law – becomes a test of civic virtue, the 'golden mean' between unquestioning obedience to the state and intolerance of all views and policies that one opposes. This is related to the Greek concept of *isonomia*, which envisions the equal participation of citizens in the exercise of communal aspirations.[10] The subject of how such citizens may be produced will be discussed later.

Our sketch here is normative, inviting attention to its distance from actual practice. Robert Putnam reminds us of that distance – and its cost in social capital – in rich empirical detail in *Bowling Alone*. Social capital is the currency of trust generated by social networks, allowing cooperation, collaboration and mobilisational channels without which citizens are unable to effectively influence governments. Putnam is quick to point out that the cohesive properties of social capital are not invariably positive; it can enable and enhance a variety of activities from benevolence to terrorism.[11] Theda Skocpol observes that the value of different types of social networks are not equal; those forms are most powerful that engage participants across class, ethnic and religious lines.[12] This is corroborated by Putnam's distinction between bonding capital and bridging capital. Bonding is what occurs when we socialize with people who are very similar to ourselves, with shared racial, religious or communal markers. This is the kind of interaction that has the most potential to fortify group identities that may be potentially isolationist or even dangerous. Bridging is the interaction among people with dissimilar backgrounds and traits that commonly occurs around a shared interest such as a sport or hobby. It is the latter variant that is essential for transcending limited personal loyalties and building social cooperation in the larger civic context.

Emphasis on difference without a counterbalancing foundation of social solidarity may disable not only opportunities for interaction and bridging capital but also a far more significant potential for the broad alliances of interest necessary to effect social change. Ethnic and cultural differences are readily evident and inescapable. They may be the source of celebrations of diversity or socio-cultural fragmentation, depending on whether any larger source of identity is available to transcend these markers of difference.

Many countries have experienced tension as a result of growing immigrant communities which have proved difficult to integrate into the host country. Britain and France both have large Muslim populations that have retained a distinct identity manifested in patterns of eating, worship and forms of dress. These populations test the meaning of national identity by forcing those who advocate integration to articulate what exactly they are supposed to be integrated into. The risk is that immigrant communities will become increasingly segregated, relying on markers of identity outside their new national context to counter a sense of alienation or exclusion.

One of the markers that frequently trumps ethnic and cultural particularities is religion. Individuals from divergent ethnicities, cultures, classes and even linguistic heritages can locate a powerful, shared identity around faith-based practices and doctrines. Religious groups and associations are also some of the most fruitful generators of social capital, because they foster networks of shared values and, frequently, resources. As we have seen, without sources of social capital there is no civil society in which citizens can play their roles. Yet the suggestion that religious identities or values can have a valuable and constructive role in active citizenship or civil society is not popular, and indeed is the frequent victim of instantaneous dismissal. Why? Because religion, in Western secular democracies, is deemed a key source of dispute, division and incivility.

Religion and Civil Society

The history of the separation of Church and State can be traced back to the 17th century and the brutal European religious wars – born of the insistence on parallel religious/political loyalties which eroded the hegemony of the Roman Catholic Church and destroyed Western Europe. The institutional partition of religion and politics into separate spheres became a vital feature of the 18th-century Enlightenment, with its emphasis on individual religious freedom and rationality. This 'disestablishment' of religion led to the secularization of the public sphere and the state.[13] Religion was relegated to the private sphere.

Sociological theories of modernity, including the well-known work of Émile Durkheim and Max Weber, predicted that while religion played a necessary role in social evolution, it would increasingly be displaced by modernity. Religion was seen as bound up with outdated ways of seeing and being in the world; modernization, then, is inexorably also secularization. This theory enjoyed great popularity, particularly in the 1950s as US modernization ideology was exported to developing countries seen as suffering under the yoke of tradition and archaic religious belief.[14] The passage of time has failed to confirm the inevitable decline of religion. In North America and in many parts of Europe, religion is resurgent in political and public debate.[15] Beyond the West, from Central and South Asia to the Middle East and sub-Saharan Africa, claims about the inverse nexus of development and public religion seem even less tenable.

In the face of these contradictions, a more nuanced definition of secularism is required to make sense of evidence that both supports and contradicts older theories of secular modernity. José Casanova offers a tripartite definition of secularization. The first kind of secularization is evident in structural differentiation, which asserts that the 'fusion of the religious and political community is incompatible with the modern principle of citizenship'. It entails the 'institutional autonomy' of the state, the economy, science and law from subservience to institutional religious norms. The second type of secularization refers to the decline in religious beliefs and practices. Finally, the third kind of secularization is the privatization of religion, which eliminates its legitimate participation in public discourse.

Casanova distinguishes between the correlation of these various strains of secularization to definitions of modernity.[16] The first kind (institutional separation) Casanova asserts is 'the valid core of the theory of secularization' and 'a general modern structural trend'.[17] I agree with this claim because one of the defining features of citizenship, essential to modern democracies, is individual agency and moral judgement. It is difficult to see how this can be feasible and efficacious outside a bona fide democratic system. When these citizen-judgements are made instead by political or religious institutions, we re-encounter manifestations of the old contest of Church and State.

The other two kinds of secularization are far less convincingly attached to theories of modernity and the democratic state. There are many examples of modern states where religious belief is highly active, and where religious groups act in civic space without limiting themselves to the performance of religious functions, such as congregational services. Most obvious is the trajectory of the United States, which cannot be easily dismissed as lagging in the drive towards modernity, and which nevertheless fails to follow the Western European paradigm of a largely agnostic or atheist society.

The evident religiosity of the American population was noted by observers as early as Alexis de Tocqueville, and remains a conspicuous feature of public life.

As we have noted, social capital, particularly 'bridging' with people who are not from one's own ethnic or cultural group, is an essential prerequisite for an effective civil society. Unless very different groups can interact in this way, they become insular communities with purely subjective interests and claims. While minority rights and group rights are a legitimate topic that has much exercised academics, the very nature of effective multicultural citizenship requires the capacity to see beyond particular personal and group interests, and engage with a larger civic good. This shared interest has the potential to unite citizens across communal lines and exert influence on the governance of their state.

What is sufficient to create this kind of cooperation? John Rawls claimed that the source of unity in modern societies is a shared conception of justice: 'although a well-ordered society is divided and pluralistic ... public agreement on questions of political and social justice supports ties of civic friendship and secures the bonds of association'.[18] While shared values are necessary, they are not sufficient to create action in civic space; shared identity is required. Kymlicka points out in comparing secessionist states with their nations of origin (he uses Swedes and Norwegians) that despite great similarities in values, no basis for cooperation or unity around a shared notion of the good is evident. He also observes that the obvious sources of shared identity – commonality of history, language or religion – are exactly what is lacking in diverse multicultural populations. Because these common factors are palpably absent, what is sufficient to produce a shared sense of loyalty and identity associated with the nation-state where no personal markers of existing commonality are broad enough? For widely disparate groups, allegiance to the larger polity is only possible if it is seen as 'the context within which their national identity is nurtured, rather than subordinated'.[19] In other words, the cohesion of a multicultural state is not founded on a pre-existing cultural or racial homogeneity, nor on an assimilationist cultural policy, but rather draws upon its capacity to provide a society in which plural histories and aspirations are possible. The effective delivery of such a promise creates a stake for diverse groups in sustaining the national and civic context in which they can exercise various liberties and realize a wide range of aspirations.

Religious identity can and does contribute to exactly this kind of national loyalty and civic engagement. The Canadian Survey of Giving, Volunteering and Participating, released in June 2006, showed that a majority of the 14 per cent of Canadians who regularly donate their time and money are religiously active.[20] Of regular church attendees 48 per cent qualified as 'top donors', whereas only 16 per cent of those who did not attend qualified in this category. These figures are not peculiar to Canada. Robert Putnam's study of civic activity in America revealed a definite link between religious affiliation and broader civic ties. He found that 75 per cent to 80 per cent of church members gave regularly to charity, compared with 50 per cent to 60 per cent of non-members. The volunteering figures showed an even broader gap: 50 per cent to 60 per cent of church members were active as compared with 30 per cent to 35 per cent of non-members. These figures do not refer to religious activities alone; Putnam found that the religious demographic was also more likely to visit friends frequently, be involved in external volunteer associations, or hold club memberships.[21] Furthermore, religious communities can foster a sense of fraternity or solidarity, a consciousness of community interest that draws the individual outside the range of his own particular concerns, which is an essential lesson for wider civic engagement.[22]

It may be argued here that religious affiliation extended beyond the private sphere can also produce sectarian tendencies, which privilege doctrinal proscriptions of the good and foster an uncivil dogmatism about public affairs. It is for this reason that the secular public sphere has been touted as a rational, objective framework for progressive public debate. This view presupposes that the secular view is neutral. Of course, this is not the case. The enforced secularism of the public sphere supposes, implicitly if not more openly, that religion is everything that secularism supposedly is not – irrational, anti-modern, divisive and violent. This assumption can only be perceived as neutral by those whose views it supports, namely those without an attachment to non-secular sources of value. In fact, tolerant civic identities and strong religious values are not broadly antithetical. In Britain, the Islamic Human Rights Commission reported that 80 per cent of British Muslims do not perceive any contradiction between being observant and being good citizens.[23]

A cursory glance at the history of the 20th century should be enough to remind us that the absence of religion is no more a guarantor of peace, unity and reason than its predecessors. The secular genocides of Nazi Germany, the Soviet Union, Cambodia, and Rwanda should be enough to dispel any illusions of a moral enlightenment in the disenchanted age. What is not required is a choice between the hegemony of state religion or state secularism in an attempt to locate the lesser evil. Any system, given exclusive authority over public life, will marginalize and oppress. Our best hope may be the kind of civil society that Ernest Gellner describes as an 'ideological stalemate'.[24] This is not an invitation to a relativist chaos, but rather the refusal to accord sole legitimacy to any particular ideology in determining the rules of civil discourse. To quote Gellner again, 'social cooperation, loyalty and solidarity do not now presuppose a shared faith. They may, in fact, presuppose the absence of a wholly shared and seriously, unambiguously upheld conviction.'[25] Once again, this does not deny the need for serious convictions – only that it is not necessary that others share their particular details in order to cooperate and share civic space.

If the existence of divergent religious convictions demanded the institutional separation of Church and State in order to live peaceably in seventeenth century Europe, where so many linguistic, historical, ethnic and cultural markers were shared, what is required of increasingly diverse nations in the 21st century? The division of religious and political authority provided space for freedom of speech, thought and eventually participation, which encouraged much scientific and cultural flourishing. Yet, contrary to the prophecies of secularism's proponents, religion has not disappeared. The institutional separation of Church and State does not entail that religion has nothing to offer the modern public sphere of civil society. As already noted, religious associations do much to engage individuals in wider circles of interest, and foster bonds of solidarity and participation, which in an atomized age are ever scarcer qualities. Given that religion shows no signs of disappearing, we will examine instances of its exclusion from the public square, and their results. We turn now to the consideration of two national contexts in which the meaning of citizenship and the role of religion in public space have shaped the experiences of Muslim citizens.

France

The French Republican model of citizenship is founded on the concept of *laïcité*, the separation of Church and State. Originally formulated to free the state from the influence of an overbearing Catholic Church, *laïcité* was intended to liberate the individual citizen and foster the exercise of his rationality. It was – and is – a secular ethic, functioning as a kind of civil religion or social bond. The individual as the bearer of rights is conceived of as autonomous and unattached, shorn of cultural, communal or religious particularities. Coupled with a faith in the uniting power of rationality, this has led to a kind of normative monoculturalism, the expectation that all groups will become homogenized as they absorb the enlightened ethos of the Republic.[26]

Whether individuals can ever be divested of their particular affiliations through the power of reason or republican rhetoric is a question I leave for the reader's consideration. Whether they should be is what I will deal with here. Even republican theory does not erase these subjective loyalties, but demands they be privatized, left behind when one enters the public sphere in order that citizens may contribute to the shared project of civic good.[27] The problem is that there must be something compelling and unifying enough about the nature of this good to inspire participation, but if the goal becomes too substantial in its detail it becomes a project with far more limited appeal, and thus loses its efficacy. As Veit Bader points out, 'There can be no viable concept of political culture without history, and the history of liberal, democratic nations is inevitably embedded in particularist ethnic histories. This reference to particular histories can be used, and is used as a criterion of exclusion.'[28]

While the official justification for state secularism is that it provides neutrality, the French model, like all others, is forged out of a particular cultural trajectory and historical experience. As a result of these past negotiations, French 'neutrality' is translated into official recognition of – though not support for – Catholic, Protestant and Jewish religious organizations. Until 2003 Muslims were not included, despite a significant influx of immigrants from the Maghreb since the 1980s.[29] The influence of cultural markers in shaping democracies is not to be denigrated, but the danger is that very subjective traditions or traits will be glorified as indispensable foundations of freedom, or constitutive elements of citizenship. This is the tension between defence of cultural distinctiveness (which has sometimes been expressed internationally as French exceptionalism) and emphasis on moral universalism, which demands cultural assimilation domestically. The broad influence of this contradiction in republican thought has been usefully outlined by Cecile Laborde.[30]

Among the most visible and dramatic examples of conflict between the new defenders of *laïcité* and French citizens who do not adhere to republican concepts of identity and public space was the *foulard* (headscarf) affair of 1989 and its aftermath. Three Muslim schoolgirls wore headscarves to public school and were asked to remove their coverings or leave. The official response at the time did not outlaw the wearing of the *foulard*; but after another such incident in 1996, and the Stasi Report of 2003, the issue culminated in legislation, passed on 3 February 2004, that banned the wearing of 'conspicuous' religious symbols in public schools. As many have observed, the apparent equality of the prohibition has selective results, since Catholics and Protestants are not frequently given to wearing items that would qualify. The legislation was clearly directed at the wearing of the *foulard*. It is not insignificant that while the 1989 and 1996 incidents generated responses privileging case-by-case decisions,[31] it was only post-September 11 that the principle of *laïcité* was reinterpreted more absolutely.

The legislation sparked extended public debate, which to outside observers may have seemed disproportionate. At the heart of the controversy were mainstream perceptions of the meaning of the headscarf itself, invoking notions of female coercion and subordination. More alarming was the suspicion that the religious expression of these students in the public space of the classroom was not a private difference alone but a deliberate challenge to the secular structure of French society by representatives of a growing immigrant population. The result was that a principle originally designed to protect freedom of conscience has been reinterpreted to proscribe certain Muslim expressions of faith.

In this reaction, France has much in common with other European democracies, though perhaps the emphasis on secularism in this case is more pointed. The suspicious perception of Muslim communities has invoked the historical particularity of these democracies, and insisted that there is something fundamentally incompatible about remaining publicly Muslim and being a European citizen. US anthropologist John R. Bowen observes that in France, immigrants who observe the *salat* may be deemed insufficiently assimilated into French society by civil servants, which could adversely impact their citizenship applications.[32] Certain civilisational theses assert that Muslims are a single, distinctive group whose priorities involve structures of law and society entirely antithetical to European norms.[33] Talk of a 'globalized *umma*' suggests a unitary transnational community with a particular socio-political agenda and shared cultural traits. Yet observant European Muslims are greatly divided in their political loyalties, and the inability of national Muslim organizations to agree or represent the views of Muslim populations makes the myth of unity a fantasy that surprises Muslims themselves.[34]

In France, this fifth column thesis finds fuel in the volatile *banlieues* (neighbourhoods) where much of the immigrant population resides. These districts suffer from unemployment rates exceeding 20 per cent; young people are disproportionately represented in this figure.[35] Alienation and violence are growing, as the riots of 2005 and 2006 clearly show. Where social mobility is impaired and economic and physical segregation from the mainstream national community are routine, the attraction of radical brands of Islam which offer an alternative to the society from which migrants feel excluded will probably increase. The meaning of religious identity here is not static, but shifts in significance depending on whether or not there is legitimate public space for Muslims *as Muslims* – or whether in excluding such identities from the national social imaginary, we play into the hands of those who define Muslim identity as solely one of alienation and defiance. Our best hope of averting this outcome is to search for shared foundations of civic value, rather than insist that the only platform for full civic participation and freedom is one rooted in wholesale adoption of mainstream national culture.

Turkey

There are a number of significant parallels between Turkey and France with regard to the conception of citizenship and public religion. Part of this is due to explicit emulation of the French republican model in the modernization process legislated by Mustafa Kemal Atatürk, and guarded by his self-proclaimed partisans, the Kemalists. Unlike France, however, Turkey has a long, indigenous Muslim history that inevitably shapes the ways in which the role of the state and the individual are understood – as well as the types of freedom and values deemed foundational to the nation. Because in this context Muslims are not immigrants, the situation reveals an assumption that runs deeper than fear of outsiders: the conviction that Islam and modernity are irreconcilable.

The Turkish term for the relationship between state and religion, *laiklik*, has often been translated as laicism, a reference to the French principle of *laïcité* that became a constitutional principle in 1937. It is seen by scholars as standing not merely for the institutional separation of Church and State denoted by secularism, but as representing the dominion of the state over religion.

This is evident in the state's control of everything from the education of religious professionals to the content of their sermons.[36] This state-run version of Islam has often been criticized for severely limiting religious freedom and failing to accommodate the beliefs of a majority of Turkish citizens – a failing evident in religious upsurges when the political climate allows more open democratic expression.[37]

It was in the 1980s that political Islamist movements became a force in Turkish politics. Previously they were allowed no formal political participation, though the popularity of various parties was influenced by the currency of religious interests among their constituents.[38] As in France, the presence of Muslim expressions in public space, designated by the state as secular, caused controversy. The Merve Kavakçı affair in 1999 (discussed at some length in Nilüfer Göle's chapter in this volume) exemplified this conflict. The state's constraints on religious displays have impacted the participation of Muslim women not only in politics but also in other domains, such as education.[39]

The question posed by the rise of political Islam is what it represents. Is it a return to tradition or a new form of political expression? Female Islamists distinguish themselves from their mothers and grandmothers as 'conscious' Muslims, emphasizing their own agency and the rights that are theirs – including family relations – on the basis of Islamic principles.[40] They are primarily an urban movement, using religious language to create political identities in civic space. Nilüfer Göle sees contemporary Islamism not as a continuation of tradition but as a new and politicized interpretation of religion used to assert a collective identity in opposition to Western modernity.[41]

Kemalists have vigorously defended the principles of secularism as foundational to freedom and progress. However, because the image of women is attached to a larger civilisational package from which modernity supposedly derives, Westernization and Westernized women in Turkey are portrayed as markers of modernity and freedom. This conjunction has defined an oppositional identity bestowed almost reflexively on ways of living and dressing that fall outside those Westernized norms. This is most evident in clashes between secularists and Islamists centred on women's bodies in public space.

What is most threatening about Islamist groups is that they assert a version of Turkish culture and modernity that challenges the validity of the Kemalist paradigm, which staked an exclusive claim on modernity as Western and secular. The secular elite who continued the Kemalist project frequently relied on top-down legislative reforms, largely untroubled by their unpopularity. In the 1950s, the Turkish government was hardly alone in supposing that it had a mandate to govern in the best interests of its people, even when the latter were incapable of recognizing those interests. Any resistance caused by lingering religious loyalties would vanish as Turkey modernised and the 'traditional' population became urbanized and educated. An irreconcilable tension was thus created in national identity: Turks were to be distinguished by a socio-cultural makeover borrowing from Europe and France in particular, yet somehow to remain distinct and separate.[42] How to achieve the latter while rejecting most of the religious and cultural elements that would make Turkish identity distinctive remains a challenge.

Islamist movements highlight forms of culture and historical symbols that are indisputably local. By refusing to remain in the 'backward' and underprivileged borders of villages and *gececondus*, they expose the limits of Kemalism in failing to reflect values and beliefs that resonate with large percentages of the population. Increasing numbers of upwardly mobile, educated and financially successful sections of the population make defining Islamist loyalties as characteristic only of the 'underdeveloped' an increasingly dubious claim.

The Kemalist reaction to the Islamists has been dictated largely by the logic of their self-definition. It is rooted in the attitude towards Islam of the first secular nationalist reformers, who categorized the thoughts and actions of religious groups as fundamentally opposed to the mission of civilization and progress. In the words of Resat Kasaba, these reformers made Islam 'an all-purpose bogey, representing everything that reform, civilization and progress were not'.[43] Yael Navaro-Yashin argues that 'secularists constructed a discursive difference between 'civilization' and 'backwardness'.[44] This opposition is part of the function of 'regulatory discourses' that rely on stigmatizing and 'othering' competing patterns of living. Ironically, this 'modernist critique' is essentially unchanged from what Kemalism was in the 1920s.[45]

Unlike Anglo-American modernity, the Turkish experience has often suppressed liberal, pluralist claims in the name of national unity.[46] Examining the history surrounding the birth of the Turkish Republic reveals multiple approaches to the concept of modernity – to say nothing of Turkish identity – and not all of them were secularist. The evidence of rising Islamist movements in Turkey demands a re-evaluation of the meaning of modernity if democracies are to continue to derive legitimacy from claims to represent their people. The supposed neutrality and equality of the secular public square is only experienced by those without religious commitments. This conceptual shift has implications beyond the Turkish Republic, given the presence of religion in the modern public domains.

Both in France and in Turkey, understandings of citizenship have been coloured by particular historical experiences. A definition of modernity as a monolithic reality derived from a fixed set of cultural characteristics and reliant on them, has been employed to exclude Muslims *as Muslims* from equal standing in the public square. They may contribute as individuals, but are obliged to leave behind their headscarves and the values and identities they represent. Such assumptions implicitly privilege Western identities and values over others. True, it is impossible to include all values and rights claims equally; this is not an argument for a civic relativism. Practices that cause measurable harm or danger to individuals cannot be tolerated, even if defended by cultural apologists. However, not everything that falls outside hegemonic Western identity or modernity can legitimately be excluded. If democracies are to reflect the principles they purport to defend, then they must offer an updated model of citizenship with the capacity to engage and include the diverse communities they serve.

The challenge facing democracies today is that of delivering maximal freedom to societies composed of groups with plural sets of values, while maintaining a sense of identity strong enough to anchor citizenship. Multicultural policies assert the compatibility of various ethnocultural identities with a broad national loyalty, often nourishing active cultural and communal expressions in the public sphere. However, the expression of particular identities and loyalties unbalanced by a sense of broader national community may lead to what critics call 'plural mono-culturalism', parallel communities that exist in the same place but do not share a sense of common identity.[47]

Two lessons can be drawn from the multicultural experience so far. First, that virtues of 'tolerance' and cultural diversity integrate immigrants effectively by not demanding that they choose between their history and their new habitus. By allowing them to incorporate older traditions and manners into the new national identity, marginalization and ghettoisation are reduced. Conversely, the exclusion of certain aspects of identity from public legitimacy has the potential to alienate. It creates a barrier that demarcates features that differentiate the Other from those included in the social imaginary of national identity. This trend has been marked in Euro-American paranoia ('Islamophobia') about Muslim communities as havens for 'enemies of freedom'.

William Galston invokes 'value pluralism' to denote different objective goods that cannot necessarily be objectively ranked. Within the limits of liberty (he does not defend an unlimited relativist position) there exists a range of legitimate variations from which permissible choices can be made.[48] Pluralism requires more than mere 'tolerance' of different groups, cultures and ideas; it demands active engagement. This is a dynamic interaction in which both sides are changed and enriched. It can take place only in a society where the rules of civility prevent groups from being deemed illegitimate civic actors by virtue merely of difference, instead of offense. Engaging religion in pluralist civic space moderates more authoritarian religious impulses because the same space that permits what some religious groups may object to is the space that allows them to exist. *It creates a 'stake' for religious groups in maintaining a plural civil society, because their own freedoms depend on it.* Competing in public for legitimacy invites peaceful engagement; exclusion generates defensive and condemnatory reactions. Attempting to restrict religious voices to the private sphere alone fails the test.

The objection that religious identity is different from cultural or ethnic markers in that it is subsuming and perhaps incapable of integration in a pluralist context has been addressed by Amartya Sen in *Identity and Violence: The Illusion of Destiny*. Sen stresses the plurality of identity markers, loyalties, interests and affiliations that contribute to an individual's identity. To reduce that identity to any one of the component characteristics creates the 'illusion of destiny', and denies the vital role of individual reasoning and choice in assigning importance to some markers over others.[49]

To insist that religious loyalties are incompatible with rational civic identity, or that strong religious belief cannot possibly be accompanied by moderate political views, creates the danger it tries to avoid. To quote Sen:

> If choices do exist and yet it is assumed that they are not there, the use of reasoning may well be replaced by uncritical acceptance of conformist behavior, no matter how rejectable it may be. Typically, such conformism tends to have conservative implications, and works in the direction of shielding old customs and practices from intelligent scrutiny.[50]

The other possible effect of the denial of reasoning and plurality in the making of identity is the 'discovery' that it is endangered, and hence warrants or justifies intolerant or violent defensive measures. Strong religious loyalties or revivalism do not necessarily entail religious fundamentalism, with all its dogmatic incompatibility.[51] To insist on treating all strong religious loyalties as incompatible is to encourage defensive, alienated and trenchant attachment to identities we have defined as oppositional. This destroys the shared sense of identity and commitment crucial to democratic civil society.

Diverse populations reflect the increasingly globalised world we inhabit. The necessity of our interaction and cooperation with people who have very different histories, cultures and beliefs from our own demands a view of individuals and societies that can incorporate such complex relationships. Idealized views of a homogenous Greek polity where citizens share most of their historical, cultural and religious identity markers fail to ground modern citizenship. An ideological discourse of modernity that pretends otherwise will merely reinforce social fragmentation and disable civic participation.

In the post-September 11 world, citizenship merits more attention than ever. It has always been true that the benefits of civil liberties and social justice are secured and retained only in the presence of active collaborators – rather than passive legal recipients of privileges, or denizens who fail to hold their states and governments accountable. Yet the modern public square, afflicted by the precipitous decline of trust fuelled by the 'War on Terror', calls particular attention to the risks of civic conformism and passivity, and of surrendering to isolationist versions of national identity. Without the bridging capital of a pluralist ethos, no version of modernity can deliver on the promise of genuine democratic discourse, which is sustained only by vibrant civic identities.

9

Globalization, Civil Imagination and Islamic Movements

Kevin McDonald

Introduction

Today the civil imagination is undergoing a profound transformation. An older social world, where clearly defined groups vied for representation in national political systems, is giving way to a new context marked by fluid networks and boundaries, new mobilities and new uncertainties around the nation-state. Older forms of social integration such as full employment, mass trade unionism and participation in political parties are giving way to concerns about fragmentation and disconnection. Fresh forms of violence appear to be emerging, no longer shaped by clear instrumental objectives. New movements and actors are emerging, but many of these no longer seek to build mass-based organizations and to claim representation in political systems on that basis. New forms of supranationalism put into question the sovereignty of nation-states, which in turn challenges the representativity of political systems. The global integration of markets, with their culture of freedom through personal choice, challenges the nature of political communities. This is amplified by the globalization of media and information exchanges, where emerging technologies such as the Internet no longer constitute mass audiences and 'publics' in the way that the national press once did in the emergence of national societies and 'public spheres'.

These questions underline the urgency of rethinking the civil sphere and the civil imagination. A civil imagination implies that we not only encounter the stranger in our own worlds, but in order to cohabit we require forms of moral imagination that allow us to see the world through the eyes of the other. How does such imagination come into being? What sustains it? What threats does it confront?

Within this wider debate, growing attention is being focused on the place of religious movements in public life. Western social sciences have directed this concern particularly at Islamic movements. In part, this reflects the dynamism of the contemporary Muslim experience, linked to new mobilities and diasporas, as well as to changing configurations of global power and conflict, from the collapse of communism to the emergence of a new form of global '*jihadi* movement'. While this movement claims to be an expression of Islam, observers such as Olivier Roy insist that it represents the triumph of a form of Third World anti-imperialism, a victory of the political over the religious.[1] Yet the Muslim experience extends far beyond these new forms of violence, and is above all present religious renewal evident in practices of piety, from acts of charity or pilgrimages, to prayer or practices such as veiling. These practices are often at the level of personal experience rather than collective organization, a clear break with older forms of state-centred movement such as the Muslim Brotherhood. As such, these emerging forms of movement are similar to others in contemporary globalization.[2]

In this chapter I explore dimensions of these practices in the light of wider debates around the civil imagination. In the process I hope to open out two questions. First, I consider the ways in which broader debates around the civil have shaped ways of thinking about emerging Islamic movements. Secondly, I explore the extent to which these movements push us to think afresh about the civil. In so doing, I wish to focus on two important approaches to civil society. One of these is the influential Kantian approach where civil society is grounded in rationality and deliberation, and privileges organizations and institutions as the locus of rational deliberation and the basis of the civic sphere. The Kantian account is associated with celebrations of cosmopolitanism and the cosmopolitan person. A second approach to civil society is equally influential, in emphasising not deliberation and rationality but rather identities, rights and claims to recognition.

This is particularly important in contemporary accounts of the 'politics of recognition'.

Both these approaches have their origins in European history and social theory – the first framed in terms of Enlightenment universalism, while the second is closely linked to the Romantic tradition. While often regarded as in tension, they both underline the centrality of autonomy to human agency and to the civil imagination, whether through the exercise of autonomous reason or through autonomy in claims to authenticity.

These traditions exercise powerful effects in framing how Western social science has attempted to think about Islamic movements, privileging two contrasting accounts: either Islam as modernity's 'Other', or Islam as an 'identity'. While at first glance these appear radically different, they both define Islamic movements in terms of Western secularism – either as a rejection of secularism or as an expression of 'identity politics'. I consider the strengths and limits of these accounts, and in the process, argue that to go beyond their limits, we need to consider Islamic movements as religious movements. This means accepting that critical dimensions of such movements are outside the liberal progressive imaginary. That leaves us with a critical question: what implications, if any, do movements outside the liberal trajectory have for the civil imagination?

The Cosmopolitan's Other

The Kantian tradition regards the autonomous rational actor as the source of the civil sphere. Influential examples of this approach range from John Rawls's attempt to articulate the rational basis of moral obligation (albeit an obligation that extends only as far as national borders),[3] to Jürgen Habermas's argument that the public sphere is grounded in the kind of rational deliberation he sees emerging in 18th-century Central European coffeehouses.[4] These traditions have been renewed and strengthened by recent theorisations of 'deliberative democracy' and the linked project of articulating 'discourse ethics', which have influenced institution-centred models of 'global civil society' as developed by authors such as David Held.[5] Such responses to an increasingly globalized world not only stress institutions and rational deliberation, they also celebrate the 'cosmopolitan person', one who is at home everywhere and can experience the unknown as a source of pleasure rather than anxiety. Implicitly or explicitly, this cosmopolitan person is constructed in opposition to an 'Other', the person tied down by the confines and constraints of tradition.

The cosmopolitan person, in my view, does not exist. He is an abstract expression of a theory of agency and subjectivity grounded in the ideal of autonomy. This is perhaps why the cosmopolitan person is so often described in terms of his opposite, the fundamentalist. While the cosmopolitan is open and curious, the fundamentalist is closed and defensive; while the cosmopolitan thrives on change, the fundamentalist fears it; while the cosmopolitan is an expression of successful modernization, the fundamentalist is the product of failed modernization. For Anthony Giddens, the heart of fundamentalism is the defence of tradition under threat.[6] Such oppositions recur in academic and popular accounts of Islamic movements. Benjamin Barber sees an emerging global conflict opposing McWorld against jihad, reflecting the principles of 'globalism' and 'tribalism'.[7] Francis Fukuyama also appears to think of Islamic practice in terms of tribalism, proposing that practices of veiling associated with Islam are best understood as a manifestation of tribal control, the means through which a collectivity limits that ability of its women to form relationships with outsiders.[8] Giddens uses a metaphor of war, arguing the 'battleground of the twenty-first century will pit fundamentalism against cosmopolitan tolerance'.[9]

These approaches to 'fundamentalism' rehearse earlier theories of 'social strain', where movements of different kinds emerge as a response to social change that they can neither control nor understand. Hence, these movements are understood as essentially reactive. Bernard Lewis, the British historian and doyen of Middle East studies in the United States, is an influential proponent of this view, describing what he calls 'Muslim rage' that he regards as an expression of frustration at the inability of Muslim-majority societies to modernize.[10] It was Lewis who revived the term 'clash of civilizations', originally used by Protestant missionaries in the Middle East in the 1920s, and later popularised by Samuel Huntington.

Anthropologist Peter van der Veer[11] notes the parallel between the 21st-century celebrations of the cosmopolitan and the account of modernization proposed by Daniel Lerner in the 1950s in his *The Passing of Traditional Society*.[12] Lerner proposed that Middle East Muslim-majority societies were confronted with a choice between 'Mecca and mechanization'. Until they freed themselves from the weight of their Islamic heritage, he argued, these societies would be unable to modernize. Lerner also celebrates a type of person, one he describes as a 'mobile personality', a person who embraces change and movement, who is free from the constraints of the past. As van der Veer notes, there is a powerful continuity between Lerner's 'mobile personality' and today's cosmopolitan person. Today's cosmopolitan expression of the civil insists not only on secularity (a dimension I will return to), but as van der Veer suggests, it extends a 'Western colonial engagement with the rest of the world',[13] one where the West is the motor of history, while the 'Other' remains defensive and inactive. It not unreasonable to regard the current celebration of 'cosmopolitan civil society' as a *lite* Kantian version of the clash of civilizations thesis.

Interpenetrations, Borders and Edges

To begin to think creatively about the civil imagination we need a more complex account than this opposition between the cosmopolitan and his 'Other'. Above all, we must recognise the extent to which civilizations interpenetrate through encounters that cannot be understood primarily in terms of conflict. Thierry Zarcone, the historian of comparative civilizations, underlines the importance of such interchange, observing that it was through the 'clash of civilizations' in the 13th century when, thanks to the Arabs and Islam, Europeans discovered the Greek heritage of philosophy, chemistry, arithmetic, astronomy and medicine.[14] The extent of this interchange goes beyond the role of Islamic civilization as a storehouse or transmitter of classical civilization. It was in 14th-century Cairo, then the intellectual capital of the world, that the North African Ibn Khaldun (1333–1406), exploring the rise and decline of various Muslim societies, developed the first conception of non-religious history. Khaldun's work marks the entry of time consciousness into the birth of modernity, above all in the Italian city-states. Zarcone also points to the 'Western' character of Islam: geographically, owing to its location vis-à-vis Asia, and culturally, in springing from Abrahamic and Greek traditions (including the nexus with the hypothetical-deductive model that shapes the architecture of Islamic law and theology). Zarcone argues that important aspects of the Islamic experience develop in buffer or intermediary civilizations, among Persians, Sassanids and the Turkish-Iranian world with its Indo-European languages and cultural locus in the West.

Zarcone also points to the encounter between Islam and the Eastern civilizations of China and Hindu India, where products of a cross-fertilization eventually made their way to the West. Additionally, important dimensions of the Muslim experience remain deeply influenced by Eastern experiences from the Confucian and Taoist roots of Chinese Muslims, the Hindu roots of Indian and Indonesian Muslims, and the Buddhist, animist and shamanist foundations of Turkish Islam that play a vital role in Sufi mysticism. Buddhist monastic architecture structured around a central courtyard gave rise to the *madrasa*; Indian yoga entered the Islamic world in the 14th century, linked to chants and breathing exercises that developed in Sufi *tariqas*. Such interpenetration continues to the present, and is not without contestation and conflict, as in debates about yoga in Egypt today.

The American historian Richard Bulliet develops a similar argument through introducing the theme of 'Islamo-Christian civilization'.[15] He argues robustly against the idea of civilizational clash, suggesting that the Muslim-majority societies of the Middle East and North Africa and the Christian-majority societies of Western Europe and America are integral to a shared civilization. The historical development of Christianity and Islam parallel each other so closely, observes Bulliet, and are so interconnected that they are best understood as part of the same 'socioreligious system'.

As with other movements that would become 'religions', the emergence and development of Islam was a dynamic process. Armando Salvatore points to the tension within the movement founded by the Prophet, where in the Qur'an the word *Allah* (God) appears 2,697 times, the word *din* (to behave duly before God) ninety-two times, while the reified term *Islam* as a noun only occurs eight times. Far more frequent is the non-reified verb *aslama*, meaning 'giving oneself in total commitment'.[16] The gradual triumph of the term 'Islam' occurs considerably later, as the result of historical processes mirroring the emergence of the concept 'religion' within Europe, amidst the rise of modern science,[17] where the axial tension between this world and the hereafter was reformulated as a contest between two spheres, the religious and the secular. It was thence that the modern notion about religion as comprising a series of personalised *beliefs* emerged, together with the generic concept of religion as a systematisation of such beliefs.[18]

Scholars of contemporary religions underline the way more recent transformations are at work in different religious traditions. The American anthropologist Robert Hefner notes important parallels between contemporary Islamic and Hindu renewal, and the renewal of Protestantism that took place early in the 20th century.[19] Olivier Roy develops a similar argument when he points to the personalisation of belief and the decline in organized religious authority in Islam, evident no less within contemporary Christianity. Bulliet suggests that key processes of innovation and transformation within Islam occur in what he calls 'edge situations' or zones of encounter with other traditions or civilizations. Such zones have played a significant role in the development of Islam in plural geographic and cultural settings.

A New Publicness

In contemporary Islam we encounter a striking example of 'global complexity', networks of flows, symbols, communications and experiences. Dale Eickelman points to the expansion of higher education, the increasing importance of travel and mobility, and the proliferation of new and old media, throughout the Muslim-majority world and beyond – ranging from print, radio, television, music, video and audio cassettes, CDs and DVD, to the Internet.[20] This is part of an explosion of Muslim popular culture, from music to pulp fiction, in particular romance fiction, breaking with the mass-media paradigm of a small number of senders and a large number of receivers, involving new vernaculars, voices and audiences. Jon Anderson sees these emerging forms of public experience as 'creole journeys'.[21] Rather than forming closed communities, these communications flows constitute fields that people enter and leave, a shift from a paradigm of community to one of contact. Such public spheres spread across Muslim majority countries, as well as between them and wider zones of diaspora.

These accounts underline the imperative of breaking free from oppositions such as 'global versus local', 'cosmopolitan versus fundamentalist', and from a priori understandings of Islamic movements as defending tradition. Instead, we encounter a wider reconfiguration where Islam, like other religions, is experiencing a process of de-institutionalisation. The authority of formal religious leaders is weakening, implying a decisive shift where meanings are increasingly constructed by political actors and cultural movements rather than religious institutions.[22] Among the most important developments in this vein is the contemporary *salafi* movement.

Neo-fundamentalism against Tradition: the *salafi* Experience

Movements of revival and reform occur in wider contexts of social, cultural and political upheaval. Religions and religious experience are vital ways of being in the world, and of experiencing the distance separating the world and the transcendent. The birth of European modernity was intimately linked to religious movements, where the vision of future redemption present within the Christian religion became secularised through the English, French and American revolutions.[23]

There is no clearer example of the misapprehension involved in regarding religious movements as defenders of tradition than the case of the contemporary *salafi* movement. The term *salafi* was used to refer to scholars and preachers advocating the way of the *salaf al-salih*, pious Muslims of the early Islamic period. This movement received impetus from the writings of Jamal al-Din al-Afghani (1839–1897), the Iranian-born philosopher and politician who spent much time in Paris and Afghanistan (as his name suggests), where he became involved in the struggle against British colonization. Al-Afghani considered Islamic civilization to be profoundly threatened by European imperialism, believing Islam had become weak and decadent through contamination by local cultures and traditions. To respond to European colonization, he argued, Muslims needed to re-engage with the Islam of the Prophet. For al-Afghani, a correct interpretation of the Qur'an and hadith (actions and sayings attributed to the Prophet) was completely compatible with modern science and rational thought; it would encourage diligence, hard work and frugality, facilitating the development of rational civilization, capitalism and democracy. Al-Afghani's core conviction was that the modernization of Islam required a return to its origins – indeed, that the modernization of Islam could only occur through its 'fundamentalisation'.[24]

The Western Debt of the *salafi*

It is important to recognise that this modernising Islam was not simply a reaction to Western domination. In fact, a more complex interpenetration of civilizations is at work here. Noah Salomon's important research in Sudan shows clearly how the British colonial regime from 1898 to 1914 wanted to remove pre-colonial social structures and culture, targeting in particular Sufi Islam and the form of government associated with it, the Mahdiyya based on the power of the mahdi ('divinely guided one'). The colonial administrators set about creating a distinction between orthodox and heterodox Islam, banning visits to the tomb of the mahdi (in fact destroying the tomb and scattering the bones), and persecuting other practices associated with the Sufi tradition. The British administrators saw Sufi practices as cruel, uncivilized and sensual, while regarding the *salafi* reform movement, present in Sudan through the Egyptian and collaborator of al-Afghani, Muhammad 'Abdu, as based on jurisprudential interpretation of scriptures. Lord Cromer, the governor of Egypt from 1883 to 1907, actively supported the development of the *salafi* movement as the version of Islam most adapted to the demands of modernization. The colonizers sought neither to secularise nor to impose Christianity, but to govern through religion:

> the establishment of a secular state necessitated not that religion retreat into the private sphere, but that religion enter the public sphere in a very different manner than it had previously. Though religion was not the foundation of law and government any longer, as it was in the Mahdist theocracy, religion was made into an important arm of disciplinary governance. It was precisely the privatisation of religion that the British feared, for that meant an Islam beyond their control. Instead, the British attempted to create a new Islamic public to supplant that of the Sufi and Messianic orders popular in the Sudan.[25]

Political Islamism

Overall the *salafi* movement took the form of a pietistic movement and did not aim at transforming political systems. Over the 20th century, however, major shifts took place that led to the constitution of today's political Islamism. Two authors in particular were instrumental in those shifts. Sayyid Abul A'la Mawdudi (1903–1979), a cleric in the region of Hyderabad, one of the principal Muslim-majority regions of India at the time of the partition, wrote and preached about what he called the decline of the Muslim population when confronted with Hindu experience. He insisted on the importance of political action and called for the end of mixing with other religions. Mawdudi performed a radical transformation in the reading of the Qur'an, introducing the modern political concept of sovereignty and arguing that 'sovereignty belongs to none but Allah'.[26] The consequence was a radical rupture: a modern understanding of the political sphere entered Islamic thought, and in the process, the political became defined in terms of the sacred.

This innovation was developed further by the Egyptian intellectual and member of the Muslim Brotherhood, Sayyid Qutb (1906–1966). Again, writing in what he experienced as a crisis situation – the triumph of Nasser's secular Arab nationalist ideology in Egypt – Qutb considered the current world to be so corrupt that it represents a state of *jahiliyyah*, the condition that the world existed in before the revelation of God through Islam. As such, Qutb radically impacted one of the core conceptual structures of Islam, the 'before' and the 'after' of prophetic revelation.

Qutb was a school inspector, Westernized, and born into a small village he later came to regard as steeped in ignorance due to superstition. His early writings, like those of al-Afghani, are imbued with the kind of Romanticism and vitalism out of which emerged European fascism. In *Social Justice in Islam* he creates a vision of an organically fused world, held together by the divine category, Will:

> [A]ll creation issuing as it does from one absolute, universal, and active Will, forms an all-embracing unity in which each individual part is in harmonious order with the remainder ... Thus, then, all creation is a unity comprising different parts; it has a common origin, a common providence and purpose, because it was produced by a single, absolute, and comprehensive Will.[27]

Aziz Al-Azmeh underlines the debt which this political Islamism owes to European culture and ideologies. Afghani developed his key themes not as a religious scholar in the holy city of Qom, but in Cairo, Istanbul and Paris, drawing heavily on the European Romantic tradition, on Herder's vitalist Romanticism and Rousseau's general will. He also drew upon the Darwinist conception of struggle for existence, arguing that one nation can grow strong only through weakening another, and saw the decline of societies as the result of being weakened by sectarianism. For al-Afghani, the classical civilization of the Muslim Arabs was weakened by esoteric sects, allowing its defeat by the Crusaders and Mongols, while the Ottoman Empire was weakened internally by Westernizing reformists. Al-Azmeh points to the similarities between this organicist, vitalist conception of the nation and the model of political action it inspired, and the development of European fascism emerging out of the same intellectual matrix.[28]

The debt to European political theory is equally evident in the work of Qutb. He theorises the role of a vanguard in the Leninist mould. There are numerous references in Qutb's writings to healthy values, degenerate nations and weakness, infertile values – expressions of his fascination with the writing of the French fascist Alexis Carrel, the author whom he cites most frequently, and from whom he adopts an overarching framework of analysis. Carrel's 'laws of life' that must be followed become the law of God, interpreted in terms of the shari'a. As Al-Azmeh notes, the shari'a is not a code, but a general concept of 'good order' similar in meaning to *nomos* or *dharma*. Qutb reframes the shari'a, Europeanising it by conceiving it as a code to be applied, and locating it within the tradition of European Romantic thought, where it becomes the equivalent of the 'laws of life'. Qutb does not seek a return to a pre-modern utopia. His writings about his time in the United States show how he is deeply affected by the extraordinary technological power of the West, as indeed was al-Afghani. He wants to separate that technological power from Western culture, and harness it to serve the transformation of the social order he envisages.

The extent of this interchange underlines just how much the idea of separate civilizational development is a myth. But this myth is powerfully supported in countries shaped by Islamist ideologies as well as by proponents of civilizational clash. The Tunisian scholar Abdelwahab Meddeb explores what he calls the enforced amnesia sweeping contemporary Muslim societies. He recounts stories of doctoral students in the humanities from Muslim-majority countries studying in European universities who are completely unaware of the interpenetration of Islamic and Western cultures. Not only is the extensive interchange between the Islamic world and the West being removed from educational curricula, so too are centuries of history and culture. Poetry of the body, sensuality and beauty, one of the great cultural achievements of 11th-century Baghdad and once a source of scandal in the West, are now burnt or destroyed. *The Thousand and One Nights*, among the treasures of the world's literary heritage, is banned in Saudi Arabia and Egypt. This amnesia extends to pre-Islamic history as well, evident in the destruction of the Buddhas at Bamiyan in Afghanistan. Likewise, Saudi funds for *madrasas* in Indonesia involve removing Indonesian history and culture from the curriculum.

There are obvious parallels between political Islamism and the Cultural Revolution in China, evident in the way the Red Guards set about destroying historical monuments and sought to obliterate China's Confucian past. Far from being a cultural movement seeking to reinstate local traditions, political Islamism is an anti-traditional modernization movement; it wants to replace customs with law (as did the British in colonial Sudan), a dimension that has strengthened in the course of the 20th century. Its founders, al-Afghani and his Egyptian collaborator, Muhammad Abduh, were clearly open to wider dimensions of the Islamic experience, such as Sufi mysticism, evidenced by the extensive correspondence between them couched in Sufi language. But as the *salafi* movement sought increasingly to purge itself of cultural impurities, it came paradoxically to depend more and more upon Western intellectual sources. There is a parallel in the way Maoism embraced another European tradition, Leninism, to modernize and purge China of its Confucian past.

Islam as Identity?

The idea of opposed civilizations that pit cosmopolitan modernizers against fundamentalist defenders of tradition appears far removed from actual Islamic movements. Should we look, then, to the other major approach shaping the civil imagination, one stressing identity, rights and recognition? Are Islamic movements best understood as 'identity movements', and if so, what are the implications for the way we approach the civil?

For those like Will Kymlicka and Charles Taylor who emphasise identity, public life is not grounded in the rationality of the individual but in communities and the 'politics of recognition', an approach associated in particular with Canadian multiculturalism and pluralism. This perspective situates the human person primarily in cultures, histories and traditions: societies are increasingly structured in terms of 'ethnocultural groups', while questions of justice are framed not within Rawlsian rationality, but in terms of 'ethnocultural justice'.[29] Kymlicka extends the model of ethnocultural groups to other marginalized groups of citizens seeking 'public affirmation of their identity', while Taylor insists upon recognition as a condition for authenticity, with a strong debt to the Romantic thought of Herder when he asserts 'just like individuals, a *Volk* should be true to itself, that is, its own culture'.[30]

At first glance this 'ethnocultural' tradition appears to be more sympathetic to Islamic movements than Kantian rationalism. Yet this sympathy brings with it an intellectual shift. Rather than locate Islam as 'Other', the politics of recognition seeks to incorporate Islam as an 'identity', the cultural expression of a community. This view is increasingly evident in anthropological studies where an earlier emphasis on ethnicity and national culture draws upon themes of 'religious community' and diaspora. Pnina Werbner convincingly demonstrates that, in Britain, Pakistanis have 'redefined themselves as a Muslim diaspora', noting that 'being a Muslim disaporan does not entail an imperative of a physical return to a lost homeland'. Those who understand themselves in this manner can assert 'their membership in a transnational moral religious community, the *umma*'.[31]

We need to give careful attention to the shift occurring here, where 'transnational ethnic worlds'[32] become redefined as 'transnational moral religious communities'. Without a doubt the emphasis on the transnational captures important dimensions of the contemporary diasporic experience, less and less defined in terms of 'homeland' and point of origin. But in the process, what was previously regarded as an 'ethnic world' becomes defined as a 'religious community'. For Werbner, this emerging transnational religious community is an expression of a wider diasporic form of 'transnational identity politics'.

We need to remember that the entry of 'identity' into the social sciences is relatively recent, taking place in the United States in the 1950s. Its development alerts us to the convergence of several processes, including a change in the status of social anxiety, from a fear of excessive conformism that motivated theories of mass society to a new fear about fragmentation in a culture defined by flux and change. The concern with identity is not only focused on the individual, but also applied to national cultures. The use of the term 'identity' in public debates was also associated with social policy debates about immigration, in the context of the creation of the concept of 'ethnic identity' in the United States.[33]

In that sense, 'identity' is a product of American culture and history, and most definitely is secular, involving no reference to tensions among the world, self and transcendence. In defining Islam as a dimension of 'transnational identity politics' we reframe religious experience as a dimension of group culture and identity, to what Werbner calls the 'performance of identity'. This has the effect of reducing religious experience to a dimension of group culture. It is a matter that is much contested in practices of veiling, with implications for our civil imagination.

Veiling: Resistance, Tradition and Modernity

Veiling and its relationship with the place of women in society has been a critical marker of the relationship between Muslim-majority societies and modernity. For secularising and Westernizing regimes, veiling has been a sign of backwardness. In Turkey, the Westernizing Kemalist government banned the traditional fez worn by men as well as the veil worn by women – deemed symbols of Ottoman backwardness – and attempted to introduce a straw hat for men and a bonnet for women. In Egypt in 1923 a movement of upper-class women involved in the nationalist struggle against British colonial power initiated a movement against veiling; indeed, urban middle-class women in Egypt wore Western dress for most of the 20th century.

Nilüfer Göle argues there is more at stake here than a simple symbol of Western modernization. Turkey's Kemalist government was aiming at drastic cultural change; if the straw hat and bonnet were not in themselves successful, the idea of fashion as a celebration of the new, of change, of the ephemeral still mattered. Westernising elites embraced modern forms of clothing and embodiment; rural women kept to the headscarf. The issue of the headscarf appeared to be framed within a wider debate about the relationship between tradition and modernization, religion and secularisation, city and provinces, elites and popular classes. From the 1980s, however, the question of veiling has re-emerged. In Turkey, as in many other countries, its social base is urban rather that rural, made up of young professional women and university students.

Arlene MacLeod's influential study of 'new veiling' among lower middle-class women in Cairo in the 1980s explores the decision to veil made by office workers in a city where veiling had not been widely practiced for decades.[34] She argues that these women are largely located in dead-end jobs in a bloated and inefficient public sector, torn between the economic imperatives of paid employment and a culture that regards the home as the appropriate place for women. MacLeod argues that they are in a 'double bind'. They make relatively limited economic gains through work, while being subjected to disapproving comments from neighbours and harassment by men in public. Adopting the veil, she argues, is a strategy to assert their centrality to family and domestic life (the veil affirming that they are in paid employment for their family's sake, not their own), without compromising their ability to leave home and earn an income. They are thus able to claim the respect accorded to women in traditional Egyptian society, while at the same time participate in employment. MacLeod proposes that the veil is neither a rejection of modern society nor a wholesale embrace of tradition, but a selective attempt to revitalize and stress some of the old ideals.

There are similarities between this attempt to identify the agency of 'new veiling' and the argument of social psychiatrist Mervat Nasser. She sees parallels between the type of agency evident in veiling and the agency present in anorexia. Both anorexia and the 'new veil' can be understood as forming systems of messages that are conveyed through the body, combining obedience and protest through conformity, moral discipline and ambivalence/refusal of the opportunities open to women. From this perspective, veiling, like anorexia, consists of 'substituting self-control for effective control of the world in which women exist'.

> Both anorexia and the veil reflect inner conflict and convey distress, symbolic of struggle that looks like resignation, rebellion that takes the shape of conformity and resistance that is dressed in complicity . . . The moral crusade of the anorexic and her strive for purity are mirrored in the young woman's voluntary return to the veil. Each pursues her externally different but psychologically analogous and culturally approved objective with fanatical and compulsive devotion. Both are symbolic of woman's self-denial, self-control as well as her search for self-validation . . . They are forms of veiled resistance adopted by women who are torn between tradition and modernity.[35]

Conversion stories posted to the Internet, in particular in Western societies (where the majority of converts to Islam are women), often attach importance to *hijab* and to the change in relationship between men and women that it produces. The constant theme running through these accounts is one where the *hijab* is understood as an instrument to negotiate male domination. They imply that a world that was not shaped by such domination would have no need of *hijab*. These accounts of agency are purely secular; any religious meaning of the practice is marginalized, with religion understood uniquely as a repository of traditional values (in the way understood by Giddens) that can be selectively mobilized to negotiate the forms of domination characterizing modernity. As such, these accounts remove the religious actor from the public sphere.

Embodied Piety, Subjectivity and the Public Sphere

Some of the most significant Islamic movements today privilege piety centred on embodied micropractices: prayer, observing rituals, negotiating public spaces, modesty, recitation and study sessions, listening to sermons, discussion of the meaning of religious texts. They often involve self-taught leaders and teachers, alerting us to the decline of traditional forms of authority centred on formally trained religious scholars. In the case of the women's mosque movement in Cairo, leaders are women themselves, most of whom do not possess recognised Islamic credentials.

Is this kind of movement an 'identity', the culture of a *volk*? Is it a defence against globalization, tradition defending itself? The anthropologist Saba Mahmood explores practices of veiling, prayer and moral cultivation emerging within this movement. Her core contention is that such practices of piety cannot be reduced to an identity claim on behalf of a community. While nationalist and Islamist parties attempt to transform the veil into a symbol of collective or national identity, Mahmood argues this is an understanding imposed from the outside, one that fails to capture critical dimensions of practices of piety. What is at stake is not veiling as a *symbol*, as representing identity, but veiling as a form of *embodied action*, part of a wider embodied process through which a pious subject is constructed, in particular through practices of prayer, recitation of the Qur'an and modest behaviour. These practices, evident especially through veiling, centre on the body; they are practices where corporeal experience is central, constituted through prayer, through movements in public, and other forms of embodiment such as learning to experience emotion and cry while praying. Such forms of corporeal practice, Mahmood argues, do 'not simply *express* the self but also *shape* the self that they are supposed to signify.[36]

This is captured by one of Mahmood's interlocutors, Amal, when she recounts her experience of veiling not in terms of representing an identity but as a way of producing a subjectivity that is 'shy' or modest:

I used to think that even though shyness [*al-haya*] was required of us by God, if I acted shyly it would be hypocritical [*nifaq*] because I didn't actually feel it inside of me. Then one day, in reading verse 25 in Surat al-Qasas ['The Story'] I realised that *al-haya* was among the good deeds, and given my natural lack of shyness, *I had to make or create it* first. I realised that making it in yourself is not hypocrisy, and the *eventually your inside learns to have al-haya* too . . . It means making yourself shy, even if it means creating it . . . And finally I understood that once you do this, the sense of shyness eventually imprints itself on your inside.[37]

Namma, another of Mahmood's interlocutors, describes what is at stake in a similar way:

In the beginning when you wear it [*hijab*], you're embarrassed and don't want to wear it because people will say you look older and unattractive, that you won't get married, and will never find a husband. But you must wear the veil, first because it is God's command, and then, with time, because your inside learns to feel shy without the veil, and if you take it off, your entire being feels uncomfortable without it.[38]

Mahmood attempts to think about what is involved in such body practices by drawing on Pierre Hadot's exploration of spiritual exercises, which he describes as 'practices which could be physical, as in dietary regimes, or discursive, as in dialogue and meditation, or intuitive, as in contemplation, but which were all intended to effect a modification and transformation of the subject who practiced them'.[39] These practices are not primarily about manifesting an identity, but are forms of work that aim at constructing or cultivating a moral or ethical self. As Mahmood argues, this understanding '*reverses the usual routing from interiority to exteriority* in which the unconscious manifests itself in somatic forms'.[40] For Talal Asad, such practice can be understood as the self, through transforming the body, transforming itself: the 'living body's materiality is regarded as an essential means for cultivating what such traditions define as virtuous conduct and for discouraging what they consider as vice. The role of fear and hope, of felicity and pain, is central to such practices. According to this view of the living body, the more one exercises a virtue the easier it becomes . . . the more one gives into vice, the harder it is to act virtuously'.[41] In that sense, there is an embodied memory constituted through corporeal practice through which embodied practice creates moral potential.

As Zarcone notes, a whole tradition of Western scholarship has regarded the body as an obstacle to be overcome, placing importance on the disembodied mind rather than on the body. Regarding the piety movement as a form of 'claiming recognition' fails to understand what is at stake in such corporeal practice. There is clearly a form of agency involved here, a form of action on the self that passes though action upon the body and its place in the world. In this case, as Mahmood argues, action does not issue from natural feelings (a personalist model), but is better understood as creating them. Outward embodied behaviour is not understood as expressing innerness. Rather, embodied behaviour is understood as an instrument to cultivate and transform inner experience. This is not based on the separation of body and mind, where inner states are represented by outer action or appearance. Instead, this is a form of action that aims at producing a form of embodied subjectivity, in a process Mahmood describes as 'a mutually constitutive relationship between body learning and body sense . . . in which the outward behaviour of the body constitutes both the potentiality and the means through which interiority is realized . . . The mosque participants do not understand the body as a sign of the self's interiority but as a means of developing the self's potentiality . . . the mosque participants treat the body as a medium for, rather than a sign of, the self.'[42] The space between the body and the self, constituting a field of ethical practice, cannot be perceived through the lens of 'identity politics' or of 'performance of identity'.

Religious Grammars

What has become the Habermasian orthodox understanding of the emergence of the public sphere ignores the central place of the religiosity of the actors involved. The Western culture out of which the Enlightenment emerged was deeply shaped by a new spirituality, evident in new forms of religious experience such as Methodism in Britain, Pietism in Germany, and in the emergence of Freemasonry – all focusing on the individual and seeking to revitalise personal commitment to Christianity. Habermas's individuals, according to the historian Margaret Jacob, are 'far too secularised . . . the by-product of an idealized, Kantian version of the Enlightenment'. Rather than embrace this vision of the secular autonomous individual, we need to understand the 'centrality of the religious transformation at work in the creation of modernity'.[43] Jacob explores the intensity of these religious movements: dialoguing with science and the new rationality; constructing new forms of sociability such as Freemasonry which emerged in the context of the collapse of older, restrictive guilds; interpenetrating with other cultural movements such as the emergence of the novel and its new way of addressing the inner person; combining themes from paganism with Christianity (in ways reminiscent of contemporary new age movements).

Other authors point to the central place of the body in the Puritan movements that emerged in this context, or the critical role of Methodism in the cultural shifts leading to a new ethic of the dignity of work, that would be decisive in the emergence of the English labour movement. These analyses all underline the importance of trying to understand religious movements as processes of social, cultural and ethical creativity. In the case of European modernity, these religious movements are not expressions of 'tradition', of defensive reactions against modernity, nor are they expressions of the culture of a people. They played a critical role in constructing ways of being in the world, as Charles Taylor has shown, of acting as 'sources of the self', constructing new forms of inwardness that had a critical role in bringing into life new forms of public culture.[44]

When thinking about emerging forms of Islamic practice, Talal Asad draws on the work of theologian John Milbank, for whom both medieval Christian and Islamic traditions recognized that complex space exists before the more simple space of the nation-state. As a result, the 'sovereign state cannot (never could) contain all the practices, relations, and loyalties of its citizens'.[45] Asad links two propositions: 'Unlike the modern, secular world of nation-states, medieval Christendom and Islam recognized a multiplicity of overlapping bonds and identities. People were not always expected to subject themselves to one sovereign authority, *nor were they themselves sovereign moral subjects.*' The emergence of the modern understanding of sovereignty was linked to the Calvinist conception of the 'community of saints', secularized by Locke. The monotheistic roots of contemporary forms of sovereignty are particularly evident in the United States, observed as early as the mid-19th century by Alexis de Tocqueville, who wrote that the people 'reign over the American political world as God rules over the universe'.[46]

Hent de Vries asks whether the political-theological origins of this form of sovereignty may not be at the roots of excesses of the use of state power that we increasingly witness today.[47] Patchen Markell suggests that a claim to sovereignty equally lies at the heart of the language of identity and its associated demand for recognition. While expressing a form of autonomy that seeks to break free of the atomism of disengaged reason, Markell insists that the theme of identity and its claims to recognition involve the utopia of a subject that can become transparent through recognition, and as such expresses a form of agency grounded in an 'aspiration to be able to act independently, without experiencing life among others as a source of vulnerability, or a site of possible alienation or self-loss'.[48]

As Asad sees it, 'the temporality of many tradition-rooted practices (that is, the time each embodied practice requires to complete and to perfect itself, the past into which it reaches, that it re-encounters, re-imagines, and extends) cannot be translated into the homogenous time of national politics. The body's memories, feelings and desires necessarily escape the rational/instrumental orientation of such politics'. Across different religious traditions, actors subject themselves to forms of suffering, including in some cases self-inflicted wounds, through which they 'seek in part to extend themselves as subjects', noting that religious traditions are able to use pain to foster spaces for moral action.[49]

Autonomy and the claims to sovereignty associated with it may be more ambiguous than the self-congratulatory celebrations of the cosmopolitan suggest. The forms of practice we have encountered cut across boundaries: the public and the private, the religious and the secular, and in the process, the boundaries of nation-states. Questions of modesty, the relationship between men and women in public, the practice of prayer, rather than remaining in the private sphere, become politicised and as the object of public debate, an obstacle to the modern state's separation of domains of private and public.[50] These movements open up new forms of public argument about ways of life characterised by relative equality of those involved (women and men are both called to be involved in *da'wa* or propagation), and cannot be understood within a liberal trajectory of tradition to modern, nor as resistance to it. Rather, as Mahmood underlines, we encounter forms of action and culture 'outside the bounds of a liberal progressive imaginary' – yet ones that represent a valuable form of human flourishing, not to be domesticated or assimilated, or regarded as an expression of a lifeworld that is provisional, destined for extinction.

To reduce emerging Islamic movements to identity politics or resistance to globalization elides the religious dimension at the centre of practices not based on a claim to autonomy. As such, they stand outside the liberal imaginary and confront us with the challenge of thinking about agency, ethics and responsibility in new ways. We may be moving into a post-secular period, one where autonomy and sovereignty (of the state and the individual) may be less and less able to respond to the questions confronting the civil. New questions and voices may be central to reconstructing the civil imaginary.

10

Reimagining the Civil: Pluralism and Its Discontents

Amyn B. Sajoo

I

Occidental constructions of modernity tie civic culture to a secular public sphere in which religion and its ethical claims are privatized. The institutions that underpin legitimacy in this civic culture – from the rule of law and independent media to associative freedom – are posited as autonomous from the control of State and Church alike. Hence, in Ernest Gellner's influential articulation,[1] a commitment to a modern pluralist civil society is incompatible with a public affinity to a community of virtue, such as the Muslim *umma*. Citizenship in this liberal perspective is about membership in a civic sphere that is distinguished by its secular identity.[2]

This picture is usefully complicated by José Casanova's sketching of public religion and its intertwining with the political and civil spheres,[3] together with the communitarian ethic of Amitai Etzioni against liberal atomism.[4] However, the events of September 11 2001 have reinforced the discourses of political modernity as, in essence, being about a commitment to secular liberal citizenship that is equal, inclusive and rational. Yes, the secular may accommodate assertive public religion, as in the United States, where it finds its way into crusading polemics in domestic as well as foreign policy. But this occurs in the context of an underlying constitutional separation between Church and State, which is anchored in an ethos of 'rational moderation' in matters public. That, at any rate, is the self-perception touted by occidental establishments, and rather stridently since the inception of the 'War on Terror'.

Quite different trajectories of civic and economic modernity provide the foundations for societies such as those of China, India, South Africa, South Korea and Turkey, as well as of Singapore and Malaysia. It is a trite observation that their historical experience of the nexus of religion and state is radically removed from the institutional tussles of church and polity that are so central to occidental narratives. Even in Turkey, where the long Ottoman encounter with institutional Islam was a central feature of public life (and the aftermath of Kemalist secular republicanism has effectively kept religion in the public square), the tussle of faith and politics is akin less to Italy or France than to India and Malaysia. Durkheim's invocation of the receding sacred in the face of industrial modernity has as little purchase in Istanbul as it does in Orhan Pamuk's rural Kars,[5] or in Mumbai, Ahmedabad or Kuala Lumpur.

Yet we are told in the wake of September 11 that what globalization alone cannot deliver through economic convergence should be pursued for reasons of 'security' through a 'rational' public sphere, where governance is the business of a secular polity that eschews religious conflict and violence, along with bureaucratic corruption. The 'public reason' that undergirds this claim – to recall John Rawls,[6] Jürgen Habermas[7] and William Galston[8] – is attached to the conditions of citizen participation and well-being. A 'reasonable' pluralism requires that only shared conceptions of the public good can support the political institutions of society: citizens may not appeal to the truths of a particular philosophy, religion or other comprehensive doctrine, but only to 'plain truths, now widely accepted, or available, to citizens generally'.[9] Otherwise, the very basis of our constitutional freedoms as expressed in the rule of law and human rights is unsustainable.

Rather inconveniently, however, liberal establishments themselves have been found seriously wanting in esteem for the rule of law and human rights in the War on Terror, and its fallout. Far from being merely episodic, this reflects a historic pattern in the officially mandated curtailment of individual and group rights in the name of the public good, even if the 'public' in question has less to do with the polity than with hegemonic segments thereof.[10] Further, they seek to advance their cause through the apparatus of public law ostensibly to protect shared values – despite the courts' reminder in 2004 that even 'a state of war is not a blank check when it comes to the rights of the Nation's citizens'.[11] As of early 2006, at least 460 inmates of 'terror camps' in Afghanistan, Iraq and elsewhere had died or been seriously abused.[12] Apart from the fact that the figure is conservative because access to inmates by independent monitors like the Red Cross is severely limited (in violation of the 1949 Geneva Conventions), there is the sheer arbitrariness of rounding up suspects on the basis of untested evidence.

This template of turning the rule *of* law into rule *by* law has also been seized upon by assorted polities, validated by the trump of 'partnership' in upholding international security against the forces of evil, viz. al-Qaeda and its countless, nameless adjuncts. Any connection to political Islam, no matter how tenuous or contrived, will serve. In India, for example, the pattern of human rights violations associated with Kashmir was subsumed into arbitrary arrests, torture and potentially grave miscarriages of justice with respect to alleged plotters in the 13 December 2001 attack on Parliament – quite literally in the shadow of the War on Terror.[13] Again, the Lebanese Shi'a movement, Hezbollah, has been equated with al-Qaeda amid rationalizations of Israel's ravaging of Lebanon in July-August 2006, in flagrant disregard of the most basic norms of international humanitarian law.[14] True, Hezbollah itself is not innocent of uncivil conduct. Yet it is the supposed 'religiously inspired' conduct of the movement that sparks the concern of Western establishments, as opposed to the brutality inflicted in the name of 'secular-rational' security by various actors.[15] The pedigree of this *Weltanschauung* includes Abu Ghraib, Guantanamo Bay, Sabra and Shatila, and erudite defences of the use of torture for the collective good.[16]

II

Now, there are many problems with a Rawlsian view of public reason as a pathway to fostering an overlapping consensus among societal groups, to form and sustain 'reasonably just democratic constitutional societies'.[17] Not the least of these, as Bryan Turner observes in his chapter, is a lack of attention to the reality of the overlapping social bonds of civil society, which require cooperation from oft-contending groups with comprehensive doctrines of the good life. It is one thing to postulate an ethic of reciprocity as a primary norm in the solidarity of civic culture; it is another to account for the practical capacity of this norm to perform the political and social task, not just the ethical one – of eliciting more than a modus vivendi in the public sphere. The dynamics of group life in plural societies, Turner argues persuasively, militate against the civic harmony that Rawls wants to elicit through reciprocity.

We have a prior hurdle, though, to overcome in that picture of 'reasonably just democratic constitutional societies' – which was the point of my excursus into the post-September 11 landscape of the condition of civil liberties. One cannot escape the sense, even in reading the revised edition of *A Theory of Justice*,[18] that it is essentially about a New England universe of contending Protestants, Catholics and Jews, salted by the revivalism of fundamentalist Christian movements. In vain does one look in this American universe for a hint of Buddhists, Hindus, Muslims, even Native Americans. Rawls embraces a politics of privatized religion, in keeping with the Durkheimian-Weberian premise of modernity, against the tide of the return of religion to a denuded public square. He does so without acknowledging the presence, much less the analytical implications, of large segments of his society that partake in lifeworlds of those other, supposedly non-Western traditions. One is reminded of Samuel Huntington's claim in *The Clash of Civilizations* that, 'A multicivilizational US will not be the US; it will be the UN . . . When Americans look to their cultural roots, they find them in Europe.'[19]

This allows a leap, post-September 11, from the interests of privileged segments of the population to that of the public at large. We are back with the problem of 'discourses of power, ideological fictions – mind-forg'd manacles – too easily made, applied and guarded'. Yes, that is Edward Said on the upshot of orientalism,[20] except that the implications of invisibility in our context here extend to minorities as well as quiescent majorities in the East and South. From Indonesia after the 2002 Bali bombings, to Malaysia, Singapore and Thailand in the past decade, and post-Soviet Tajikistan, Uzbekistan and Kyrgyzstan, Muslim societies are rapidly being reduced by scholars and policy analysts to the familiar clamour of forces seen to dominate public religion in the postmodern West. These are fundamentalism and cosmopolitan spirituality, both tied to globalism and its information network.[21]

What is missing in this perspective is the middle ground between the text/rule-centric drive of fundamentalism, and the relaxed, relativistic impulses of urban spiritualism. This hybrid-middle has been explored with regard to the wider Middle East in the work of Dale Eickelman, among others, and shown to involve a dense 're-intellectualization' of Islamic discourses through new global media.[22] Among the key features of the terrain are neo-*ijtihad* in a pluralist entwining of particularist and universalist readings of texts, gender and minority inclusion, and a renewed commitment to ethics beyond traditional rule-bound understandings. A similar unfolding in Southeast Asian Buddhist and even Japanese civic bonding tied to religion have been explored of late.[23] Despite the conspicuous attention accorded to isolationist clusters, it turns out that engagement with civic mainstreams is the more common mode for religious communities and movements. This is especially true for diasporic Muslims in Europe and North America, where the re-intellectualization of traditional legal-ethical precepts and the discourse of human rights has meant that civic citizenship trumps separatism.[24]

An appreciation of this middle ground has the merit of avoiding the slippage that the fundamentalism-versus-cosmopolitan spirituality reduction can lead to. For if the main challenge is seen as the intrusion of institutionalized religion via fundamentalism, and the 'irrational' (or 'non-rational') worldview of spirituality against the 'public reason' of the civitas, then why shouldn't we fully privatize religion in public policy? Welcome back, Rawls. But if the middle terrain is recognized as real and promising in drawing on traditional bonds of faith as well as modern communicative action in creating social capital, there is a different ethos that public policy must contend with. Pluralist religious actors and institutions engage mutually and with secular counterparts. Exit Rawls?

Not if Bryan Turner is right in warning here that the habitus[25] of a religious ethos is fraught with 'rituals of intimacy' that are exclusionary in their reinforcing of sectarian identities and of patriarchal dominance. Certainly, when it comes to fundamentalist drives for a restoration of orthodoxy, notably through tighter compliance with shari'a-centric codes, then pluralist public space is compromised. In this case, the closer we hew to a constitutional separation of religion and state, the greater the promise of at least a modus vivendi, perhaps even an overlapping Rawlsian consensus. But there is far too much evidence of a 'middle habitus' to bear out the case for fundamentalist dominance. Indeed, can we assume that all fundamentalisms are static in their appetite for anti-pluralist codes? If so, how do we account for sharp swings of the pendulum between rigid and milder forms of Buddhist, Catholic, Hindu, Jewish and Protestant fundamentalisms in the past century?

III

The ethical lifeworld of religion, like any secular lifeworld, is a complex habitus in which the rituals of intimacy are both inclusive *and* exclusive. Wearing a headscarf in a specific style, reciting the Qur'an in a favoured tonal-gestural manner and discouraging intermarriage all appear to be exclusionary. Yet in the dietary prohibition of pork and alcohol, the performance of the *hajj* and the rendering of *zakat*, the primacy of the global *umma* prevails over the particularism of the local. Or consider the institution of *waqfs* for socio-religious welfare, which defies a neat public/private or local/global division. Likewise, in a diverse marketplace, *halal* beef in a downtown Singapore foodcourt, *kosher* lamb in a Paris supermarket, or vegan burgers in a Vancouver restaurant, no longer cater to tidy cliques of Muslims, Jews or health-food trendies. *Halal* beef in Singapore is also marketed as 'Malay cuisine.' Muslims shop for *kosher* meat as a favoured choice where the available *halal* options are limited. 'Mad cow' disease and the avian-flu virus have turned many into vegans . . . which happens to be in keeping with strict Hindu dietary preferences!

We inhabit a global bazaar, even if we shop in local stalls. What happens in one stall, no matter how clamorous, does not necessarily reflect the entire habitus of the bazaar. Take the case of apostasy (*ridda*), about which the world heard so much when an Afghan convert to Christianity of many years, Abdul Rahim, was abruptly caught in a post-Taliban powerplay in 2006. Apostasy, like blasphemy, has long been more a political than a theological issue.[26] Ultimately, the disposition of Rahim's fate was not determined by his persecutors but rather by Muslim public officials in Kabul who arranged for his freedom, in an overlap of political and ethical concerns. It also turns out that he was not quite the 'Christian martyr' depicted in Western media at the time, but a severely disturbed man whose account was found to be 'contradictory and unbelievable' by an official in Germany where he received asylum (a finding endorsed by Rahim's brother).[27]

Attending to the outward form of rituals alone leaves out the ethos and context; it is to observe the habitus without the benefit of the 'social imaginary' that accompanies it (about which more below). In the same vein, to perceive ethics in Islamic contexts as no more than a shari'a-centric code, attached to jihad as identity-purification, is to privilege the narrowest of interpretations. It fails to do justice to the historical and contemporary contours of pluralist lifeworlds of Muslim ethical praxis.[28] Militant Wahhabism or the Taliban may cast the shari'a as an austere code – much like some Protestant revivalists favour reading the Old Testament as a blueprint for the militancy of US foreign policy in the Middle East. But these literalist approaches to religion are the target of sustained attack by activist intellectuals, including Muslims. Their jihad is intrinsically pluralist, not purist, and their antecedents in history are abundant.[29]

Ibn al-'Arabi of Andalus (1165–1240) was among those ante-cedents, his influence extending to Damascus and the Arabian Penisinsula. It is true that his native Andalusia provided a cosmo-politan habitus for the flowering of al-'Arabi's thought. But his ability to envision the legitimacy of diverse faith revelations was coupled with a firm conviction about the 'unity of being' (*wahdat-al-wujud*).[30] In this, he trekked the Sufi gnosis and intellectualism of the Persian Ibn Sina (980–1037), and the Central Asian al-Farabi (879–950). There was also al-'Arabi's even more adven-turous contemporary, Ibn Rushd (1126–89), whose reflections on reason and revelation in his commentaries on Aristotle and Plato not only challenged orthodoxy at home, but were to shape the European Renaissance.[31] This line of cosmopolitan thought, and the praxis that it inspired, attest to pluralist commitments that are bound-up with Muslim ethics. If we are to pit al-'Arabi against Rawls, the habitus must be understood in all its complexity of *din wa duniya*, sacred and secular.

There are prominent contemporary bearers of that brand of cosmopolitan religiosity even in 'distant' Southeast Asia, including Nurcolish Madjid, Ahmad Saefuddin, Chandra Muzzafar, Zainah Anwar and Abdurrahman Wahid.[32] The region hosts public insti-tutions such as MUIS (the Islamic Religious Council of Singapore), whose statutory mandate since the 1968 Administration of Muslim Act in Singapore reflects a commitment to expressing faith-inspired public ethics in concrete welfarist terms, including the administration of *zakat, waqf, madrasa*s, certification of *halal* foods, outreach and organizational development and poor relief. As with ICMI (the Islamic Intellectuals Association of Indonesia), a 1990 creation of the Suharto Government, the formal associa-tion of religion and state might be perceived by Western analysts as problematic from the standpoint of civil society. Yet formal autonomy can also make civic actors, individual and institu-tional, irrelevant, while appearing to uphold the norm of being 'extrapolitical'. It is the effective generation of social capital that is the weightier issue.

I will return to the role of Muslim public intellectuals in fostering pluralist politics in the next section. The argument at this juncture is that without a discourse of public ethics where religion plays a dynamic role, vital commitments to civic life are in fact jeopardized. These include social citizenship and democratic accountability,[33] as well as nonviolent discourse. I locate ethics within civil society, girded by human rights.[34] The admixture of overlap and divergence in how societies encounter modernity leads me to propose that the trajectories that undergird public religion are optimally explored through the underlying 'social imaginary'. As elucidated by Charles Taylor, the social imaginary is a background repository of images and narratives that shape how citizens envision their shared spaces *as a moral order,* 'making possible common practices and a widely accepted sense of legitimacy'.[35]

Like Cornelius Castoriadis who invoked this concept with a view to challenging the determinism of Marxist theories of social change,[36] Taylor locates the social imaginary between the embodied practices of the habitus, on the one hand, and formal doctrines or theories, on the other. Castoriadis and Taylor stress the *agency* of ordinary men and women who shape a social imaginary and its moral order. This allows a symbolic idiom such as that of democracy – and social capital – to emerge from the habitus of practices. It also keeps the imaginary grounded in the ordinary, rather than belonging to elites who create theory and doctrine. Varied imaginaries yield 'multiple modernities', rather than that of the West alone. Their locus in secular time is, for Taylor, not about the absence of religion but its centrality to 'the personal identities of individuals or groups, and hence a defining constituent of political identities.'[37]

IV

What does a social imaginary in which public ethics plays a vital role in the exercise of pluralist citizenship look like? A growing number of Muslim intellectuals within the Islamic world and its diaspora have averred that civil society shorn of public religion and ethics falls short of the ideals of civility embodied in their heritages.[38] They follow in the wake of colonial-era engagement with a hegemonial European modernity by the likes of Shah Walliullah, Namik Kemal Bey, Ali 'Abd al-Raziq, and Muhammad Iqbal. In this vein, leading voices in our time include Fazlur Rahman, Abdolkarim Soroush, Abdulaziz Sachedina, Abdullahi An-Na'im, Tariq Ramadan, Ebrahim Moosa and Amina Wadud, and Nobel laureate Shirin Ebadi, in addition to those cited in the previous section. What Nilüfer Göle has called the 'forbidden modern' in reference to the challenge that headscarf-wearing, highly educated, professional Muslim women pose to secularist assumptions, is about a clash of imaginaries within Muslim public spheres.[39]

For Indonesia's Nurcolish Madjid, liberal political toleration is not far removed from that of Muslim religiosity; indeed, it is rooted in his reading of the Qur'an and *sunna*, albeit in historical context. Madjid has successfully straddled the turbulent divides of state and politics in the Suharto era and its aftermath, as a member of ICMI and the legislature, as well as the founder of a private foundation committed to interfaith welfarism. Like Göle's critique of Kemalist republicanism in Turkey (old and new), his insistence on a public ethics of inter-faith accommodation and welfare as well as gender makes room for a non-exclusive religiosity. Amid recent interethnic and interreligious violence in Ambon and Sulawesi, Madjid's voice has been heard as consistently as it was during the Suharto era; and he was not alone in this invocation of what might be called 'confessional reason' against the anti-pluralism of the Majlis Ulama Indonesia (MUI).[40] This recourse, it would seem, is more likely than a separationist stance to engender the dialogue necessary for an overlapping consensus of social actors.

For those who join the occidental critique, *a fortiori* post-September 11, theocracies such as Taliban-led Afghanistan and Iran, or the hardline orthodoxy of Saudi Arabia, are easily disposed of. Their versions of 'modernity' are contested robustly enough by vast sectors of their own populations.[41] Rather, it is the presence of 'political Islam' in civil society that is problematic, as articulated in the works of Amin Maalouf, Azar Nafisi and Orhan Pamuk, among others. The conjoining of religion and civic identity is, for them, a recipe for a Hobbesian universe of conflict and violence, or as Mohammed Arkoun casts it, religious imaginaries trapped in a 'closed official corpus'.[42] Yet pathologies of political violence are a salient facet of the secular habitus, in liberal and authoritarian settings. Pluralism is not a default mode of occidental civic culture.

All pluralist social imaginaries, religious *and* secular, must navigate their impulses of univocal, exclusive and often violent modes of public discourse in fostering civil society. The limits of secular human rights as a redoubt against incursive officialdom, manifest in the post-September 11 period, suggest that public ethics have a critical role in civic space and that religion, suitably framed in relation to public reason, is more likely than its absence to support that role. This imaginary entails cultural as well as political expressions, from education, architecture, the arts and journals of opinion, to institutions of governance, religion, and, indeed, of the sciences.[43] Only then can citizenship and the rule of law attract a widely accepted democratic legitimacy.

A vital feature of this legitimacy is the capacity of a society to accommodate the 'competing affiliations' of cultural and political identity, in which individuals and communities are not reduced to single ethnic, religious, sexual, ideological or other social markers.[44] Multiple and overlapping affiliations allow for recognition of civic sharing and empathy that finds expression in common citizenship. Singular/exclusive affiliations involving Buddhists, Christians, Hindus, Jews or Muslims simply lapse into tribal discourses and practices in the 'clash of civilizations' mode. True, individual and communal choices of identities are not unlimited: we are significantly predisposed to particular affiliations by dint of genetic, cultural, economic and social heritages and habitus. Yet the degree to which public space allows us to choose our priorities among alternative affiliations is vital – so is the capacity to retain the integrity of particular ethical commitments, without which pluralism erodes into relativism. The scope for the freedom to choose is, in our time, felt to be the domain of human rights law in an appropriate constitutional framework. But again there are limits to what human rights norms can do in fostering an ethos that privileges pluralist identities.

Like M. R. Menocal in her study of cosmopolitan civility in Muslim Spain,[45] Amartya Sen draws upon Mughal India in the 16th and 17th centuries to illustrate the mediation of multiple ethno-religious affiliations. The mediation turned out to be successful to a degree that demolishes the myth of occidental, secular modernity as uniquely tolerant, or of Islamdom as reflexively intolerant. Like Abbasid Baghdad and Fatimid Cairo, Cordoba under the Umayyad rule of 'Abd al-Rahman III (r. 912–961) revelled in trading networks of Christians, Jews and Muslims, enormous multilingual libraries, innovative science and graceful public architecture, in short a universe 'where piety and observance were not seen as inimical to an intellectual and "secular" life and society'.[46] Civil ecumenism in Mughal India under Akbar (r. 1556–1605) engaged Hindus, Jains, Sikhs, Catholics, Muslims and even atheists in *rahi 'aql* or 'the path of reason'. Indeed, Akbar drew doctrinal inspiration from the Andalusian Ibn al-'Arabi's encompassing *wahdat-al-wujud*. Early in his reign he abolished the *jizya* or poll tax on non-Muslims (long before the liberalizing Ottomans); a proclamation from Agra in the 1590s held that 'anyone is to be allowed to go over to a religion that pleases him'; and translations of Hindu epic texts were commissioned for Akbar's own edification. It should be noted that a pre-existing milieu of socio-religious pluralism under the Mughals allowed Akbar's ecumenism to thrive[47] – and that this was not novel either. More than a millennium earlier, edicts of the the Mauryan emperor Ashoka (r. 273–232 BC) affirmed not only reverence for all sects but also engagement among them that extended to marginalized peoples.

Faith commitments, then, may be folded into a civic imaginary that engenders a more rather than less inclusive ethos. But attempting to fold religious commitments into narrow ideological agendas of the state is a different matter. While both these approaches involve the engineering of public policy, the former engages with civil society as a democratic actor in advancing a shared interest; the latter approach curtails the autonomy of civil society, often straying into authoritarianism. Failing to appreciate the distinction has serious implications for our post-September 11 age:

> The basic recognition of the multiplicity of identities would militate against trying to see people in exclusively religious terms, no matter how religious they are . . . What religious extremism has done to demote and downgrade the responsible political action of citizens has been, to some extent, reinforced rather than eradicated by the attempt to fight terrorism by trying to recruit the religious establishment on 'the right side'. In the downplaying of political and social identities as opposed to religious identity, it is civil society that has been the loser, precisely at a time when there is a great need to strengthen it.[48]

Even where public policy engages with civil society as an autonomous actor in a pluralist setting, striking a balance between collective and individual as well as secular and religious identities is a key challenge for modern citizenship. A practical illustration is provided by a recent episode concerning the Muslim diasporic community in Canada. Civic issues ranging from access to justice and expressive religious autonomy to gender and minority rights came to the fore when the province of Ontario was faced with the use of its Arbitration Act by a community of Muslims. In essence, the idea was to apply processes of alternative dispute resolution (ADR) in matters of inheritance, matromonial and other family disputes by using the personal law norms of the Shari'a. This would occur under the aegis of the Islamic Institute of Civil Justice (IICJ), established by a retired lawyer, Syed Mumtaz Ali, in late 2003.[49] A stormy public debate ensued, pitting the proponents of the IICJ against those who saw the Shari'a as inherently problematic for the rights of women, though all rulings would be subject to meeting the constitutional standards of Canada's federal Charter of Rights and Freedoms.

In a public review of how Ontario's Arbitration Act would square with the notion of religiously based arbitration, and particularly the IICJ (with which the provincial government had no connection), strong representations were made about the perils of such recourse. While Christians, Jews and the Ismaili Muslim community already had ADR processes under the province's Arbitration Act, the new Institute was cast as different; this was because of its more 'exclusive' aspirations in relation to secular law, and the perceived nature of the shari'a as rigid and insensitive to gender equity.[50] The public review, conducted by a former Ontario attorney-general with marked feminist leanings, was thoroughgoing and incisive. Meanwhile, the debate had become national, then Euro-Canadian; its focus was not on the merits of religious-based arbitration in relation to norms of human rights and social justice (including on gender and access to justice), but rather on the shari'a as an Islamic code of ethics and law.[51] It attests to the acuity of the public review that it was able to sift through the barrage of submissions (and public demonstrations) that painted the IICJ initiative as akin to a beach-head for the Taliban.

Subject to carefully drawn legislative and practical safeguards, the review recommended that the 'Arbitration Act should continue to allow disputes to be arbitrated using religious law'[52] in effect, that the IICJ should receive equal treatment with other faith-based arbitral initiatives. Such was the negative response from those opposed to the initiative, who successfully lobbied the women's caucus in the province's ruling party, that the government backed away from the outcome of its own review. On 14 February 2006 amendments to the Arbitration Act outlawed all forms of religious arbitration, allowing only the use of provincial or national law in family-related ADR, whose impact was also borne by the Jewish community.[53] An opportunity to test innovative ways in which faith-based arbitral processes could serve communal as well as societal expectations of equity and justice became a casualty of a 'secular absolutism'. This stance, in the tradition associated with France, holds that separation of Church and State entails an exclusive role for the state in matters 'regulated elsewhere by state law'.[54] The rationale is that secular law is neutral and treats all citizens equally, even if some have far closer ties to the mainstream ethos.

Yet fidelity to democratic values surely requires the recognition of religious as well as secular identities that 'intersect', in their fragmented complexity, in the individual citizen.[55] To insist that this complexity can be captured by a fixed boundary between public and private is untenable. Evidently, the Ontario Muslims who were prepared to use the Arbitration Act and national human rights laws as enabling instruments for ADR sought to engage with the state in furthering their objectives. Judicial oversight of the Institute's rulings guaranteed an institutionalized overlap not only of process and systems but also ultimately of religious and civic identities. In blocking this avenue, the state must bear its share of responsibility for any resulting 'enclaving' of society, instead of fostering a pluralist engagement towards effective citizenship, with proper safeguards. The cost of this failure may well be the highest for vulnerable members of religious communities who lose the benefit of state-supported human rights protections in an integrated arbitral system; from domestic violence to single parenthood in poverty, those vulnerabilities are no small matter in diasporic Ontario.[56] Ironically, it was in the name of such disadvantaged women that much of the vocal opposition to the IICJ was purportedly launched.

The lesson that secular absolutism is no less capable than its religious counterpart of pitting itself against the overlapping collective and individual identities of citizens is hard-earned in modern democracies of various stripes. Consider the results of two recent surveys of religiosity in Turkey and Britain – both involved extensive and independent polling, respectively by the Turkish Economic and Social Studies Foundation (TESEV) and the *Guardian* newspaper. In Turkey, 45 per cent identified themselves first as Muslim, while 19 per cent said that they were 'Turkish first'; the figures were up from 36 and 21 per cent respectively in 1999.[57] Only 25 per cent favoured political parties that are religious, however, down from 41 per cent in 1999; and just 9 per cent favoured the idea of a shari'a-based constitution, down from 21 per cent. In Britain, two-thirds said they were not religious, with 43 per cent never attending religious services; 82 per cent actually deemed religion a divisive force in society.[58]

Not surprisingly, for a country whose French-style constitutional secularism has defined itself in direct opposition to Islam, the Turkish survey's findings were taken as evidence of the success of Mustapha Kemal's modernist legacy. The Western press weighed in reassuringly on this Europeanizing trend,[59] also holding that 'pious Islam and political Islam are not the same thing'.[60] While noting this 'paradox', the *New York Times* cautioned that 'increased religiosity, or at least identification with religion, could eventually present a serious problem for Turkish society'.[61] None saw fit to remark that the survey pushed a reductive choice between being Muslim and being Turkish, as if the identities could have no parity. Nor did the seriousness of a declining identification with Turkish identity as a mark of shared citizenship elicit comment (though the *New York Times* reported that a robust economy had 'eased the integration of religious Turks into the country's secular society'). The prime concern was the familiar contest of 'Muslim' and 'secular' identities, and how closely this mirrored the Western experience of modernity. Of special interest was the fact that only 11 per cent of women favoured the headscarf, down from 16 per cent in 1999; most 'secular' Turks had thought the opposite was true, in their apprehension of political Islam.

A telling detail in that survey was that 13 per cent of ultra-secular and ultra-nationalist Turks sympathized with suicide bombing, compared with 9 per cent of supporters of the ruling Islamist party. Only weeks after the survey, the prominent Armenian-Turkish journalist, Hrant Dink, was assassinated by extreme nationalists over his public censure of the country's record on the treatment of Armenians in the early part of the 20th century.[62] Dink had been found culpable in 2005 for 'insulting Turkishness' under Article 301 of the Turkish Penal Code, a provision that human rights monitors in and outside the country have rightly found deeply offensive. In effect, the legislation allows one to be 'Turkish' solely as prescribed by the strident secularism of Kemalist ideology. This might go some way towards explaining both the weak public appeal of Turkish citizenship and the motivations for political violence.

Again, there was no dearth of reductive analysis about the British survey. Under the banner 'Beyond Belief', a *Guardian* editorial saw the poll as 'an important corrective to the impression that religion increasingly colours our sense of identity'.[63] Insofar as the target was politicians for whom 'religion can be a flag of convenience, a way of categorising people that avoids more difficult issues of race and class', the editorial rightly noted the complexity of British identity. But it also claimed that 'people regard language, law and institutions, not religion, as the defining aspects of their Britishness', and that 'politicians create the climate that elevates religion's significance'. The assumption: left to its own devices, religion will fade not only from the public domain and civil society, but also from the private sphere, judging by the declining attendance at services and of self-identification as 'religious'. Still, two-thirds identified themselves as Christian, a marker whose significance cannot but be contextualised in the wake of September 11 2001, the history of Irish Republican Army (IRA) bombings, and the London transport attacks of 7 July 2005.[64] Amid a staple of news reports that blithely link religion to violence, how willingly may the average citizen confess to religious conviction ?

V

On a civic landscape where individualist 'expressivist' modes of religiosity that stress spirituality over institutional creeds vie with a 'post-Durkheimian' order in which institutional affiliations are ever more fractured, the meaning of what it is to be religious is deeply contested.[65] This landscape is more variegated and pluralist than the 'civil religion' sketched by Robert Bellah with regard to the United States;[66] nor is it confined to liberal democracies. It extends to civic landscapes ranging from Turkey and India to Malaysia, Indonesia, ex-Soviet Central Asia and parts of the Middle East. The received modernity of the occident overlaps with the vernacular to engender alternative modernities and practices of citizenship. Reductive definitions of religiosity of the kind thrown up by the opinion surveys noted above fail to enlighten on where we are and the new imaginaries of civic identity in our globalised age.

More broadly, the upshot of the perspective offered in this chapter is that whether in the context of growing ethno-religious plurality or post-September 11 security, public policy must contend with the growing national and transnational role of civil society as a legitimate 'driver' of civic modernities. An exclusively top-down approach *ipso facto* fails the test of democratic legitimacy, quite apart from the issue of effective governance. A purely adversarial view of state-civil society actors fails the test of a purposive commitment to enhancing social capital. A variegated public is more likely than a homogenous one to bolster civil society, and hence provide legitimate partnership in governance. Ethno-political conflicts in post-Cold War contexts where authoritarian or totalitarian control gave the impression of successful policy management – as in ex-Yugoslavia, Central Asia – attest to the need for mediatory civil society in governance.

Claims on behalf of 'secular' public space as the appropriate canvas for modern governance can no longer retreat into assumptions about the 'irrationality' of non-religious public discourse as the primary choice for 'liberal neutrality'. Occidental civic cultures have been compelled to revisit the contours of Church–State separation as constituted through 20th-century constitutional accords. Formulaic civic strategies derived from Western narratives of modernity have not succeeded in building democratic polities in post-Cold War Afghanistan, Chechnya, Haiti, Rwanda and Somalia, to name but a few instances – having struggled also in Northern Ireland. The recent record in Iraq is hardly reassuring on prospects for the export of neoconservative models.

Pluralist legitimacy requires attention to markers of citizen identity, participation and dignity in the midst of multiple/inclusive identities. Public religions with sound ethical commitments may serve the objectives of citizenship, where public trust and solidarity trump the perils of fragmentation and incivility. The ancient ideal of *isonomia* – equality stirred with equity – today requires, as Eva Schubert argues in this volume, citizens as 'active collaborators' in defence of a pluralist ethos. The ethics of engaged citizenship cannot be reduced, in the instance of Islam, to fixed shari'a codes or *fiqh* rulings; Muslim history does not support such a reading. Mediatory avenues of moral reasoning come into play, aided by the institutions of civil society as a central tenet of democratic culture. This is not to suggest that civil society *ipso facto* guarantees public accountability. Appropriate institutions and norms are required, whose renewal is always a matter of concern, as attested in the aftermath of the 'War on Terror'. Political violence, whether secular or religious, is an embedded feature of the habitus and social imaginary of modern societies. Hence the permanent need for the safeguards of human rights and the rule of law – even in readings of scripture, as Bruce Lawrence cogently argues in his chapter. Religious ethics can be mobilized to enhance the legitimacy of those constraints on uncivil conduct. Only then will the abjuring of uncivil means of seeking change be grounded in an enduring consensus, rather than a purely tactical modus vivendi. At the same time, the persistent failure of the international community to attend to issues of social and distributive justice, and of political self-determination (as in Palestine, Chechnya, Kashmir), will exacerbate the tendency to feed single/exclusionary identities at the expense of civic ones.

Democratic governance requires a commitment to pluralism that in most societies cannot tidily be sequestered from public religion. The success of this nexus is tied to public ethics as a source of civic solidarity/citizenship (and as constraining uncivil/violent conduct), through avenues that are not merely political but also socio-cultural. These encompass a broad spectrum of instruments of education, socialization and engagement for the general welfare, which also serve to countervail the more exclusive rituals of denominational membership. Within and across geo-cultural boundaries, a hegemonial modernity that is exclusively technocentric, individualist and secular is untenable. Modes of governance must come to terms with accountabilities in this new landscape.

Transnational migration enhanced by globalization has spurred citizen diasporas that test the fidelity of host polities to democratic values, while challenging old assumptions about constitutional norms of governance. In areas such as personal law, dispute resolution and religious expression, creative approaches to the nexus of public and private are required. If the contemporary record on access to justice, distributive equity, expressive freedoms and gender/minority rights is to be improved, civil society and the state must shun the pitfalls of both secular and religious absolutism that ultimately subvert citizenship. This, as Tariq Ramadan insists, is not about territorial but imaginative citizenship, a domain not of culture but of spirit.[67] The quest is for landscapes that allow for multiple, if overlapping, social imaginaries in modernity's shadow.

Notes

1. Introduction

1   *Talaye sorkh* in the original Persian, produced and directed by Jafar Panahi, written by Abbas Kiarostami; with festival awards at Cannes, Chicago, Tbilisi and Valladoid.

2   Richard Tapper, ed., *The New Iranian Cinema: Politics, Representation and Identity* (London & New York, 2002); Hamid Dabashi, *Close-Up: Iranian Cinema, Past, Present, Future* (London & New York, 2002); Hamid Reza Sadr, *Iranian Cinema: A Political History* (London & New York, 2006).

3   Jacques Le Goff, *History and Memory,* trans. S. Rendall and E. Claman (New York, 1992), p. 40 ('Antique (Ancient)/Modern').

4   Charles Baudelaire, *The Painter of Modern Life and Other Essays,* trans. and edited by Jonathan Mayne (London, 1964), p. 5.

5   Michel-Rolph Trouillot, 'The Otherwise Modern', pp. 220–237, in Bruce M. Knauft, ed., *Critically Modern* (Bloomington & Indianapolis, IN, 2003), at p. 227. For Trouillot, there is rich paradox in Baudelaire being at once wedded to a modern sense of time yet 'resolutely antimodernist' in his distaste for 'the management of places and populations' that signified French modernisation at home and in the colonies.

6   Marilyn Ivy, *Discourses of the Vanishing: Modernity, Phantasm, Japan* (Chicago, 1995), pp. 4–5.

7   Marshall Berman, *All that is Solid Melts into Air: The Experience of Modernity* (New York, 1982), p. 16. Again, consider Lawrence Cahoone's expansive (albeit provisional) definition of modernity as 'the ideas, principles and patterns of interpretation, of diverse kinds ranging from the philosophic to the economic, on which western and central European and American society and culture, from the sixteenth through to the twentieth centuries, increasingly to be found

itself to be based': *The Dilemma of Modernity: Philosophy, Culture and Anti-Culture* (Albany, NY, 1988), p. 1.

8 Paul Rabinow, ed., *The Foucault Reader* (New York, 1984), p. 39. Likewise for the anthropologist Donald Donham: 'To invoke the modern involves . . . a way of experiencing time and historicity, with a certain structure of progressive expectations for the future. The past is separated from the present and expectations are reoriented to the future' : 'On Being Modern in a Capitalist World', pp. 241–257, in Knauft, *Critically Modern*, at p. 244.

9 Tilo Schabert, 'Modernity and History 1: What is Modernity?', pp. 9–21, in Athanasios Moulakis, ed., *The Promise of History* (Berlin, 1985), at pp. 17–18.

10 Keith Watenpaugh, *Being Modern in the Middle East: Revolution, Nationalism, Colonialism and the Arab Middle Class* (Princeton & Oxford, 2006), p. 15.

11 John D. Kelly, 'Alternative Modernities or an Alternative to "Modernity": Getting Out of the Modernist Sublime', pp. 258–286, in Knauft, *Critically Modern*, at p. 262.

12 Ibid., p. 279. See further his, 'U.S. Power, after 9/11 and before It: If Not an Empire, Then What?', *Public Culture*, 15:2 (Spring 2003), pp. 347–70.

13 In this vein see also Watenpaugh, *Being Modern in the Middle East*, pp. 12–14.

14 See Jonathan Friedman's remarks on Kelly's critique, 'Modernity and Other Traditions', pp. 287–313, in Knauft, *Critically Modern*, at pp. 292–293.

15 Ibid., p. 293.

16 Marshall Hodgson, *The Venture of Islam: Conscience and History in a World Civilization*, 2 (Chicago, 1974), p. 375. See further the various essays in Stuart Hall *et al.*, ed., *Modernity: An Introduction to Modern Societies* (Oxford, 1996).

17 Jürgen Habermas, *The Philosophical Discourse of Modernity*, trans. F. Lawrence. (Cambridge, MA, 1990). His other principal works are *The Structural Transformation of the Public Sphere: An Enquiry into a Category of Bourgeois Society*, trans. T. Burger & F. Lawrence (Cambridge, MA, 1989) and *The Theory of Communicative Action*, 2 vols (Boston, 1984). See generally W. Outhwaite, ed., *The Habermas Reader* (Cambridge, 1996).

18 Principally in *Elementary Forms of the Religious Life* (1912) and *The Division of Labor in Society* (1893). See generally, Steven Lukes, *Émile Durkheim: His Life and Work, A Historical and Critical Study*

(Stanford, 1985); and Anthony Giddens, *Durkheim on Politics and the State* (Stanford, 1986).

19 See Owen Chadwick, *The Secularisation of the European Mind in the Nineteenth Century* (Cambridge & New York, 1990); Rajeev Bhargava, ed., *Secularism and Its Critics* (Delhi, 1998); Talal Asad, *Formations of the Secular: Christianity, Islam, Modernity* (Stanford, 2003); Robert Coles, *The Secular Mind* (Princeton, 1999).

20 Charles Taylor, *Sources of the Self: The Making of the Modern Identity* (Cambridge, MA, 1989); Anthony Giddens, *Modernity and Self-Identity: Self and Society in the Late Modern Age* (Stanford, 1991); Asad, *Formations of the Secular*.

21 Adopted by General Assembly Resolution 217A(III) (10 Dec 1948). Text at http://www.unhchr.ch/udhr/lang/eng.htm. All UN member states are required to affirm the Declaration.

22 See Micheline R. Ishay, ed., *The Human Rights Reader* (New York, 1997); Ian Carter *et al.*, ed., *Freedom: A Philosophical Anthology* (Oxford, 2007); Matthew J. Gibney, ed., *Globalizing Rights: The Oxford Amnesty Lectures* (Oxford & New York, 2003).

23 See Derek Heater, *Citizenship: The Civic Ideal in World History, Politics and Education*, 3rd ed. (Manchester, 2004); David Copp, J. Hampton and J. E. Roemer, ed., *The Idea of Democracy* (Cambridge & New York, 1993). On rule of law in particular, see John Rawls, *A Theory of Justice*, rev. ed. (Oxford, 1999), pp. 206–213; and Thomas Carothers, 'The Rule of Law Revival', *Foreign Affairs*, 77:3 (Mar/Apr 1998), pp. 95–106.

24 *Democracy in America* (1835). See generally Seymour Drescher, *Dilemmas of Democracy: Tocqueville and Modernization* (Pittsburgh, PA, 1968); Cheryl Welch, *The Cambridge Companion to Tocqueville* (Cambridge, 2006).

25 Ernest Gellner, *Conditions of Liberty: Civil Society and Its Rivals* (London, 1994); Thomas Janoski, *Citizenship and Civil Society: A Framework of Rights & Obligations in Liberal, Traditional, and Social Democratic Regimes* (Cambridge, 1998); Michael Edwards, *Civil Society* (Cambridge, 2004). On the social capital of civil society, see Robert Putnam, *Bowling Alone: The Collapse and Revival of American Community* (New York, 2000); Barbara Arneil, *Diverse Communities: The Problem with Social Capital* (Cambridge, 2006).

26 Anthony Giddens, *The Consequences of Modernity* (1990) and *Modernity and Self-Identity: Self and Society in the Late Modern Age* (Stanford, 1991).

27 *Modernity at Large: Cultural Dimensions of Globalization* (Minneapolis, MN, 1996), pp. 32–33.

28 See generally Arif Dirlik, 'Is There History after Eurocentrism? Globalism, Postcolonialism, and the Disavowal of History', *Cultural Critique*, 42 (1999), pp. 1–34; and his *The Postcolonial Aura: Third World Criticism in the Age of Global Capitalism* (Boulder, CO, 1998). On the limits of technology in civic culture, see Darin Barney, *Prometheus Wired* (Vancouver & Toronto, 2000).

29 Felipe Fernández-Armesto, *Civilizations: Culture, Ambition and the Transformation of Nature* (London, 2000); Amartya Sen, 'Civilizational Confinement', pp. 40–58, in his *Identity and Violence: The Illusion of Destiny* (New York & London, 2006); Edward Said, 'The Clash of Ignorance', *The Nation* (New York), 22 October 2001.

30 Allen Pred's *Recognizing European Modernities: A Montage of the Present* (London, 1995) takes this claim to the hegemonial heart.

31 Michel Foucault, *Power/Knowledge: Selected Interviews and Other Writings*, ed. Colin Gordon (New York, 1980). See generally Perry Anderson, *The Origins of Postmodernity* (London, 1998); Thomas Docherty, ed., *Postmodernism: A Reader* (New York, 1993).

32 See Michael Kelly, ed., *Critique and Power: Recasting the Foucault/Habermas Debate* (Cambridge, MA, 1994).

33 Arturo Escobar, *Encountering Development: The Making and Unmaking of the Third World* (Princeton, 1995); Nils Gilman, *Mandarins of the Future: Modernization Theory in Cold War America* (Baltimore, MD, & London, 2003).

34 Bernard Yack, *The Fetishism of Modernities: Epochal Self-Consciousness in Contemporary Social and Political Thought* (Notre Dame, IN, 1997), p. 138.

35 Giddens, *The Consequences of Modernity*, p. 38.

36 Ulrich Beck, Anthony Giddens and Scott Lash, ed. *Reflexive Modernization: Politics, Tradition and Aesthetics in the Modern Social Order* (Cambridge, 1994), p. 58.

37 See Masoud Kamali, *Multiple Modernities, Civil Society and Islam: The Case of Iran and Turkey* (Liverpool, 2006), pp. 18–19.

38 See Bruce M. Knauft, pp. 1–54, in *Critically Modern*, at p. 22.

39 A distinction not heeded in Knauft, above. See further Diana Eck, *A New Religious America* (San Francisco, 2001), pp. 70–71; and Amir Hussain, 'Muslims, Pluralism, and Interfaith Dialogue', pp. 251–269, in Omid Safi, ed., *Progressive Muslims: On Justice, Gender, and Pluralism* (Oxford, 2003), at pp. 251–252.

40 Gellner, *Conditions of Liberty*, pp. 15–29; Şerif Mardin, 'Civil Society

and Islam', pp. 278–300, in John A. Hall, ed., *Civil Society: Theory, History, Comparison* (Cambridge, 1995).

41 Amyn B. Sajoo, ed., *Civil Society in the Muslim World: Contemporary Perspectives* (London & New York, 2002), pp. 1–34; John Keane, *Civil Society: Old Themes, New Visions* (Cambridge, 1998), pp. 27–31; Michael Edwards, *Civil Society*. On civilisational roots in Muslim context, see Ellis Goldberg, 'Private Goods, Public Wrongs, and Civil Society in Some Medieval Arab Theory and Practice', pp. 248–271, in Ellis Goldberg *et al.*, ed., *Rules and Rights in the Middle East* (Seattle, WA & London, 2003).

42 John Rawls, *A Theory of Justice*, p. 340, and *The Law of Peoples* (Cambridge, MA, 1999), p 16.

43 See David Held, 'Democracy: From City-States to a Cosmopolitan Order?', pp. 14–52, in his *Prospects for Democracy* (Cambridge, 1993); Richard Falk, *Law in an Emerging Global Village: A Post-Westphalian Perspective* (Ardsley, NY, 1998) and *Religion and Humane Global Governance* (New York, 2001).

44 Charles Taylor, *Modern Social Imaginaries* (Durham, NC & London, 2004), pp. 3–30, quotes at p. 22. See also his 'Two Theories of Modernity', pp. 172–196, in D.P. Gaonkar, ed., *Alternative Modernities* (Durham, NC & London, 2001); and D.P. Gaonkar, 'Toward New Imaginaries: An Introduction', *Public Culture*, 14:1 (2002), pp. 1–19. Taylor builds on the seminal work of Cornelius Castoriadis on imaginaries in history in *The Imaginary Institution of Society*, trans. K. Blamey (Cambridge, MA, 1987; French orig. 1975); on the idea of 'habitus' as repository of 'embodied practice' developed by Pierre Bourdieu, notably in *Outline of a Theory of Practice* (Cambridge, 1977; French orig. 1972); and on Benedict Anderson's *Imagined Communities: Reflections on the Origin and Spread of Nationalism* (London & New York, 1983; rev. ed., 2006).

45 Taylor, 'Two Theories of Modernity', p. 189; Gaonkar, 'Toward New Imaginaries', pp. 10–11.

46 *Modern Social Imaginaries*, p. 196. Invoking Dipesh Chakrabarty's *Provincializing Europe* (Princeton, 2000), Taylor argues for finally getting over 'seeing modernity as a single process of which Europe is the paradigm'. See further his *A Secular Age* (Cambridge, MA & London, 2007), notably Part V.

47 *Modernity at Large*, p. 31. 'No longer mere fantasy (opium for the masses whose real work is elsewhere), no longer simple escape (from a world defined principally by more concrete purposes and structures), no longer elite pastime (thus not relevant to the lives of ordinary

people), and no longer mere contemplation (irrelevant for new forms of desire and subjectivity), the imagination has become an organized field of social practices, a form of work (in the sense of both labor and culturally organized practice) . . .'

48 See Charles Taylor, *The Ethics of Authenticity* (Cambridge, MA, and London, 1991).

49 Edward Said, *Orientalism* (New York, 1978), and *Covering Islam*, rev. ed. (New York, 1997).

50 Aziz al-Azmeh, *Islams and Modernities* (London & New York, 1993), pp. 22, 23–24.

51 Mohammed Arkoun, *Rethinking Islam: Common Questions, Uncommon Answers*, trans R. D. Lee (Boulder, CO, 1994), notably pp. 6–14, 86–105. See also his *The Unthought in Contemporary Islamic Thought* (London, 2002).

52 Arkoun sees postcolonial ideologies as resulting in 'the triumph of a social imaginary that is termed "Islamic" but that in fact sacralizes an irreversible operation of political, economic, social, and cultural secularization' (*Rethinking Islam*, p. 13). But his primary focus remains on the making and results of the religious dimensions of the imaginary.

53 See Pippa Norris and Ronald Inglehart, ed., *Sacred and Secular: Religion and Politics Worldwide* (New York, 2004), notably chapter 6 ('Religion and Politics in the Muslim World'); Abdelwahab El-Affendi, 'On the State, Democracy and Pluralism', pp. 172–194, in Suha Taji-Farouki and B. Nafi, ed., *Islamic Thought in the Twentieth Century* (London & New York, 2004).

54 Andrew Davison, *Secularism and Revivalism in Turkey: A Hermeneutic Reconsideration* (New Haven & London, 1998), p. 196. See also Talal Asad, *Formations of the Secular*, especially p. 25.

55 See Ahmad Dallal, 'Science, Medicine, and Technology', pp. 155–213, in John L. Esposito, ed., *The Oxford History of Islam* (Oxford & New York, 1999); Mark Graham, *How Islam Created the Modern World* (Beltsville, MD, 2006).

56 Muhammad Iqbal, *Six Lectures on the Reconstruction of Religious Life in Islam* (Lahore, 1930), at p. 20.

57 See generally see Mircea Eliade, *Images and Symbols: Studies in Religious Symbolism*, trans. Philip Mairet (Princeton, 1991); Robert Detweiler and David Jasper, *Religion and Literature: A Reader* (Louisville, KY, 2000); Robert Coles, *The Call of Stories: Teaching and the Moral Imagination* (Boston, 1989).

58 See John Seyller, ed., *The Adventures of Hamza* (Washington, 2002),

which accompanied a travelling exhibition in 2002–2003 of the manuscripts of the *Hamzanama*.

59 See generally, E. Allworth, ed., *Central Asia: 130 Years of Soviet Dominance* (Durham, NC, 1994); Shirin Akiner, *Islamic Peoples of the Soviet Union* ((London & Boston, 1983); Pauline Jones Luong, ed., *The Transformation of Central Asia: States and Societies from Soviet Rule to Independence* (Ithaca, NY, 2004).

60 Maria-Rosa Menocal, *Ornament of the World: How Muslims, Jews and Christians Created a Culture of Tolerance in Medieval Spain* (Boston & London, 2002); Salma K. Jayyusi, ed., *The Legacy of Muslim Spain* (Leiden, 1992); Bernard F. Reilley, *The Medieval Spains* (Cambridge & New York, 1993).

61 Or for that matter Asmaa Abdol-Hamid aspiring to do so in Denmark: see Ian Traynor, 'Feminist, Socialist, Devout Muslim: Woman Who Has Thrown Denmark into Turmoil', the *Guardian*, 16 May 2007.

62 William C. Chittick, *Imaginal Worlds: Ibn al-'Arabi and the Problem of Religious Diversity* (New York, 1994). See also Roxanne L. Euben, 'Contingent Borders, Syncretic Perspectives: Globalization, Political Theory, and Islamizing Knowledge', *International Studies Review* 4:1, (2002) pp. 23–48.

63 See Onora O'Neill, *Bounds of Justice* (Cambridge & New York, 2000); Joshua Parens, 'Multiculturalism and the Problem of Particularism', *The American Political Science Review*, 88:1 (1994), pp. 169–181.

64 A. Sen, *Identity and Violence: The Illusion of Destiny* (New York, 2006), pp. 12–17.

65 As depicted in, for example, A. Giddens, *Runaway World* (London, 1999); Benjamin Barber, *Jihad vs. McWorld: How Globalism and Tribalism are Reshaping the World* (New York, 1995); Francis Fukuyama, 'Voile et contrôle sexuel', *Le Monde*, 4 Feb 2004.

66 Charles Taylor, *Sources of the Self*, and *Varieties of Religion Today: William James Revisited* (Cambridge, MA & London, 2002). See also Saba Mahmood, *Politics of Piety: The Islamic Revival and the Feminist Subject* (Princeton, 2004).

67 Including within more orthodox quarters: Maha Azzam, 'Islamism Revisited', *International Affairs*, 82: 6 (2006), pp. 1119–32; Madawi Al-Rasheed, *Contesting the Saudi State* (Cambridge, 2007); Ziba Mir-Hosseini and Richard Tapper, *Islam and Democracy in Iran* (London & New York, 2006).

68 Nikki Keddie, *Sayyid Jamal al-Din al-Afghani: A Political Biography* (Berkeley, CA, 1972); Antony Black, *The History of Islamic Political Thought* (New York, 2001).

69 Ebrahim Moosa, *Ghazali and the Poetics of Imagination* (Chapel Hill, NC & London, 2005), which sees the *dihliz* as 'the critical intermediate space between outside and inside, between exoteric (*zahir*) and esoteric (*batin*) . . . a welcoming space' (p. 48), that ultimately allowed Ghazali to navigate clashing discursive traditions within Islam. More generally see W. Montgomery Watt, *Muslim Intellectual: A Study of al-Ghazali* (Edinburgh, 1963).

70 See generally Amyn B. Sajoo, *Muslim Ethics: Emerging Vistas* (London & New York, 2004); Margaret Somerville, *The Ethical Imagination: Journeys of the Human Spirit* (Toronto, 2006). On the ethics of technology see Darin Barney, *Prometheus Wired*; on social citizenship see especially Ayse Bugra, 'Poverty and Citizenship: An Overview of the Social Policy Environment in Republican Turkey', *International Journal of Middle East Studies*, 39 (2007), pp. 33–52, and Robert W. Hefner, *Civil Islam: Muslims and Democratisation in Indonesia* (Princeton, NJ, 2000).

71 See Stefano Bianca and Philip Jodidio, ed., *Cairo: Revitalising a Historic Metropolis* (Turin, 2004).

72 These include the 14th-century Umm Sultan Shaban Mosque, the Khayrbek complex with its medieval palace, mosque and Ottoman house, and the Darb Shoughlan School.

73 See http://www.akdn.org/agency/aktc_hcsp_cairo.html#contact.

74 See generally Uma Kothari and Martin Minogue, ed., *Development Theory and Practice: Critical Perspectives* (London, 2002); Michael E. Latham, *Modernization as Ideology* (Chapel Hill, NC & London, 2000).

75 See Kenneth Frampton, ed., *Modernity and Community: Architecture in the Islamic World* (London, 2001); and Sherban Cantacuzino, *Architecture in Continuity: Building in the Islamic World Today* (New York, 1985), highlighting the priorities of the AKTC's Aga Khan Award for Architecture.

76 Elisabeth B. MacDougall and Richard Ettinghausen, ed., *The Islamic Garden* (Washington, DC, 1976); Emma Clark, *The Art of the Islamic Garden* (Ramsbury, UK, 2004). See also Jeff Albert, M. Bernhardsson and R. Kenna, ed., *Transformations of Middle Eastern Natural Environments: Legacies and Lessons* (New Haven, CT, 1998).

77 Charles E. Beveridge and Paul Rocheleau, *Frederick Law Olmsted: Designing the American Landscape* (New York, 1998); Witold Rybczynski, *A Clearing in the Distance: Frederick Law Olmsted and North America in the Nineteenth Century* (New York, 1999).

78 Hassan Fathy, *Architecture for the Poor: An Experiment in Rural Egypt* (Chicago, 1976); James Steele, *An Architecture for People: The Complete Works of Hassan Fathy* (London, 1997); Malcolm Miles' 'Utopias of

Mud? Hassan Fathy and Alternative Modernisms', *Space and Culture*, 9 (2006), pp. 115–139.
79 Sami Zubaida, 'Max Weber's *The City* and the Islamic City', *Max Weber Studies*, 6:1 (January 2006), pp. 111–118; Janet Abu-Lughod, 'The Islamic City: Historical Myth, Islamic Essence, and Contemporary Relevance', *International Journal of Middle East Studies*, 19 (May 1987), pp. 155–176; Albert Hourani and S.M. Stern, ed., *The Islamic City: A Colloquium* (Oxford, 1970).

2. Scripture, History and Modernity: Readings of the Qur'an

1 Ludwig Wittgenstein, *Philosophical Investigations I*, #203 (London, 1958), p. 82.
2 Charles M . Wood, *Theory and Understanding: Critique of the Hermeneutics of Joachim Wach* (Chicago, 1975), p. 85.
3 Leo Tolstoy, *Resurrection* (London, 1904), p. 123. 'Mysticism without poetry is superstition, while poetry without mysticism is prose.'
4 William E. Connolly, *Pluralism* (Durham, NC, 2005), p. 59.
5 Ibid., p. 64.
6 Charles Taylor, *The Varieties of Religion Today: William James Revisited* (Cambridge, 2002), p. 79
7 Dale F. Eickelman, 'Islam and Modernity', in Eliezer Ben-Rafael and Yitzhak Sternbeg, ed. *Identity, Culture and Globalization* (Leiden, 2002), pp. 101–103.
8 See Bruce Lincoln, *Holy Terrors: Thinking About Religion after September 11* (Chicago, 2003), p.7 ff.
9 Abdullahi An-Na'im, *The Future of Shari'a: Secularism from an Islamic Perspective*, Introduction (Cambridge, MA, forthcoming).
10 These are questions that I raise and consider to be axial for any consideration of the Noble Qur'an as a scriptural resource for charting social and political ideals: Bruce Lawrence, *The Qur'an: A Biography* (London, 2006), pp. 14–15.
11 These fifteen principles are cited in their fullest form, with Arabic technical terms at several points, in Christian Troll, *Sayyid Ahmad Khan: A Reinterpretation of Muslim Theology* (New Delhi, 1978), pp. 276–278.
12 Ibid., p. 229.
13 For a discussion of the limits to Sir Sayyid's approach to science, see Muzaffar Iqbal, *Islam and Science* (Burlington, 2002), pp. 244–253.
14 All these citations from Iqbal's classical poem rely on Khushwant Singh, trans., *Shikwa o-Jawab-i Shikwa* (New Delhi, 1981).

15 This translation, along with multiple insights into Iqbal's lyrical genius, comes from Mustansir Mir, *Tulip in the Desert: A Selection of the Poetry of Muhammad Iqbal* (Montreal, 2000).

16 Numerous reprints have appeared of this classic. The best analytical study of Iqbal's engagement with images and passages from the Qur'an remains Annemarie Schimmel, *Gabriel's Wing: A Study into the Religious Ideas of Sir Muhammad Iqbal* (Leiden, 1963). It is usefully to be supplemented by Iqbal Singh, *The Ancient Pilgrim: An Introduction to the Life and Work of Muhammad Iqbal* (Oxford, 1997).

17 Translation from Mir, *Tulip in the Desert*.

18 See *Messages to the World: The Statements of Osama Bin Laden*, ed. Bruce Lawrence and Howarth James (London, 2005).

19 An astute analysis of Bin Laden's reliance on Ibn Taymiyyah and other medieval exegetes is to be found in Rosalind Gwynne, 'Al-Qa'ida and al-Qur'an: The "Tafsir" of Usamah bin Laden' online at http://www.utk.edu/~warda/bin_laden_and_quran.htm.

20 Lawrence and James, *Messages to the World*, p. 183.

3. *Heroic Themes: An Invitation to Muslim Worlds*

1 Marshall Hodgson, *The Venture of Islam*, 1 (Chicago, 1974), p. 58.

2 See John Renard, *Islam and the Heroic Image: Themes in Literature and the Visual Arts* (Columbia, SC, 1993), pp. 43–119.

3 Allessandro Bausani, 'Elementi Epici Nell Letterature Islamiche', in *La Poesia Epica e la sua Formazione* (Rome, 1970), pp. 759–68. See also Daniel Biebuyck, 'The Epic as Genre in Congo Oral Literature', in Richard M. Dorson, *African Folklore*, p. 269 f, on applying DeVries' criteria for the heroic lifecycle pattern as link to other heroic traditions; and K. Kailasapathy, *Tamil Heroic Poetry*, p. 229 f, on 'The World of the Heroes', where the author compares Homeric Greek and Tamil literature to show how both are reflections of a 'Heroic Age'. One might extend the comparison to include several other heroic traditions, as does Kassim Ahmad, *Characterization in Hikayet Hang Tuah*, pp. 1–5. On comparisons between Persian and Arthurian traditions, see J.C. Coyajee, 'Studies in the Shahnameh', in *Journal of the K.R. Cama Oriental Institute*, 33 (1939), pp. 13–307.

4 Mounah Khouri and Hamid Algar, *An Anthology of Modern Arabic Poetry* (Berkeley, 1975), pp. 143–149.

5 Ibid., pp. 175–179, at p. 179; 181–191, at p. 187.

6 Matthias Vereno, 'On the Relations of Dumezilian Comparative

Indo-European Mythology to History of Religions in General', in *Myth in Indo-European Antiquity*, ed. Gerald L. Larson (Berkeley, CA, 1974), p. 182 ff. Dumezil's three-part structure of sacred, military, and mercantile functions relates myth/epic characters to actual historical settings. Sacred function is related to 'sovereignty' – when these split, the problem of a power struggle arises: 'The more complete the transfer of sovereignty from the first to the second function in any given culture at any given time, the sharper the distinction between the sacred and secular.'

7 Lode F. Brakel, 'Persian Influence on Malay Literature', in *Abr Nahrain*, 9 (1969–1970), pp. 14–15, quoting Winstedt's translation. Brakel further defines the function of the *hikayat* in Malay culture as 'power-strengthening, enhancing the *mana* of whoever participates in the act of reciting, be it as reader or as listener . . . [Furthermore] to recite it or to have it recited is a meritorious act which atones for sins'. (pp. 6–7).

8 See 'The Re-examination of the Soviet Asian Epics,' in *Soviet Epics*, in *Central Asia Review*, 4 (1956), pp. 66–71, on the ideological implications of epic changes and the insertion of religious elements (e.g. making Köroghlu a saint who wins by God's power, etc.).

9 Francisco Marcos Marin, *Poesia Narrativa Arabe y épica hispanica: Elementos Arabes en los origines de la epica hispanica* (Madrid, 1971), pp. 237–269. See also Julie Scott Meisami, *Medieval Persian Court Poetry* (Princeton, 1987), p. 134 ff. on hero as model; Harry T. Norris, *The Adventures of Antar* (Warminster, 1980), p. 69, on Antar and Islam and development beyond pre-Islamic forms and values; and Bridget Connelly, *Arab Folk Epic and Identity* (Berkeley, CA, 1986), chapters 8–10, on related issues in Hilali saga.

10 Norris, *Adventures of Antar*, pp. 14–22.

11 Sayyid H. Hurreiz, *Ja'iliyyin folktales An Interplay of African, Arabian and Islamic Elements* (Bloomington, IN, 1977), p. 34.

12 Reuben Levy, *The Epic of Kings* (selections) (London, 1967), p. 152ff.

13 *Iskandarnamah: A Persian Medieval Alexander-Romance*, tr. Minoo Southgate (New York, 1985), pp. 54, 57.

14 Levy, *Epic of Kings*, pp. 350–351.

15 Ibid., p. 5.

16 Ignaz Goldziher, 'What Is Meant by "al-Jahiliyya?"', *Muslim Studies*, 1 (London, 1967), pp. 11–44; and 'Muruwwah and Din', ibid., 1, pp. 203–208.

17 Toshihiko Izutsu, *Ethico-Religious Concepts in the Qur'an* (Montreal, 1966).

18 M. M. Bravmann, *The Spiritual Background of Early Islam* (Leiden, 1972), p. 2.

19 Helmer Ringgren, *Fatalism in Persian Epics* (Uppsala, 1952), p. 130.

20 Soewito Santoso, 'The Islamization of Indonesian/Malay Literature in Its Earlier Period', *Journal of the Oriental Society of Australia*, 8 (1971), p. 9.

21 Ibid., pp. 9–10.

22 Ibid., pp. 16–18.

23 R. O. Winstedt, 'Hikayat Hang Tuah', *Journal of the Malayan Branch Royal Asiatic Society*, 83 (1921), p. 121 and *passim*.

24 Santoso, 'The Islamization of Indonesian/Malay Literature, pp. 20–24.

25 Bausani, 'Elementi Epici', pp. 759–68; schematic diagram, p. 768.

26 Lode F. Brakel, 'On the Origin of Malay Hikayat', *Review of Indonesian and Malaysian Affairs*, 13 (1979), pp. 21–22. He makes a similar argument for the introduction of the Islamicate genres known as *kitab* and *sya'ir* in 22 ff. See also Brakel, 'Persian Influence on Malay Literature', on Persian influence.

27 William L. Hanaway, 'Persian Popular Romances Before the Safavid Period', Ph.D. dissertation (Columbia University, NY, 1970), p. 265.

28 Ibid., 263–269.

29 See J. J. Ras, *Hikayat Bandjar: A Study of Malay Historiography* (The Hague, 1968), p. 133 and *passim*, for parallels with other stories. See also Aly Mazaheri, 'L'Iran de Ferdovsi et le héros culturel Rustam', *Zamam*, 1 (1979), pp. 4–20, and Sorush Soroudi, 'Islamization of the Iranian National Hero Rustam as Reflected in Persian Folktales', *Jerusalem Studies in Arabic and Islam*, 2 (1980), pp. 365–383, on Islamization of Rustam and the Persianization of Ali.

30 Ismail Hamid, *Arabic and Islamic Literary Tradition* (Kuala Lumpur, 1982), p. 130 ff.

31 Ahmad, *Characterization in Hikayat Hang Tuah*.

32 Shaharuddin B. Maaruf, *Concept of a Hero in Malay Society* (Singapore, 1984), p. 48.

33 Summarized from Maaruf, pp. 9–16. With feudalism, says Maaruf, the other ingredient in the distortion of the heroic image is materialism, the archetype of which is J. Paul Getty.

34 Joseph L. Mbele, 'The Identity of the Hero in the Liongo Epic', *Research in African Literature*, 17 (Winter 1986), pp. 464–471; 'Women in the African Epic,' *Research in African Literatures*, 37 (Summer 2006), pp. 61–67

35 Marcos, *Poesia Narrativa Arabe*, p. 314.

36 See Claude Cahen, 'Futuwwa/Pre- and Early Islamic', *Encyclopedia of Islam EI2*, vol. 3, pp. 961–965; Franz Taeschner, 'Futuwwa/ Post-Mongol Period', Ibid., vol. 3, pp. 966–69; and 'Ayyar', ibid., vol. 1, p. 794.

37 See J. Christoph Bürgel, 'Die Frau als Person in der Epik Nizamis', *Asiatische Studien*, 42 (1988), pp. 137–155.

38 Thomas Winner, *The Oral Art and Literature of the Kazakhs of Russian Central Asia* (Durham, 1958), pp. 75–78.

39 On this and related heroic imagery in Saddam's public art program, see Kanan Makiya, *The Monument: Art and Vulgarity in Saddam Hussein's Iraq* (London & New York, 2004).

40 As suggested by visual imagery in Afghan calendar art. See, for instance, Pierre Centilivres and Micheline Centiliveres-Demont, 'Les martyrs afghans par le texte et l'image (1978–1992)', in Catherine Mayeur-Jaouen, *Saints et Heros du Moyên-Orient Contemporain* (Paris, 2002), pp. 285–300.

41 David B. Edwards, *Heroes of the Age: Moral Fault Lines on the Afghan Frontier* (Berkeley, CA, 1996), esp. 'The Lives of an Afghan Saint', pp. 128–171.

4. *An Andalusian Modernity in Narratives of Women*

1 Charles Taylor, *Multiculturalism and 'The Politics of Recognition'* (Princeton, NJ, 1992), p. 42.

2 Duncan Brown, *Oral Literature and Performance in South Africa* (Oxford, Capetown & Athens, OH, 1999), pp. 2–3.

3 Quoted in Leslie Fiedler, *Love and Death in the American Novel* (New York, 1992), p. 40.

4 See Gayatri Chakravorty Spivak, *Death of a Discipline* (New York, 2003), pp. 101–102. A welcome exception is María Rosa Menocal's *The Ornament of the World: How Muslims, Jews and Christians Created a Culture of Tolerance in Medieval Spain* (New York & London, 2002).

5 Dilip Gaonkar, 'Toward New Imaginaries: An Introduction', *Public Culture*, 14 (2002), pp. 1–19, at p. 10.

6 María Rosa Menocal, *The Arabic Role in Medieval Literary History: A Forgotten Heritage*, rev. ed. (Philadelphia, PA, 2004), pp. 56–57.

7 Jürgen Habermas, *The Structural Transformation of the Public Sphere: An Enquiry into a Category of Bourgeois Society*, rev. ed. (Cambridge, MA, 1992), p. 9.

8   Manuela Marín in *Mujeres en Al-Ándalus*, (Madrid, 2000), p. 22, notes that the extant verse of Walláda, Hafsa bint al Hajy and other women poets amply confirms the liberty enjoyed by Andalusian women.

9   Roger Boase, *The Origin and Meaning of Courtly Love: A Critical Study of European Scholarship* (Manchester, 1977), p. 2.

10 The tradition of women involved in Andalusian music has survived in Moroccan cities such as Tetouan and Shefchaouen which still have all-female orchestras of Andalusian musicians.

11 Julia Kristeva, 'Postmodernism?', in Harry R. Gavin, ed. *Romanticism, Modernism, Postmodernism* (London & Toronto, 1980), pp. 136–141, at p. 140.

12 Leila Ahmed, *Women and Gender in Islam* (New Haven, CT, & London, 1992), p. 84.

13 Abdellah Laroui, *The History of the Maghrib* (Princeton, NJ, 1977), p. 212.

14 Muhammad Ibn 'Aazzouz Hakeem, *al-Jadeed fee tareekh Titwan: aljuz' al-'awal : hukkam Titwan min sanat 888 ila sanat 1375 (1483–1956)* (Tetouan, 2000), p. 32.

15 Jean-Louis Miège, M'hammad Benaboud and Nadia Erzini, *Tétouan: Ville andalouse marocaine* (Paris, 1996), p. 28.

16 Ibid., p. 29.

17 Whereas in Meknes, for example, the term used for such a tale is *hajia*, in Tetouan the term is *khurafa*, the same term which according to Marín (*Mujeres en Al-Andalus*, pp. 630–31) was used in al-Andalus to denote tales told by women in the evening while they were spinning. Spinning and storytelling, she notes, were activities specifically associated with women, and considered too lacking in prestige to be incorporated into written records more associated with men.

18 Ibid., pp. 113–114.

19 Ibid., pp. 253–311.

20 See Álvaro Machordom Comins, *La Expulsión de Los Moriscos: Proceso Histórico a Felípe III* (Spain, 2000), *passim*.

21 Miége *et al.*, *Tétouan: Ville andalouse marocaine*, p. 30.

22 Jean-Louis Miège, *Tétouan à travers les siècles* (Tetouan, 1996), p. 7.

23 See Dolores López Enamorado, *Cuentos Populares Marroquíes* (Madrid, 2000), p. 15.

24 One 17th-century Tetouani woman left an endowment for storks to be healed by *jbeeras* when they broke their legs. See Muhammad Ibn 'Aazzouz Hakeem, *Titwaniyat fi dhakirat at-tareekh* (Tetouan, 2001), p. 15.

25 Ibid., *passim.*
26 See Muhammad Ibn 'Azzouz Hakeem, *as-Sit al-Hurra, hakimat Titwan: bint al-'amir mulay 'Ali ibn Rasheed* (Rabat, 1983), *passim.*
27 Marín in *Mujeres en Al-Ándalus,* p. 717, defines *jaria* (pl. *jawari*) as a young woman, a slave girl or a slave who is a singer. However, 'slave' in English fails to capture the status of women more akin to indentured labour, sometimes brought by their parents to large households where they were expected to be trained in a more sophisticated way of life.
28 Ibid. In al-Andalus they belonged mainly to the more sophisticated milieus and tended to be good looking and highly educated, particularly in the liberal arts and music. Their ability to excel in these arts could increase their value considerably, as was the case of the singer Tara, who was offered for sale to the emir al-Mundir. On hearing her he was so satisfied with her singing that he paid her twice the amount asked (p. 42). *Jawari* often took part in poetic gatherings organized by their patrons, where they responded to the verses of males with poetry which they improvised themselves (p. 643).
29 This is similar to the situation that prevailed in the Middle East, as Leila Ahmed explains: 'To us, with our notions of slavery grounded in the history of American society, the very idea that slaves constituted the upper classes is so counterintuitive as to seem almost nonsensical. But in the Middle East, slaves and slave origins were so fundamentally part of aristocratic and royal life that for over a thousand years nearly all caliphs, kings, and sultans in the region were the sons of slave mothers.' Leila Ahmed, *A Border Passage From Cairo to America: A Woman's Journey* (Harmondsworth, 1999), p. 98.
30 Linda Hutcheon, *A Poetics of Postmodernism* (New York & London, 1991), p. 89.
31 In Moroccan *dareeja* (a dialect of Arabic) this tale is a *jmila*, which is both the diminutive and the feminine of 'camel', and a pun on the feminine of 'beautiful'.
32 According to Lacan's *The Four Fundamental Concepts of Psychoanalysis* (Harmondsworth, 1977), p 197, the child at first is what he calls (in one of his many plays on words) an 'hommelette', a little man and a broken egg, which spreads without defined limitations. The child at this stage is grounded in the real, the world of real objects and ideas unmediated by the structuring potential of language. Thus Lacan claims, 'C'est le monde des mots qui crée le monde des choses' – the reality of the things we appear to perceive are 'created' by language: *Écrits 1* (Paris, 1966), p. 155. This is why it is necessary, according to

Lacan, to traverse the other two stages, the imaginary and the symbolic. The first is the pre-oedipal identification of the child with its mirror image in which it begins to acquire a gendered subjectivity. However, the individual only becomes a sexual being upon entering the symbolic, the order of language, which comes under the law of the father (*Écrits 1*, pp. 167–168).

33 Fatima Mernissi, *The Veil and the Male Elite: A Feminist Interpretation of Women's Rights in Islam* (Cambridge, MA, 1991), p. 93.

34 Ibid., p. 94.

35 Habermas, *Structural Transformation*, p. 4.

36 According to Marin, in the towns of al-Andalus the river was considered a woman's space, where they at times went to wash clothes. *Mujeres en Al-Andalus*, pp, 291–292.

37 Bakhtin, *Rabelais and His World* (Bloomington, IN, 1984), p, 7.

38 Gaonkar, 'Toward New Imaginaries', p. 11.

39 See Habermas, *Structural Transformation*, p. 19. A similar emergence of the private economy within the public sphere occurred in Tetouan, where until the beginning of the early 20th century numerous households bred silk worms and the women spun, dyed and wove the silk as they did the wool. Once this process was relegated to the public sphere, and to distant locales both in Morocco and Europe, the women lost the economic autonomy with which it had endowed them and the art of storytelling which formed an integral part of the spinning.

40 Bakhtin, *Rabelais and His World*, p. 9.

41 See Lacan, *The Four Fundamental Concepts of Psychoanalysis*, p. 74.

42 Bakhtin, *Rabelais and His World*, pp. 19–20.

43 Homi K. Bhabha, *The Location of Culture* (New York & London, 1994), p. 30.

44 See Taylor, *Multiculturalism and 'The Politics of Recognition'*, pp. 32–33.

45 Gaonkar, 'Toward New Imaginaries', p. 15.

46 Ibid., p. 7.

47 Julia Kristeva, 'Women's Time', *Signs*, 1 (1981), pp. 13–35, p. 16.

48 Ibid., p. 23.

49 Jacques Lacan, *Ecrits 2* (Paris, 1971), p. 111.

50 See Lacan, *Ecrits 1*, pp. 167–168.

51 Kristeva, 'Postmodernism?', p. 136.

52 Lacan, *The Four Fundamental Concepts of Psychoanalysis*, p. 188.

53 Kristeva, 'Women's Time', p. 17.

54 Ibid.

55 Benedict Anderson, *Imagined Communities: Reflections on the Origins*

and Spread of Nationalism, rev. ed. (New York & London, 2006), p. 205.

56 Kristeva, 'Women's Time', p. 34.

57 Bhabha, *The Location of Culture*, p. 153.

58 Gaonkar, 'Toward New Imaginaries', p. 9.

59 See Menocal, *The Arabic Role in Medieval Literary History*, ch. 1.

60 Ibid, ch. 5.

6. Forbidden Modernities: Islam in Public

1 In speaking of Islamism, one differentiates between *Muslim* (which expresses religious identity) and *Islamist* (which refers to a social movement through which Muslim identity is collectively reappropriated as a basis for an alternative social and political project). Thus Islamism implies a critique and even a discontinuity with the given categories of Muslim identity.

2 Farhad Khosrokhavar and Olivier Roy, *Iran: Comment sortir d'une révolution religieuse* (Paris, 1999); Fariba Adelkhah, *Être moderne en Iran* (Paris, 1998).

3 Olivier Roy, *L'Echec de l'Islam politique* (Paris, 1992); Gilles Kepel, *Jihad: Expansion et déclin de l'Islamisme* (Paris, 2000).

4 On historical semantics, see Reinhart Koselleck, *Vergangene Zukunft: Zur Semantik geschichtlicher Zeiten* (Frankfurt am Main, 1979).

5 Sudipta Kaviraj, 'Filth and the Public Sphere: Concepts and Practices about Space in Calcutta', *Public Culture*, 10 (1997), p. 98.

6 Cornelius Castoriadis, *The Imaginary Institution of Society*, tr. Kathleen Blamey (Cambridge, 1987), p. 238.

7 Ibid., pp. 367–368.

8 Shmuel N. Eisenstadt and Schluchter Wolfgang, 'Introduction: Paths to Early Modernities – A Comparative View', *Daedalus*, 127:3 (1998), pp. 4–7.

9 Nilüfer Göle, 'Global Expectations, Local Experiences, Non-Western Modernities', in *Through a Glass, Darkly: Blurred Images of Cultural Tradition and Modernity over Distance and Time*, ed. Wil Arts (Leiden, 2000).

10 Charles Taylor, *Modern Social Imaginaries* (Durham, NC, & London, 2004), pp. 23–30.

11 'The Revolt of Women', *Hürriyet* (4 May 1999), p. 1. According to a survey on political and social values conducted in October 1999 by the Political Science Foundation in Istanbul (IMV-SAM), 61 per cent of the

Turkish population thinks that Kavakçi should have taken off her headscarf while in the Parliament. Another covered woman deputy, from the Nationalist Party (MHP), had taken off her headscarf to attend the National Assembly and was applauded while giving her oath.

12 Nicole Pope, 'Parliament Opens amid Controversy', TurkeyUpdate (www.turkeyUpdate.com) (3 May 1999).

13 'The Revolt of Women', 1.

14 Nicole Pope, 'Islamist Deputy Stripped of Her Turkish Citizenship', TurkeyUpdate (www.turkeyUpdate.com) (17 May, 1999).

15 David Frisby, *Fragments of Modernity: Theories of Modernity in the Work of Simmel, Kracauer, and Benjamin* (Cambridge, 1985) p. 6.

16 Clifford Geertz, 'Thick Description: Toward an Interpretative Theory of Culture', in *The Interpretation of Cultures: Selected Essays* (New York, 1973).

17 Jacques Revel, 'Micro-analyse et construction du social', in *Jeux d'échelles: La micro-analyse a l'éxperience*, ed. J. Revel (Paris, 1996).

18 Revel, *Jeux d'échelle*, p. 36. Revel uses this example to establish a parallel with microhistory. Rather than privileging one over the other, he argues that the methodological principle is the variation between them.

19 Nilüfer Göle, *The Forbidden Modern: Civilization and Veiling* (Ann Arbor, MI, 1996).

20 For an analysis of 'the foreigner' in terms of distance from/proximity to the social group, see Simmel's notion of 'l'étranger': Georg Simmel, 'Digressions sur l'étranger', in *L'école de Chicago: Naissance de l'écologie urbaine*, ed. Yves Grafmeyer and Isaac Joseph (Paris, 1979). For an English translation, see *The Sociology of Georg Simmel*, tr. Kurt Wolff (New York, 1950).

21 Simonettea Tabboni, 'Le multiculturalisme et l'ambivalence de l'étranger', in *Une société fragmentée?: Le multiculturalisme en débat*, ed. Michel Wieviorka *et al.* (Paris, 1997) pp. 239–240.

22 On global circulations and modern social imaginaries, see Arjun Appadurai, *Modernity at Large* (Minneapolis, MN, 1996).

23 Erving Goffman, *Les cadres de l'éxperience* (Paris, 1991), p. 417; originally published as *Frame Analysis: An Essay on the Organization of Experience* (New York, 1974).

24 Victor Turner, *The Anthropology of Performance* (New York, 1986), p. 24.

25 On the public sphere in the West, see Jürgen Habermas, *The Structural Transformation of the Public Sphere: An Enquiry into a Category of Bourgeois Society* (Cambridge, 1989); on the public sphere in a

Muslim context, see Nilüfer Göle, 'The Gendered Nature of the Public Sphere', *Public Culture*, 10 (1977) pp. 61–81.

26 Danilo Martuccelli, *Sociologies de la modernité: L'itinéraire du XXe siècle* (Paris, 1999) p. 447.

27 Alain Touraine, *Critique de la modernité* (Paris, 1992), p. 337.

28 On reflexivity and modernity, see Ulrich Beck, Anthony Giddens and Scott Lasch, *Reflexive Modernization: Politics, Tradition, and Aesthetics in the Modern Social Order* (Cambridge, 1994).

29 The title of the Turkish edition of my book on veiling, *The Forbidden Modern* is *Modern Mahrem*.

30 Craig Calhoun, 'Habitus, Field, and Capital: The Question of Historical Specificity', in C. Calhoun, Edward LiPuma and Moishe Postone, ed., *Bourdieu: Critical Perspectives* (Chicago, 1993), pp. 61–89.

31 Richard Sennett, *Flesh and Stone: The Body and the City in Western Civilization* (New York, 1996).

32 Ibid., p. 370.

33 Scott Lash, *Another Modernity: A Different Rationality* (Oxford, 1999), p. 4.

34 Castoriadis, *Imaginary Institution*, p. 367.

35 *Modern Social Imaginaries*, p. 196.

7. *Revivalism and the Enclave Society*

1 John Urry, *Sociology Beyond Societies: Mobilities for the Twenty First Century* (New York, 2000).

2 Arjun Appadurai, *Modernity at Large: Cultural Dimensions of Globalization* (Minneapolis, MN, 1996).

3 Arjun Appadurai, ed., *Globalization* (Durham, NC & London, 2001).

4 Dilip P. Gaonkar, 'Toward New Imaginaries: An Introduction', *Public Culture*, 4 (2002), pp. 1–19.

5 Michel Foucault, 'Governmentality', in G. Burchell, C. Gordon, and P. Miller, ed., *The Foucault Effect: Studies in Governmentality* (London, 1991), pp. 87–104.

6 John Torpey, *The Invention of the Passport: Surveillance, Citizenship and the State* (New York, 1999).

7 Saskia Sassen, *Guests and Aliens* (New York, 1999).

8 Olivier Roy, *Globalised Islam: The Search for the New Ummah* (New York, 2004).

9 Saba Mahmood, *Politics of Piety: The Islamic Revival and the Feminist Subject* (Princeton, NJ & Oxford, 2005).

10 John Rawls, *The Law of Peoples* (Cambridge, MA, 1999).

11 Jeff Spinner-Halev, 'Hinduism, Christianity, and Liberal Religious Tolerance', *Political Theory*, 33 (2005), pp. 28–57.
12 Bryan S. Turner, *Vulnerability and Human Rights* (Philadelphia, PA, 2006).
13 Nicholas Abercrombie, Stephen Hill and Bryan S. Turner, *The Dominant Ideology Thesis* (London, 1980).
14 Bryan S. Turner, *Citizenship and Capitalism: The Debate over Reformism* (London, 1986).
15 Daniel Bell, *The Coming of Post-Industrial Society: A Venture in Social Forecasting* (New York, 1973).
16 Jean-françois Lyotard, *The Postmodern Condition: A Report on Knowledge*, tr.
   G. Bennington and B. Massumi (Minneapolis, MN, 1984).
17 Peter L. Berger, ed., *The Desecularization of the World* (Michigan, 1999).
18 Herfried Münkler, *The New Wars* (Cambridge, 2005).
19 Bryan S. Turner, 'Historical Sociology of Religion: Politics and Modernity', in G. Delanty and E. F. Isin, ed., *Handbook of Historical Sociology* (London, 2003), pp. 349–363.
20 Yolanda Chin and Norman Vasu, *Rethinking Racial Harmony in Singapore* (Singapore, 2006), pp. 1–3.
21 Kathryn Spellman, *Religion And Nation: Iranian Local And Transnational Networks in Britain* (Oxford, 2005).
22 Karen Armstrong, *The Battle for God: Fundamentalism in Judaism, Christianity and Islam* (London, 2001); P. L. Berger, ed., *The Desecularization of the World*; M. Juergensmeyer, ed., *Global Religions: An Introduction* (Oxford, 2003).
23 Bryan S. Turner, 'Cosmopolitan virtue, globalization and patriotism', *Theory Culture & Society*, 19 (2002), pp. 45–63.
24 Rawls, *The Law of Peoples*, p. 16.
25 Ibid., p. 136.
26 Ibid., p. 137.
27 Emile Benveniste, *Indo-European Language and Society* (Coral Gables, FL, 1973).
28 Rawls, *The Law of Peoples*, p. 6.
29 Tamotsu Shibutani, *Society and Personality* (Englewood Cliffs, NJ, 1961).
30 Zainah Anwar, 'What Islam, Whose Islam? Sisters in Islam and the Struggle for Women's Rights', in R. W. Hefner, ed., *The Politics of Multiculturalism: Pluralism and Citizenship in Malaysia, Singapore and Indonesia* (Honolulu, 2001), pp. 227–252.
31 Kyai Hajji Abdurrahman Wahid, 'Extremism isn't in Islamic Law', *Washington Post* (23 May 2006).
32 Jason Tedjasukmana, 'Indonesia's Skin Wars', *Time Magazine* (10 April 2006).

33 Erving Goffman, *The Presentation of Self in Everyday Life* (Harmondsworth, 1959).

34 Marshall G. Hodgson, *The Venture of Islam* (Chicago, 1974).

35 Marwan Ibrahim Al-Kaysi, *Morals and Manners in Islam: A Guide to Islamic Adab* (London, 1989).

36 Peter Mandaville, *Transnational Muslim Politics* (London & New York, 2001).

37 Olivier Roy, *The Failure of Political Islam* (Cambridge, MA); *Globalized Islam: The Search for a New Ummah*.

38 Pierre Bourdieu, *Outline of a Theory of Practice* (Cambridge, 1977).

39 Christian Joppke, 'The Retreat of Multiculturalism in the Liberal State: Theory and Policy', *British Journal of Sociology*, 55 (2004), pp. 237–257.

40 Melford E. Spiro, *Buddhism and Society: A Great Tradition and its Burmese Vicissitudes* (New York, 1970); B. S. Turner, *Weber and Islam* (London & New York, 1998); M. Weber, *Sociology of Religion* (London, 1966).

41 Immanuel Kant, *Religion within the Limits of Reason Alone* (New York, 1960).

42 Ronald Lukens-Bull, *A Peaceful Jihad: Negotiating Identity and Modernity in Muslim Java* (New York, 2005).

43 Max Weber, *The Protestant Ethic and the Spirit of Capitalism* (London, 2002).

44 Harvey Cox, 'Christianity' in Mark Juergensmeyer, ed., *Global Religions: An Introduction* (Oxford, 2003), pp. 17–27.

45 Elaine Combs-Schilling, *Sacred Performances: Islam, Sexuality and Sacrifice* (New York, 1989).

46 Ernest Gellner, *Muslim Society* (Cambridge & New York, 1981).

47 Graham Warde, 'The Future of Religion', *Journal of the American Academy of Religion*, 74 (2006), pp. 179–186.

48 James Beckford, *Social Theory and Religion* (Cambridge, 2003).

49 Wade Clark Roof, *A Generation of Seekers: The Spiritual Journeys of the Baby Boom Generation* (San Francisco, CA, 1993).

50 Stephen Hunt, *Religion and Everyday Life* (London & New York, 2005).

51 Thierry Paquot, 'Through the Gates and Over the Wall', *Le Monde Diplomatique* (October 2006), pp. 14–15.

52 Gabriel A. Almond, R. Scott Appleby and Emmanuel Sivan, *Strong Religion. The Rise of Fundamentalism Around the World* (Chicago & London, 2003).

53 Noorhaidi Hasan, *Laskar Jihad: Islam, Militancy and the Quest for Identity in Post-New Order Indonesia* (Ithaca, NY, 2006).

54 Joel Migdal, *State in Society: Studying How States and Societies Transform and Constitute One Another* (New York, 2001).

55 David Lehmann and Batia Siebzehner, *Remaking of Israeli Judaism: The Challenge of Shas* (London, 2006).

56 Cynthia Hamilton, 'Multiculturalism as a Political Strategy', in Avery Gordon and Christopher Newfield, ed., *Mapping Multiculturalism* (Minneapolis, MN, 1996), pp. 167–176.

57 M. M. Sharif, *A History of Muslim Philosophy* (Wiesbaden, 1963).

58 William C. Chittick, *Imaginal Worlds: Ibn al-'Arabi and the Problem of Religious Diversity* (New York, 1994); S. H. Nasr, *Sufi Essays* (Albany, NY, 1972).

59 Douglas Hartmann and Joseph Gerteis, 'Dealing with Diversity: Mapping Multiculturalism in Sociological Terms', *Sociological Theory*, 23 (2005), pp. 218–240; Joshua Parens, 'Multiculturalism and the Problem of Particularism', *American Political Science Review*, 88 (1994), pp. 169–181.

8. *Modern Citizenship, Multiple Identities*

1 Amartya Sen, *Identity and Violence: The Illusion of Destiny* (London, 2006), p. 16.

2 Frederick Cooper, *Colonialism in Question: Theory, Knowledge, History* (Berkeley, CA, 2005), pp. 113–114.

3 Will Kymlicka, *Multicultural Citizenship* (Oxford, 1995), p. 2.

4 Derek Heater, *Citizenship: The Civic Ideal in World History, Politics, and Education*, 3rd ed. (New York, 2004), pp. 4–5.

5 Thomas Janowski, *Citizenship and Civil Society: A Framework of Rights and Obligations in Liberal, Traditional, and Social Democratic Regimes* (Cambridge, 1998), pp. 10–11.

6 Michael Walzer, *Spheres of Justice* (Oxford, 1983), p. 19, cited in Heater, *Citizenship*, p. 341.

7 Ruth Lister, *Citizenship: Feminist Perspectives* (London, 1997), p. 66.

8 Charles Taylor, *Modern Social Imaginaries* (Durham, NC, London, 2004), p. 90.

9 Heater, *Citizenship*, pp. 200–205.

10 Jean-Pierre Vernant, *The Origins of Greek Thought* (New York, 1982), p. 61.

11 Robert Putnam, *Bowling Alone: The Collapse and Revival of American Community* (New York, 2000), pp. 21–24.

12 Theda Skocpol, *Diminished Democracy: From Membership to Management in American Civic Life* (Oklahoma City, 2003), cited in Michael Edwards, *Civil Society* (Oxford, 2004), pp. 77–80.

13 José Casanova, *Public Religions in the Modern World* (Chicago, 1994), pp. 213–214.

14 Hugh Heclo, 'An Introduction to Religion and Public Policy', pp. 3–7, and Wilfred M. McClay, 'Two Concepts of Secularism', p. 32, in H. Heclo and W. M. McClay, ed. *Religion Returns to the Public Square: Faith and Policy in America* (Baltimore, MD, 2003).

15 Casanova, *Public Religions*, pp. 3–5

16 Ibid, pp. 212–215.

17 Ibid, p. 212.

18 Cited in Kymlicka, *Multicultural Citizenship*, p. 187.

19 Kymlicka, *Multicultural Citizenship*, pp. 188–189.

20 Canadian Survey of Giving and Volunteering (www.imaginecanada.ca), at www.givingandvolunteering.ca/pdf/SGVP_Highlights_2004_en.pdf, p. 15.

21 Putnam, *Bowling Alone*, pp. 66–67.

22 Heater, *Citizenship*, p. 191.

23 Faisal Bodi, 'Incoherent on Cohesion', the *Guardian*, 1 Sept 2006; Arun Kundani, 'Report finds no contradiction in being British and Muslim', *Independent Race and Refugee News Network* (7 Dec 2004).

24 Ernest Gellner, *Conditions of Liberty: Civil Society and its Rivals* (London, 1994), p. 78.

25 Ibid., p. 96.

26 Jeremy Jennings, 'Citizenship, Republicanism, and Multiculturalism in Contemporary France', *British Journal of Political Science*, 30 (2000), pp. 575–598, at pp. 579, 584. For a thorough examination of the notion of equality as assimilation with reference to Muslim communities in France, Turkey and the UK, see Ellen Wiles, 'Headscarves, Human Rights, and Harmonious Multicultural Society: Implications of the French Ban for Interpretations of Equality', *Law & Society Review*, 3 (2007), pp. 699–736.

27 Cecile Laborde, 'The Culture(s) of the Republic: Nationalism and Multiculturalism in French Republican Thought', *Political Theory*, 29 (2001), pp. 716–735, at p. 721.

28 Veit Bader, 'The Cultural Conditions of Transnational Citizenship: On the Interpenetration of Political and Ethnic Cultures', *Political Theory*, 25 (1997), pp. 771–813, at p. 780.

29 Riva Kastoryano, 'National Institutions and Transnational Identities', *Inroads*, 15 (2004), p. 63.

30 Laborde, 'The Culture(s) of the Republic, p. 721.

31 Elaine R. Thomas, 'Keeping Identity at a Distance: Explaining France's New Legal Restrictions on the Islamic Headscarf', *Ethnic and Racial Studies*, 29 (2006), pp. 237–259, at pp. 1, 7.

32 Jytte Klaussen, *The Islamic Challenge: Politics and Religion in Western Europe* (Oxford, 2005), p. 21.

33 Ibid., pp. 3–4.

34 Ibid., pp. 24–28.

35 Kastoryano, *National Institutions*, pp. 64–65.

36 Jenny White, 'The Political Economy of Culture', in *Islamist Mobilization in Turkey* (Seattle, WA, 2002), p. 35.

37 Thomas W. Smith, 'Between Allah and Ataturk: Liberal Islam in Turkey', *The International Journal of Human Rights*, 9 (2005), pp. 307–325, at pp. 8, 17.

38 Ibid., pp. 10–13.

39 Ibid., p. 11.

40 Ayse Saktanber, 'Becoming the "Other" as a Muslim in Turkey: Turkish Women vs. Islamist Women', *New Perspectives on Turkey*, 11 (2004), pp. 107–21.

41 Nilüfer Göle, 'The Quest for the Islamic Self within the Context of Modernity', in Sibel Bozdogan and Resat Kasaba, ed, *Rethinking Modernity and National Identity in Turkey* (Washington, 1997), pp. 87–89.

42 Resat Kasaba, 'Kemalist Certainties and Modern Ambiguities', in *Rethinking Modernity and National Identity in Turkey*, pp. 24–29.

43 Ibid., p. 28.

44 Yael Navaro-Yasin, 'The Historical Construction of Local Culture: Gender and Identity in the Politics of Secularism versus Islam', in Caglar Keyder, ed., *Istanbul Between the Local and the Global* (Lanham, MD, 1999), pp. 73–74.

45 Sabrina Tavernise, 'In Turkey, Fear About Religious Lifestyle', *New York Times* (30 April 2007); Paul de Bendern, 'Turks Seek Solace in Ataturk at Time of Tension', *Reuters* (10 April 2007).

46 Erik Jan Zurcher, 'Young Turks, Ottoman Muslims, and Turkish Nationalists: Identity Politics 1908–1938', in *Ottoman Past and Today's Turkey*, ed. Kemal H. Karpat (Boston, 2000), pp. 177–179.

47 Amartya Sen, *Identity and Violence: The Illusion of Destiny* (New York, 2006), pp. 154–160.

48 William Galston, *The Practice of Value Pluralism* (Cambridge, 2005), pp. 11–12.

49 Sen, *Identity and Violence:* p. 17.

50 Ibid., p. 9.

51 Klaussen, *The Islamist Challenge*, pp. 101–102.

9. *Globalization, Civil Imagination, and Islamic Movements*

1 Olivier Roy, *Globalized Islam: The Search for a New Ummah* (London, 2004).

2 Kevin McDonald, *Global Movements: Action and Culture* (Oxford, 2006).

3 John Rawls, *A Theory of Justice* (Cambridge, MA, 1991).

4 Jürgen Habermas, *The Structural Transformation of the Public Sphere* (Cambridge, MA, 1991).

5 Daniel Held, 'Principles of Cosmopolitan Order', in G. Brock and H. Brighouse, ed., *The Political Philosophy of Cosmopolitanism* (Cambridge, 2005).

6 Anthony Giddens, *Runaway World* (London, 1999).

7 Benjamin Barber, *Jihad vs. McWorld: How Globalism and Tribalism are Reshaping the World* (New York, 1995).

8 Francis Fukuyama, 'Voile et contrôle sexuel', *Le Monde* (4 February 2004).

9 Giddens, *Runaway World*, p. 4.

10 Bernard Lewis, 'The Roots of Muslim Rage', *The Atlantic Monthly*, 266 (September 1990), pp. 47–60.

11 Peter van der Veer, 'Cosmopolitan Options', *Etnográfica*, 6 (2002), pp. 15–26.

12 Daniel Lerner, *The Passing of Traditional Society: Modernizing the Middle East* (Glencoe, IL, 1958).

13 Van der Veer, 'Cosmopolitan Options', p. 16.

14 Theirry Zarcone, 'View from Islam, View from the West', *Diogenes*, 50 (2003), pp. 49–59.

15 Richard Bulliet, *The Case for Islamo-Christian Civilization* (New York, 2004).

16 Armando Salvatore, *Islam and the Political Discourse of Modernity* (Reading, 1997).

17 Talal Asad, *Genealogies of Religion: Discipline and Reasons of Power in Christianity and Islam* (Baltimore, MD, 1993).

18 Talal Asad, *Formations of the Secular: Christianity, Islam, Modernity* (Stanford, CT, 2003).

19 Robert Hefner, 'Multiple Modernities: Christianity, Islam and Hinduism in a Globalizing Age', *Annual Review of Anthropology*, 27 (1998), pp. 83–104.

20 Dale F. Eickelman, 'Islam and the Languages of Modernity', *Daedalus*, 129 (2000), pp. 119–133; D. Eickelman and Jon Anderson, ed. *New Media in the Muslim World: The Emerging Public Sphere*, 2nd ed. (Bloomington and Indianapolis, IN, 2003).

21 Jon W. Anderson, 'New Media, New Publics: Reconfiguring the Public Space of Islam', *Social Research*, 70 (2003), pp. 887–906.

22 Nilüfer Göle, 'Islam in Public: New Visibilities and New Imaginaries', *Public Culture*, 14 (2002), pp. 173–190.

23 Shmuel N. Eisenstadt, *Fundamentalism, Sectarianism and Revolution: The Jacobin Dimension of Modernity* (Cambridge, 1999).

24 Bryan Turner, 'Cosmopolitan Virtue: Religion in a Global Age', *European Journal of Social Theory*, 4 (2001), pp. 131–52.

25 Noah Salomon, 'Undoing the Mahdiyya: British Colonialism as Religious Reform in the Anglo-Egyptian Sudan, 1898–1914', *Society for the Anthropology of Religion* (2003), pp. 1–32, at p. 23.

26 Abdelwahab Meddeb, *La maladie de l'Islam* (Paris, 2002).

27 Sayyid Qutb, *Social Justice in Islam* (New York, 1953), p. 39.

28 Aziz Al-Azmeh, *Islams and Modernities* (New York 1996).

29 Will Kymlicka, *Politics in the Vernacular: Nationalism, Multiculturalism and Citizenship* (New York, 2001).

30 Charles Taylor, 'The Politics of Recognition', in A. Gutman, ed., *The Politics of Recognition* (Princeton, NJ, 1994).

31 Pnina Werbner, 'The Place which is Diaspora', *Journal of Ethnic and Migration Studies*, 28 (2002), pp. 119–133, at p. 129.

32 Pnina Werbner, 'Global Pathways: Working Class Cosmopolitans and their Creation of Transnational Ethnic Worlds', *Social Anthropology*, 17 (1999), pp. 17–35.

33 For an excellent exploration of the entry of 'identity' into the social sciences, see Philip Gleason, 'Identifying Identity: A Semantic History', *Journal of American History*, 69 (1983), pp. 910–931.

34 Arlene Macleod, *Accommodating Protest: Working Women, the New Veiling, and Change in Cairo* (New York, 1991).

35 Merrat Nasser, 'The New Veiling Phenomenon', *Journal of Community and Applied Social Psychology*, 9 (1999), pp. 410–411.

36 Saba Mahmood, 'Ethical Formation and Politics of Individual Autonomy in Contemporary Egypt', *Social Research*, 70 (2003), p. 842 (emphasis in original).

37 Saba Mahmood, *Politics of Piety: The Islamic Revival and the Feminist Subject* (Princeton, 2004), pp. 156–157.

38 Ibid., p. 157.

39 Pierre Hadot, 'What is Ancient Philosophy?' in S. Mahmood, *Politics of Piety* (Cambridge, 2002), p. 122.

40 Mahmood, *Politics of Piety*, p. 122 (emphasis added).

41 Asad, *Genealogies of Religion*, pp. 89–90.

42 Mahmood, *Politics of Piety*, p. 166.

43 Margaret C. Jacob, 'Private Beliefs and Public Temples: The New Religiosity in the Eighteenth Century', *Social Research*, 59 (1992), p. 77.

44 Charles Taylor, *Sources of the Self: The Making of the Modern Identity* (Cambridge, 1989).

45 John Milbank, *The Word Made Strange* (Oxford, 1997).

46 Alexis de Tocqueville, *Democracy in America* (New York, 1999), p. 392.

47 Hent de Vries, 'Before, Around and Beyond the Theologico-Political', in H. de Vries and L. Sullivan, eds., *Political Theologies: Public Religions in a Post-Secular World* (New York, 2006).

48 Patchen Markell, *Bound by Recognition* (Princeton, NJ, 2003), p. 12.

49 Asad, *Formations of the Secular*, pp. 179, 78.

50 Charles Hirschkind, 'Civic Virtue and Religious Reason: An Islamic Counter Public', *Cultural Anthropology*, 16 (2001), pp. 3–34.

10. *Reimagining the Civil: Pluralism and Its Discontents*

1 Ernest Gellner, *Conditions of Liberty: Civil Society and Its Rivals* (London & New York, 1994).

2 Thomas Janoski, *Citizenship and Civil Society* (Cambridge & New York, 1998); Derek Heater, *Citizenship: The Civic Ideal in World History, Politics and Education* (Manchester & New York, 2004); Ruth Lister, *Citizenship: Feminist Perspectives* (London, 1997).

3 José Casanova, *Public Religions in the Modern World* (Chicago, 1994).

4 Amitai Etzioni, *New Communitarian Thinking: Persons, Virtues, Institutions, and Communities,* (Charlottesville, VA, 1995).

5 Orhan Pamuk, *Snow: A Novel*, trans. Maureen Freely (New York, 2004).

6 John Rawls, *Political Liberalism* (New York, 1993); *The Law of Peoples* (Cambridge, MA, 1999).

7 Jürgen Habermas, *The Structural Transformation of the Public Sphere* (Cambridge, MA, 1991); *Between Facts and Norms: Contributions to a Discourse Theory of Law and Democracy* (Cambridge, MA, 1996).

8 William Galston, *The Practice of Value Pluralism* (Cambridge, 2005); 'Religious Pluralism and The Limits of Public Reason', *How Naked a Public Square? Reconsidering the Place of Religion in American Public Life,* Princeton University Conference, Oct 22–23, 2004: http://web. princeton.edu/ sites/jmadison/events/conferences/religion/religion.htm.

9 Rawls, *Political Liberalism*.

10 Ronald Dworkin, 'The Threat to Patriotism', pp. 273–284, in C. Calhoun *et al.*, ed., *Understanding September 11* (New York, 2002);

T. Clay Arnold, 'Executive Power, the War on Terrorism, and the Idea of Rights', *Politics & Policy*, 34:4 (2006), pp. 670–88; Cynthia Brown, ed. *Lost Liberties: Ashcroft and the Assault on Personal Freedom* (New York, 2003).

11 *Hamdi v. Rumsfeld*, 524 U.S. 507 (2004), at p. 536. The US Supreme Court further observed in this regard: 'It is during our most challenging and uncertain moments that our Nation's commitment to due process is most severely tested; and it is in those times that we must preserve our commitment at home to the principles for which we fight abroad.' (p. 532). A similar warning was issued to the British Government in a House of Lords ruling against arbitrary detention under the Anti-Terrorism, Crime and Security Act of 2001. 'The real threat to the life of the nation, in the sense of a people living in accordance with its traditional laws and political values', Lord Hoffman observed, 'comes not from terrorism but from laws such as these': 'British Court Says Violate Rights', *New York Times*, 17 Dec 2004. See generally, Bruce Ackerman, *Before the Next Attack: Preserving Civil Liberties in an Age of Terrorism* (New Haven, CT, 2006).

12 Detainee Abuse and Accountability Project, *By the Numbers: Findings* (New York, April 2006): http://hrw.org/reports/2006/ct0406/index.htm. The project is run by a coalition of US academics and human rights monitors.

13 See Arundhati Roy, 'India's Shame', *Guardian*, 15 Dec 2006; extended version in her introduction to *13 December – A Reader: The Strange Case of the Attack on the Indian Parliament* (New Delhi, 2006).

14 Human Rights Watch, 'Israel/Lebanon: Israeli Indiscriminate Attacks Killed Most Civilians', 6 Sept. 2007 (New York/Jerusalem): http://hrw.org/english/docs/2007/09/06isrlpa16781.htm; Amnesty International, *Deliberate destruction or 'collateral damage'? Israeli attacks against civilian infrastructure* (MDE 18/007/2006) (London, 2006): http://web.amnesty.org.library/index/engmde180072006; Ken Silverstein, 'Parties of God', *Harper's*, 314:1882 (March 2007), pp. 33–44, at pp. 40–43.

15 See Yitzhak Laor, 'You Are Terrorists, and We Are Virtuous', *London Review of Books*, 28:16 (17 August 2006): http://www.lrb.co.uk/v28/n16/laor01_.html. Former US president, Jimmy Carter, characterised the situation thus: 'I don't think that Israel has any legal or moral justification for their massive bombing of the entire nation of Lebanon. What happened is that Israel is holding almost 10,000 prisoners, so when the militants in Lebanon or in Gaza take one or two soldiers, Israel looks upon this as a justification for an

attack on the civilian population of Lebanon and Gaza'. 'The US and Israel Stand Alone', Interview with *Spiegel*, 15 Aug 2006: http://www.spiegel.de/international/spiegel/0,1518,431793,00.html.

16 Sanford Lewinson, ed., *Torture: A Collection* (Oxford & New York, 2004); Human Rights Watch, *The Road to Abu Ghraib* (New York, 2004): http://hrw.org/reports/2004/usa0604/.

17 Rawls, *Law of Peoples*, p. 6.

18 John Rawls, *A Theory of Justice*, revised ed. (Oxford & New York, 1999); original edition published in 1971.

19 Samuel Huntington, *The Clash of Civilizations and the Remaking of World Order* (New York, 1996), pp. 306–307.

20 Edward Said, *Orientalism* (New York, 1979), p. 328.

21 Malise Ruthven, *Fundamentalism: The Search for Meaning* (Oxford & New York, 2004); Karen Armstrong, *The Battle for God* (New York, 2000); Charles Taylor, *Varieties of Religion Today: William James Revisited* (Cambridge, MA, 2002).

22 Dale Eickelman, 'Islam and Ethical Pluralism', pp. 115–134, in Sohail Hashmi, ed., *Political Ethics* (Princeton, 2002); Dale Eickelman and Jon Anderson, *New Media in the Muslim World: The Emerging Public Sphere*, 2nd ed (Bloomington & Indianapolis, IN, 2003).

23 See Kuah-Pearce Khun Eng, *State, Society and Religious Engineering: Towards A Reformist Buddhism* (Singapore, 2003); Eiko Ikegami, *Bonds of Civility: Aesthetic Networks and the Political Origins of Japanese Culture* (Cambridge & New York, 2005).

24 Abdullah Saeed, 'Muslims in Secular States: Between Isolationists and Participants in the West', *MUIS Occasional Paper Series*, 1 (Singapore, 2005).

25 As sketched by Pierre Bourdieu, *Outline of a Theory of Practice* (Cambridge, 1977).

26 See Abdulaziz Sachedina, 'Freedom of Conscience and Religion in the Qur'an', pp. 53–90, in D. Little *et al.*, ed., *Human Rights and the Conflict of Cultures* (Columbia, SC, 1988).

27 'The Troubled Odyssey of Abdul Rahman', *Spiegel*, 3 April 2006: http://www.spiegel.de/international/spiegel/0,1518,409650,00.html.

28 Amyn B. Sajoo, *Muslim Ethics: Emerging Vistas* (London & New York, 2004).

29 Omid Safi, ed., *Progressive Muslims: On Justice, Gender, and Pluralism* (Oxford, 2003); Khaled Abou El Fadl, *Speaking in God's Name: Islamic Law, Authority and Women* (Oxford, 2001); Akbar S. Ahmed, *Islam Under Siege: Living Dangerously in a Post-Honor World* (Cambridge & Oxford, 2003); Khaled Abou El Fadl, ed., *The Place of Tolerance in*

Islam (Boston, MA, 2002); Richard Falk, *Religion and Humane Global Governance* (New York, 2001).

30 See generally William Chittick, *Imaginal Worlds: Ibn al-'Arabi and the Problem of Religious Diversity* (Albany, NY, 1994); S.H. Nasr, *Three Muslim Sages* (Cambridge, MA, 1964).

31 Majid Fakhry, 'Philosophy and Theology', pp. 268–303, in John L. Esposito, ed., *The Oxford History of Islam* (Oxford & New York, 1999).

32 Suha Taji-Farouki, ed., *Modern Muslim Intellectuals and the Qur'an* (Oxford & New York, 2004); Howard M. Federspiel, *Indonesian Muslim Intellectuals of the 20th Century* (Singapore, 2006); Greg Fealy and Virginia Hooker, ed., *Voices of Islam in Southeast Asia: A Contemporary Sourcebook* (Singapore, 2006); Amyn B. Sajoo, *Pluralism in 'Old Societies and New States'* (Singapore, 1994).

33 Engin Isin and Bryan S. Turner, *Handbook of Citizenship Studies* (London, 2002).

34 Sajoo, *Muslim Ethics*; and 'Ethics in the Civitas', pp. 214–246, in A.B. Sajoo, ed., *Civil Society in the Muslim World: Contemporary Perspectives* (London & New York, 2002).

35 Charles Taylor, *Modern Social Imaginaries* (Durham, NC, 2004) pp. 23–30 (quote at p. 34). See also his, 'Two Theories of Modernity', pp. 172–196, in D. P. Gaonkar, ed., *Alternative Modernities* (Durham, NC, 2001).

36 Cornelius Castoriadis, *The Imaginary Institution of Society*, trans. Kathleen Blamey (Cambridge, MA, 1987).

37 Taylor, *Modern Social Imaginaries*, pp. 193–194.

38 Seyyid Hossein Nasr, *Islam and the Plight of Modern Man* (London & New York, 1975); Fazlur Rahman, *Islam and Modernity: Transformation of an Intellectual Tradition* (Chicago, 1982); Farish Noor, *New Voices of Islam* (Leiden, 2002); Ibrahim Abu-Rabi, *Contemporary Islamic Intellectual History: A Theoretical Perspective* (MUIS Occasional Paper Series, #2), (Singapore, 2006).

39 Nilüfer Göle, *The Forbidden Modern: Civilization and Veiling* (Ann Arbor, MI, 1997). See also her, 'Islam in Public: New Visibilities and New Imaginaries', *Public Culture*, 14:1 (2002), pp. 173–190.

40 *Voices of Islam in Southeast Asia*, especially pp. 453–456 (Madjid), pp. 461–462 (MUI). Again, Indonesia's constitutional court has upheld the legal constraint on polygamy – requiring the consent of prior spouses before a religious court can approve an application for further marriages – as properly protective of 'the basic rights of wives and prospective wives': 'Indonesia blocks polygamy demand', BBC News, 3 Oct. 2007: http://news.bbc.co.uk/go/pr/fr/-2/hi/asia-pacific/7025593.stm.

41 See, *inter alia,* Madawi Al-Rasheed, *Contesting the Saudi State: Islamic Voices from a New Generation* (Cambridge, 2007); Ziba Mir-Hosseini and Richard Tapper, *Islam and Democracy in Iran* (London & New York, 2006); *Iran: Between Tradition and Modernity,* ed. Ramin Jahanbegloo (Lanham, MD & Oxford, 2004).

42 Mohammed Arkoun, *Rethinking Islam* (Boulder, CO, 1994), pp. 35–40. See also his *The Unthought in Contemporary Islamic Thought* (London, 2002).

43 See R. C. Lewontin, *Biology as Ideology: The Doctrine of DNA* (Toronto, 1991).

44 See Amartya Sen, *Identity and Violence: The Illusion of Destiny* (New York & London, 2006), notably chapters 2 and 4.

45 María-Rosa Menocal, *Ornament of the World: How Muslims, Jews and Christians Created a Culture of Tolerance in Medieval Spain* (Boston & London), 2002.

46 Ibid., p. 87.

47 John F. Richards, *The Mughal Empire* (Cambridge & New York), 1993.

48 Sen, *Identity and Violence,* p. 83.

49 Anna C. Korteweg, 'The Sharia Debate in Ontario', *ISIM Review* (International Institute for the Study of Islam in the Modern World, Leiden, Netherlands), No. 18 (Autumn 2006), pp. 50–51: http://www.isim.nl/files/Review_18/Review_18–50.pdf; Marion Boyd, 'Dispute Resolution in Family Law: Protecting Choice, Promoting Inclusion', *Report to the Attorney General and Minister Responsible for Women's Issues,* Ontario (Canada), 20 Dec 2004: http://www.attorneygeneral.jus.gov.on.ca/english/about/pubs/boyd/.

50 Boyd, 'Dispute Resolution'.

51 Korteweg, 'The Sharia Debate'.

52 Boyd, 'Dispute Resolution', p. 133.

53 Korteweg, 'The Sharia Debate'.

54 Ayelet Shachar, *Multicultural Jurisdictions: Cultural Differences and Women's Rights* (Cambridge & New York, 2001), p. 73.

55 Boyd, 'Dispute Resolution', pp. 91–92.

56 As attested in Korteweg, 'The Sharia Debate', and Boyd, 'Dispute Resolution'.

57 Mustafa Akyol, 'No real threat to secularism, says TESEV', *Turkish Daily News,* 22 November 2006: http://www.turkishweekly.net/news.php?id=41217.

58 Julian Glover and Alexandra Topping, 'Religion Does More Harm Than Good – Poll', *Guardian,* 23 Dec 2006: http://www.guardian.co.uk/religion/Story/0,,1978045,00.html.

59 Doug Saunders, 'Papal Visit Underlines Turkish Take on Faith', *Globe and Mail*, 30 Nov 2006.

60 'A Chance to Get Friendlier: The Pope's Controversial Trip to Turkey', *The Economist*, 27 Nov 2006.

61 Sabrina Tavernise, 'Allure of Islam Signals a Shift Within Turkey', *New York Times*, 28 Nov 2006.

62 Suna Erdem, 'Murdered Journalist's Funeral is a Silent Rally of Defiance', *The Times* (London), 24 Jan 2007; Gareth Jenkins, 'Editor Hated by Turkish Right Gunned Down', *Sunday Times* (London), 21 Jan 2007.

63 23 Dec 2006: http://www.guardian.co.uk/commentisfree/story/0,,1978092,00.html.

64 Mukul Devichand, 'Telling Muslim Tales', *Open Democracy* (London), 29 Dec 2006: http://www.opendemocracy.net/conflict-terrorism/muslim_tales_4219.jsp.

65 Taylor, *Varieties of Religion Today*, notably chapters 3 and 4. See further his *A Secular Age* (Cambridge, MA & London, 2007), notably Part V.

66 Robert Bellah, *Beyond Belief: Essays on Religion in a Post-Traditional World* (New York, 1970), chapter 9.

67 Tariq Ramadan, *Western Muslims and the Future of Islam* (Oxford, 2004), chapter 10. In the same vein, Aziz Al-Azmeh assails the 'culturalist differentialism' that obscures and essentialises in the name of 'authenticity' in *Islams and Modernities* (London, 1993), pp. 4–10.

Select Bibliography

Abou El Fadl, Khaled, ed. *The Place of Tolerance in Islam.* Boston, 2002.

Abu-Lughod, Janet, 'The Islamic City – Historical Myth, Islamic Essence, and Contemporary Relevance', *International Journal Middle East Studies,* 19 (1987) pp. 155–176.

Adelkhah, Fariba. *Being Modern in Iran,* tr. J. Derrick. London, 1999.

Ahmed, Akbar S. *Postmodernism and Islam: Predicament and Promise.* London & New York, 2004.

Albert, Jeff, Magnus Bernhardsson and Roger Kenna, ed., *Transformations of Middle Eastern Natural Environments: Legacies and Lessons.* New Haven, CT, 1998.

Almond, G.A., R.S. Appleby, and E. Siva, *Strong Religion: The Rise of Fundamentalism Around the World.* Chicago & London, 2003.

Anderson, Benedict. *Imagined Communities: Reflections on the Origin and Spread of Nationalism.* Rev. ed., New York, 2006.

An-Na'im, Abdullahi Ahmed. *Toward an Islamic Reformation: Civil Liberties, Human Rights, and International Law.* Syracuse, NY, 1990.

Appadurai, Arjun. *Modernity at Large: Cultural Dimensions of Globalization.* Minneapolis, MN, 1996.

Appiah, Kwame Anthony. *Cosmopolitanism: Ethics in a World of Strangers.* New York, 2006.

Arkoun, Mohammed. *Rethinking Islam: Common Questions, Uncommon Answers,* tr. Robert D. Lee. Boulder, CO, 1994.

_____ *The Unthought in Contemporary Islamic Thought.* London, 2002.

Asad, Talal. *Formations of the Secular: Christianity, Islam, Modernity.* Palo Alto, CA, 2003.

Al-Azmeh, Aziz. *Islams and Modernities.* London, 1993.

Azzam, Maha. 'Islamism Revisited', *International Affairs* (London), 82:6 (2006), pp. 1119–32.

Baderin, Mashood A. *International Human Rights and Islamic Law.* Oxford & New York, 2003.

Bakhtin, Mikhail. *Rabelais and His World*, tr. H. Iswolsky. Bloomington, IN, 1984.

Barney, Darin. *Prometheus Wired: The Hope for Democracy in the Age of Network Technology.* Vancouver & Toronto, 2000.

Beck, Ulrich, Anthony Giddens and Scott Lash, ed. *Reflexive Modernization: Politics, Tradition and Aesthetics in the Modern Social Order.* Cambridge, 1994.

Beckford, J. *Social Theory and Religion.* Cambridge, 2003.

Bellah, Robert. *Beyond Belief: Essays on Religion in a Post-Traditional World.* New York, 1970.

Berger, P. L. ed. *The Desecularization of the World.* Michigan, 1999.

Berman, Marshall. *All That Is Solid Melts into Air: The Experience of Modernity.* New York, 1988.

Bhabha, Homi K. *The Location of Culture.* New York & London, 1994.

Bhargava, Rajeev, ed. *Secularism and its Critics.* New Delhi, 1998.

Bianca, Stefano and Philip Jodidio, ed. *Cairo: Revitalising a Historic Metropolis.* Turin, 2004.

Black, Antony. *The History of Islamic Political Thought.* New York, 2001.

Bourdieu, Pierre. *Outline of a Theory of Practice.* Cambridge, 1977.

Boyd, Marion. 'Dispute Resolution in Family Law: Protecting Choice, Promoting Inclusion.' Report to the Attorney General and Minister Responsible for Women's Issues, Ontario (Canada), 20 December 2004: http://www.attorneygeneral.jus.gov.on.ca/english/about/pubs/boyd/.

Bozdogan, Sibel and Resat Kasaba, ed. *Rethinking Modernity and National Identity in Turkey.* Washington, DC, 1997.

Brown, Nathan J. and Clark B. Lombardi. 'The Supreme Constitutional Court of Egypt on Islamic Law, Veiling and Civil Rights: An Annotated Translation of Supreme Constitutional Court of Egypt *Case No. 8 of Judicial Year 17* (18 May, 1996)', *American University International Law Review*, 21 (2006), pp. 437–60.

Bulliet, Richard. *The Case for Islamo-Christian Civilization*. New York, 2004.

Bunt, Gary. *Virtually Islamic: Computer-Mediated Communication and Cyber Islamic Environments*. Cardiff, 2000.

Calhoun, Craig. ed. *Habermas and the Public Sphere*. Cambridge, MA, 1992.

_____ , Paul Price and Ashley Timmer. ed. *Understanding September 11*. New York, 2002.

Cantacuzino, Sherban, ed., *Architecture in Continuity: Building in the Islamic World Today*. New York, 1985.

Carter, Ian, Matthew H. Kramer and Hillel Steiner, ed. *Freedom: A Philosophical Anthology*. Oxford, 2007.

Casanova, José. *Public Religions in the Modern World*. Chicago & London, 1994.

Castoriadis, Cornelius. *L'institution imaginaire de la société*. Paris, 1975; English trans., *The Imaginary Institution of Society*, tr. Kathleen Blamey. Cambridge, MA, 1987.

Chadwick, Owen. *The Secularisation of the European Mind in the Nineteenth Century*. Cambridge & New York, 1990.

Chakrabarty, Dipesh. *Provincializing Europe: Postcolonial Thought and Historical Difference*. Princeton, 2000.

Chatterjee, Partha. *The Nation and its Fragments: Colonial and Postcolonial Histories*. Princeton, 1993.

Chittick, William C. *Imaginal Worlds: Ibn al-'Arabi and the Problem of Religious Diversity*. Albany, NY, 1994.

Clark, Emma. *The Art of the Islamic Garden*. Ramsbury, UK, 2004.

Connelly, Bridget. *Arab Folk Epic and Identity*. Berkeley, 1986.

Connolly, William E. *Pluralism*. Durham, NC, 2005.

Cooke, Miriam and Bruce Lawrence, ed. *Muslim Networks: From Hajj to Hip Hop*. Chapel Hill, NC & London, 2005.

Cooper, Frederick. *Colonialism in Question: Theory, Knowledge, History*. Berkeley, CA, 2005.

Dabashi, Hamid. *Close-Up: Iranian Cinema, Past, Present, Future.* London & New York, 2002.

_____, ed. *Dreams of Nation: On Palestinian Cinema.* London & New York, 2006.

_____. *Iran: A People Interrupted.* New York, 2007.

Davison, Andrew. *Secularism and Revivalism in Turkey: A Hermeneutic Reconsideration.* New Haven & London, 1998.

D'Entrèves, Maurizio Passerin and Seyla Benhabib, ed. *Habermas and the Unfinished Project of Modernity: Critical Essays on the Philosophical Discourse of Modernity.* Cambridge, MA, 1997.

Dirlik, Arif. 'Is There History after Eurocentrism? Globalism, Postcolonialism, and the Disavowal of History', *Cultural Critique*, 42 (1999), pp. 1–34

Doubleday, Veronica. *Three Women of Herat.* London, 2006.

Edwards, David B. *Heroes of the Age: Moral Fault Lines on the Afghan Frontier.* Berkeley, CA, 1996.

Edwards, Michael. *Civil Society.* Oxford, 2004.

Eickelman, Dale F. 'Islam and Modernity', in Eliezer Ben-Rafael and Yitzhak Sternberg, ed., *Identity, Culture and Globalization.* Leiden, 2002, pp. 93–104.

_____ and Jon Anderson. *New Media in the Muslim World: The Emerging Public Sphere.* 2nd ed., Bloomington & Indianapolis, IN, 2003.

Eisenstadt, S. N. *Fundamentalism, Sectarianism and Revolution: The Jacobin Dimension of Modernity.* Cambridge, 1999.

Eliade, Mircea. *Images and Symbols: Studies in Religious Symbolism,* tr. Philip Mairet. Princeton, NJ, 1991.

Escobar, Arturo. *Encountering Development: The Making and Unmaking of the Third World.* Princeton, NJ, 1995.

Esposito, John L., ed. *The Oxford History of Islam.* Oxford & New York, 1999.

Falk, Richard. *Religion and Humane Global Governance.* New York, 2001.

Fathy, Hassan. *Architecture for the Poor: An Experiment in Rural Egypt.* Chicago, 1976.

Federspiel, Howard. *Indonesian Muslim Intellectuals of the 20th Century.* Singapore, 2006.

Fernández-Armesto, Felipe. *Civilizations: Culture, Ambition and the Transformation of Nature.* London, 2000.

Frampton, Kenneth, ed. *Modernity and Community: Architecture in the Islamic World.* London, 2001.

Gaonkar, Dilip P., ed. *Alternative Modernities.* Durham, NC, 2001.

_____ , 'Toward New Imaginaries: An Introduction,' *Public Culture,* 14:1 (2002), pp.1–19.

Gavin, Harry R., ed. *Romanticism, Modernism, Postmodernism.* London & Toronto, 1980.

Gellner, Ernest. *Conditions of Liberty: Civil Society and its Rivals.* London, 1994.

Gibney, Matthew J., ed. *Globalizing Rights: The Oxford Amnesty Lectures, 1999.* Oxford, 2003.

Giddens, Anthony. *The Consequences of Modernity.* Stanford, CA, 1990.

Gleason, Philip. 'Identifying Identity: A Semantic History', *Journal of American History,* 69:4 (1983), pp. 910–31.

Goffman, Daniel. *The Ottoman Empire and Early Modern Europe.* Cambridge, 2002.

Goldberg, Ellis *et al.,* ed. *Rules and Rights in the Middle East: Democracy, Law, and Society.* Seattle, WA & London, 2003.

Göle, Nilüfer. *The Forbidden Modern: Civilization and Veiling.* Ann Arbor, MI, 1996.

_____ 'Islam in Public: New Visibilities and New Imaginaries', *Public Culture,* 14:1 (2002), pp. 173–90.

Gonzalez, Valérie. *Beauty and Islam: Aesthetics in Islamic Art and Architecture.* London & New York, 2001.

Graham, Mark. *How Islam Created the Modern World.* Beltsville, MD, 2006.

Habermas, Jürgen. *The Structural Transformation of the Public Sphere: An Enquiry into a Category of Bourgeois Society,* tr. T. Burger and F. Lawrence. Cambridge, MA, 1989.

_____ . *The Philosophical Discourse of Modernity,* tr. F. Lawrence. Cambridge, MA, 1990.

Hall, Stuart, *et al.,* ed. *Modernity: An Introduction to Modern Societies.* Oxford, 1996.

Hamid, Ismail. *Arabic and Islamic Literary Tradition.* Kuala Lumpur, 1982.

Hasan, N. *Laskar Jihad: Islam, Militancy And the Quest for Identity in Post-New Order Indonesia.* Ithaca, NY, 2006.

Hashmi, Sohail, ed. *Islamic Political Ethics.* Princeton, NJ, 2002.

Hawley, John, ed., *The Postcolonial Crescent: Islam's Impact on Contemporary Literature.* New York, 1998.

Heater, Derek. *Citizenship: The Civic Ideal in World History, Politics and Education.* Manchester & New York, 2004.

Hefner, Robert. 'Multiple Modernities: Christianity, Islam and Hinduism in a Globalizing Age', *Annual Review of Anthropology,* 27 (1998), pp. 83–104.

_____ , ed. *The Politics of Multiculturalism: Pluralism and Citizenship in Malaysia, Singapore and Indonesia.* Honolulu, 2001.

Hirschkind, Charles. 'Civic Virtue and Religious Reason: An Islamic Counter Public', *Cultural Anthropology,* 16 (2001), pp. 3–34.

Hobsbawm, Eric and Terence Ranger, ed. *The Invention of Tradition.* Cambridge, 1983.

Hourani, Albert and S. M. Stern, ed. *The Islamic City: A Colloquium.* Oxford, 1970.

_____ *Arabic Thought in the Liberal Age, 1798–1939.* Cambridge, 1983.

Huntington, Samuel P. *The Clash of Civilizations and the Remaking of World Order.* New York, 1996.

Hutcheon, Linda. *The Poetics of Postmodernism: History, Theory, Fiction.* New York & London, 1988.

Inayatullah, Sohail and Gail Boxwell, ed. *Islam, Postmodernism, and other Futures: A Ziauddin Sardar Reader.* Sterling, VA, 2003.

Jahanbegloo, Ramin, ed. *Iran: Between Tradition and Modernity.* Lanham, MD & Oxford, 2004.

Johansen, Baber. *Contingency in a Sacred Law: Legal and Ethical Norms in the Muslim Fiqh.* Leiden, 1999.

Kamali, Masoud. *Multiple Modernities, Civil Society and Islam: The Case of Iran and Turkey.* Liverpool, 2006.

Karim, K. H., ed. *The Media of Diaspora.* New York & London, 2002.

Karpat, Kemal H., ed. *Ottoman Past and Today's Turkey.* Boston, 2000.

Keddie, Nikki. *Women in the Middle East: Past and Present.* Princeton, 2007.

Khalid, Adeeb. *Islam after Communism: Religion and Politics in Central Asia.* Berkeley, CA, 2007.

Knauft, Bruce M., ed. *Critically Modern: Alternatives, Alterities, Anthropologies.* Bloomington & Indianapolis, IN, 2002.

Kristeva, Julia. 'Women's Time', *Signs,* 1 (1981), pp. 13–35.

Kymlicka, Will. *Multicultural Citizenship: A Liberal Theory of Minority Rights.* Oxford, 1995.

___ *Politics in the Vernacular: Nationalism, Multiculturalism and Citizenship.* Oxford, 2001.

Laborde, Cecile. 'The Culture(s) of the Republic: Nationalism and Multiculturalism in French Republican Thought', *Political Theory,* 29 (2001), pp. 716–35.

Laroui, Abdellah. *The History of the Maghrib: An Interpretive Essay,* tr. Ralph Manheim. Princeton, 1977.

Latham, Michael E., *Modernization as Ideology: American Social Science and 'Nation Building' in the Kennedy Era.* Chapel Hill, NC & London, 2000.

Lawrence, Bruce, *The Qur'an: A Biography.* London, 2006.

Lebbady, Hasna. 'Of Women-Centered Moroccan Tales and their Imagined Communities', *The Muslim World,* 95 (2005), pp. 217–30.

Lerner, Daniel. *The Passing of Traditional Society: Modernizing the Middle East.* Glencoe, IL, 1958.

Lewis, Bernard. *The Emergence of Modern Turkey.* Oxford, 1968.

Lewontin, R.C. *Biology as Ideology: The Doctrine of DNA.* Toronto, 1991.

Luong, Pauline Jones, ed. *The Transformation of Central Asia: States and Societies from Soviet Rule to Independence.* Ithaca, NY, 2004.

Maalouf, Amin. *In the Name of Identity: Violence and the Need to Belong,* tr. B. Bray. New York, 2000.

Macleod, Arlene. *Accommodating Protest: Working Women, the New Veiling, and Change in Cairo.* New York, 1991.

Mahmood, Saba. 'Ethical Formation and Politics of Individual

Autonomy in Contemporary Egypt', *Social Research*, 70:3 (2003), pp. 1501–30.

_____. *Politics of Piety: The Islamic Revival and the Feminist Subject.* Princeton, NJ & Oxford, 2004.

Maaruf, Shaharuddin B. *Concept of a Hero in Malay Society.* Singapore, 1984.

MacDougall, Elisabeth B. and Richard Ettinghausen, ed. *The Islamic Garden.* Washington, DC, 1976.

Mayeur-Jaouen, Catherine. *Saints et héros du moyên-orient contemporain.* Paris, 2002.

McDonald, Kevin. *Global Movements: Action and Culture.* Oxford, 2006.

Meisami, Julie Scott. *Medieval Persian Court Poetry.* Princeton, NJ, 1987.

Menocal, María Rosa. *The Arabic Role in Medieval Literary History: A Forgotten Heritage.* Philadelphia, PA, 1987.

_____ *Ornament of the World: How Muslims, Jews and Christians Created a Culture of Tolerance in Medieval Spain.* Boston & London, 2002.

Mernissi, Fatima. *The Veil and the Male Elite: A Feminist Interpretation of Women's Rights in Islam*, tr. M. J. Lakeland. Cambridge, MA, 1991.

Miège, Jean-Louis. *Tétouan à travers les siècles.* Tetouan, Morocco, 1995.

Migdal, J. *State in Society: Studying How States and Societies Transform and Constitute One Another.* New York, 2001.

Miles, Malcolm, 'Utopias of Mud? Hassan Fathy and Alternative Modernisms', *Space and Culture*, 9 (2006), pp. 115–39.

Mir, Mustansir. *Tulip in the Desert: A Selection of the Poetry of Muhammad Iqbal.* Montreal, 2000.

Mir-Hosseini, Ziba and Richard Tapper. *Islam and Democracy in Iran: Eshkevari and the Quest for Reform.* London & New York, 2006.

Mitchell, Timothy. *Rule of Experts: Egypt, Techno-politics, Modernity.* Berkeley, CA, 2003.

Moosa, Ebrahim. *Ghazali and the Poetics of Imagination.* Chapel Hill, NC & London, 2005.

Nasr, Seyyid Hossein. *Islam and the Plight of Modern Man*. London & New York, 1975.

Nasser, Mervat. 'The New Veiling Phenomenon', *Journal of Community and Applied Social Psychology*, 9:6 (1999), pp. 407–12.

Navaro-Yasin, Yael. 'The Historical Construction of Local Culture: Gender and Identity in the Politics of Secularism versus Islam' in Caglar Keyder, ed., *Istanbul Between The Local and The Global*. Lanham, MD, 1999, pp. 60–74.

Norris, Pippa and Ronald Inglehart, ed., *Sacred and Secular: Religion and Politics Worldwide*. New York, 2004.

Outhwaite, William, ed. *The Habermas Reader*. Cambridge, 1996.

Pamuk, Orhan. *Snow: A Novel*, tr. Maureen Freely. New York, 2004.

Putnam, Robert D. *Bowling Alone: The Collapse and Revival of American Community*. New York, 2000.

Qutb, Sayyid. *Social Justice in Islam*. New York, 1953.

Rahman, Fazlur. *Islam and Modernity: Transformation of an Intellectual Tradition*. Chicago, 1982.

Ramadan, Tariq. *Western Muslims and the Future of Islam*. Oxford & New York, 2004.

Al-Rasheed, Madawi. *Contesting the Saudi State: Islamic Voices from a New Generation*. Cambridge, 2007.

Rawls, John. *A Theory of Justice*. Rev. ed., Oxford & New York, 1999.

Renard, John. *Islam and the Heroic Image: Themes in Literature and the Visual Arts*. Columbia, SC, 1993.

Roy, Olivier. *Globalized Islam: The Search for a New Ummah*. London, 2004.

Ruthven, Malise. *Fundamentalism: The Search for Meaning*. Oxford & New York, 2004.

Sachedina, Abdulaziz. *The Islamic Roots of Democratic Pluralism*. New York, 2001.

Sadr, Hamid Reza. *Iranian Cinema: A Political History*. London & New York, 2006.

Sadri, M. and A. Sadri, ed. and tr. *Reason, Freedom and Democracy in Islam: Essential Writings of Abdolkarim Soroush*. Oxford & London, 2004.

Said, Edward. *Orientalism*. New York, 1978.

_____ *Covering Islam: How the Media and the Experts Determine How We See the Rest of the World*. Rev. ed., New York, 1997.

_____ 'The Clash of Ignorance', *The Nation*, 22 October 2001 (http://www.thenation.com/doc/20011022/said).

Sajoo, Amyn B. *Pluralism in Old Societies and New States*. Singapore, 1994.

_____ , ed. *Civil Society in the Muslim World: Contemporary Perspectives*. London & New York, 2002.

_____ *Muslim Ethics: Emerging Vistas*. London & New York, 2004.

Salvatore, Armando and Dale Eickleman, ed. *Public Islam and the Common Good*. Leiden, 2004.

Santoso, Soewito. 'The Islamization of Indonesian/Malay Literature in its Earlier Period', *Journal of the Oriental Society of Australia*, 8 (1971), pp. 9–27.

Schaebler, Birgit and Leif Stenberg, ed. *Globalization and the Muslim World: Culture, Religion, and Modernity*. Syracuse, NY, 2004.

Sen, Amartya. *Identity and Violence: The Illusion of Destiny*. New York & London, 2006.

Silverstein, Ken. 'Parties of God', *Harper's*, 314:1882 (March 2007), pp. 33–44.

Smith, Thomas W. 'Between Allah and Ataturk: Liberal Islam in Turkey', *The International Journal of Human Rights*, 9 (2005), pp. 307–25.

Somerville, Margaret. *The Ethical Imagination: Journeys of the Human Spirit*. Toronto, 2006.

Soroudi, Sorush. 'Islamization of the Iranian National Hero Rustam as Reflected in Persian Folktales', *Jerusalem Studies in Arabic and Islam*, 2 (1980), pp. 365–83.

Taji-Farouki, Suha, ed. *Modern Muslim Intellectuals and the Qur'an*. Oxford & New York, 2004.

Tapper, Richard, ed. *The New Iranian Cinema: Politics, Representation and Identity*. London & New York, 2002.

Taylor, Charles. *Sources of the Self: The Making of the Modern Identity*. Cambridge, MA, 1989.

_____ *The Ethics of Authenticity*. Cambridge, MA, & London, 1991.

_____ *Varieties of Religion Today: William James Revisited.* Cambridge, MA & London, 2002.

_____ *Modern Social Imaginaries.* Durham, NC & London, 2004.

_____ *A Secular Age.* Cambridge, MA & London, 2007.

Thomas, Elaine R. 'Keeping Identity at a distance: Explaining France's New Legal Restrictions on the Islamic Headscarf', *Ethnic and Racial Studies,* 29 (2006), pp. 237–59

Troll, Christian. *Sayyid Ahmad Khan: A Reinterpretation of Muslim Theology.* New Delhi, 1978.

Turner, Bryan S. *Weber and Islam.* London & New York, 1998.

_____ 'Cosmopolitan Virtue: Religion in a Global Age', *European Journal of Social Theory,* 4:2 (2001), pp. 131–52.

_____ *Vulnerability and Human Rights.* Philadelphia, PA, 2006.

Urry, J. *Sociology Beyond Societies: Mobilities for the Twenty First Century.* New York, 2000.

Vahdat, Farzin. 'Post-Revolutionary Islamic Discourses on Modernity in Iran: Expansion and Contraction of Human Subjectivity', *International Journal of Middle East Studies,* 35 (2003), pp. 599–631.

Warde, G. 'The Future of Religion', *Journal of the American Academy of Religion,* 74:1 (2006), pp. 179–86.

Watenpaugh, Keith. *Being Modern in the Middle East: Revolution, Nationalism, Colonialism, and the Arab Middle Class.* Princeton, NJ, 2006.

Werbner, Pnina. 'Global Pathways: Working Class Cosmopolitans and their Creation of Transnational Ethnic Worlds', *Social Anthropology,* 17:1 (1999), pp. 17–35.

_____ 'The Place which is Diaspora', *Journal of Ethnic and Migration Studies,* 28:1 (2002), pp. 119–33.

White, Jenny. *Islamist Mobilization in Turkey: A Study in Vernacular Politics.* Seattle, WA, 2002.

Wiles, Ellen. 'Headscarves, Human Rights, and Harmonious Multicultural Society: Implications of the French Ban for Interpretations of Equality', Law & Society Review, 4:3 (2007), pp. 699–735.

Winner, Thomas. *The Oral Art and Literature of the Kazakhs of Russian Central Asia.* Durham, NC, 1958.

Yack, Bernard. *The Fetishism of Modernities: Epochal Self-Consciousness in Contemporary Social and Political Thought*. Notre Dame, IN, 1997.

Zarcone, Thierry. 'View from Islam, View from the West', *Diogenes*, 50 (2003), pp. 49–59.

Zubaida, Sami. 'Max Weber's *The City* and the Islamic City', *Max Weber Studies*, 6:1 (2006), pp. 111–18.

Index

Abd al-Wahhab, Muhammad 154
Abd as-Sabur, Salah 55
Abd-al Raziq, Ali 216
Abduh, Muhammad 192, 195
Abdurashidov, Abduvali 111
absolutists 29, 220, 221, 226
Abu Ghraib 209
Aga Khan Development Network (AKDN) 16,
    94, 98, 99
Aga Khan Music Initiative in Central Asia
    (AKMICA) 16, 93–5, 98–117
Aga Khan Trust for Culture (AKTC) 21, 22, 98,
    104
agency 6, 7, 8, 10, 12, 17, 18, 19, 86, 98, 136,
    166, 169, 177, 185, 186, 198, 199, 202,
    204, 205, 215
Ahmad, Kassim bin 66–7
Akbar, civil ecumenism of 218
al-Afghani, Jamal al-Din 20, 191–2, 193, 194,
    195
al-Andalus 16–17, 74–8
al-'Arabi, Muhammad ibn 18, 141, 159–60, 214,
    218
Al-Azhar Park (Cairo) 21–3
Al-Azmeh, Aziz 13–14, 193, 194
al-Ghazali, Abu Hamid 20
al-Kaysi, M. I. 151
al-Muizz (Fatimid Imam-Caliph)
al-Qaeda 47, 209
Alexander see Iskandar
Alhambra 15
'Ali (ibn Abu Talib) 62, 69
Almatov, Almas 105
Alovatov, Aqnazar 111
alternative dispute resolution (ADR) 219, 220,
    221
An-Na'im, Abdullahi 27, 216
Andalusia/Andalusians 73–8, 90–1
Andalusian music 75, 76, 89, 92
anomie 6, 25
Antonioni, Michelangelo 125
Anwar, Zainah 214
apostasy 149–50, 213
Appadurai, Arjun 8, 12, 137

Appiah, Anthony 116
architecture for the poor 22
Arkoun, Mohammed 14, 217
as-Sit al-Hurra (The Free Lady) 77
Asad, Talal 201, 203–4
Atatürk, Mustafa Kemal 17, 176
authenticity 13, 14, 132, 185, 196
autonomy 7, 19, 25, 90, 97, 169, 173, 185, 186,
    203, 204, 205, 214, 218, 219

Bader, Veit 174
Bakhtin, Mikhail, theory of narrative 86
Barber, Benjamin 186
Baudelaire, Charles 2, 3
Bausani, Allessandro 62, 64
Bell, Daniel 143
Bellah, Robert 223
Berman, Marshall 4
Bhabha, Homi K. 242, 243, 260
Blow-up (1966, Antonioni film) 125
Boase, Roger 75
Bourdieu, Pierre 133, 152
Bowen, John R. 175
Brakel, Lode F. 56, 64
Bravmann, M. M. 60
Bulliet, Richard 188, 189

Carrel, Alexis 194
Casanova, José 169, 207
Castoriadis, Cornelius 90–1, 121, 122, 135, 215
cinema 1–3
citizenship 7–8, 14, 18, 20, 25, 130, 131, 139–40,
    143, 161–82, 207, 211, 215, 217, 219,
    221, 222, 224, 226
civil imagination 183–5, 187, 195, 197, 205
civil society 18–19, 20, 25, 85, 130, 145, 148, 164,
    165–6, 168, 170, 173, 180–2, 184, 185,
    187, 207, 210, 215, 217, 218–19, 224–6
clash of civilisations 9, 152, 186–7, 194, 210,
    217
colonialism 120, 122, 187, 191, 197
communitarian ethic 166, 207
Comte, Auguste 142
Connolly, William 25–6

Cooper, Frederick 163
Cordoba 218
cosmopolitanism 19, 145, 147, 155–7, 159, 160, 184, 185–7, 204
   cosmopolitan religiosity 20, 211, 214

Danielou, Alain 93
Darb al-Ahmar (Cairo) 21
Darwin, Charles 30, 38
Davison, Andrew 14
de Vries, Hent 204
Dink, Hrant 222
Durkheim, Émile 6, 153, 168, 208, 210, 223

Ebadi, Shirin 216
Edwards, David B. 71–2
Eickelman, Dale 26–7, 189–90, 211
Eisenstadt, Shmuel N. 122
enclave society 18, 137, 155–7
Enlightenment 6, 9, 10, 159, 168, 185, 202
ethical imagination 20
Etzioni, Amitai 207
evangelism 143, 146

Fathy, Hassan 22
Fatimids 218
feudal conservatism 67–8
feudal romanticism 67
fiqh 224
Firdawsi 59, 65
Foucault, Michel 4, 9, 13
Fukuyama, Francis 186
fundamentalism 19, 29, 49, 124, 140, 143, 145, 146, 147, 148, 151, 153, 154–5, 158, 160, 163, 176, 181, 186, 190–1, 195, 210, 211, 212
futuwwa 57, 68

Galston, William 180, 208
Gaonkar, Dilip 84
Gellner, Ernest 11, 172, 207
gendered space 121, 133
ghazal 63
Giddens, Anthony 8, 186, 199
   and reflexivity 10
Glazer, Nathan 139
globalism 8, 9, 186
globalization 20, 137–9, 154–5, 161, 181, 183–6, 189–90, 200, 205, 208, 212–13, 223, 225
Goffman, Erving 128, 151
Goldziher, Ignaz 60
Governance 6, 12, 17, 28, 163, 170, 192, 208, 217, 224, 225
   democratic governance 7–8, 11, 225
Guantanamo Bay 209

Habermas, Jürgen 6, 9, 25, 75, 133, 185, 202–3, 208
habitus 51, 122, 123, 131, 132, 133, 152, 155, 180, 212–13, 214, 215, 217, 225
Hadot, Pierre 201
Hamid, Ismail 66

Hamza 16, 62
Hamzanama (Adventures of Hamza) 15–16, 54
Hanaway, William 64–6
Hang Tuah 51, 61–2, 66–7
headscarf/*foulard* 17, 119, 124, 125, 126, 127, 135–6, 174–5, 179, 198, 212, 216, 222
Hefner, Robert 189
Held, David 186
Hezbollah 157, 209
hijab 78–9, 82–4, 199, 200
hikayat (Malay narratives) 64, 66, 67
hilm 57
Hodgson, Marshall 5, 52–3
human rights 7, 25, 27, 160, 166, 208, 211, 215, 217–18, 221, 222
Huntington, Samuel 187, 210
Hurreiz, Sayyid 58–9
Hussein, Saddam 71

Ibn Hazm 75, 91
Ibn Khaldun 14, 188
Ibn Rushd (Averroes) 74, 75, 91, 214
Ibn Sina 214
Ibn Taymiyyah 46
Ibn Tufayl 75
imaginary
   civic 218
   hybrid 51
   Islamic 157–60
   liberal 19, 205
   public 123
   religious 14, 119, 141, 217
   secular 119, 129, 131, 217
   social 13, 14, 20–1, 73–4, 75, 82, 84–6, 87, 90, 91, 120, 121–3, 127, 128, 129, 130, 131, 135, 155, 162, 176, 180, 213, 215, 217, 225, 226
   and moral order 215
indigenization 52, 59, 62, 132–3
individualism 7, 120, 155
interiority3 201, 202
Iqbal, Muhammad 15, 28, 29, 35–41, 49, 216
Iranian Revolution 1, 56, 119
ird 57
Iskandar (Alexander) 16, 54, 59, 61, 62, 66
Iskandarnama (Book of Alexander) 69
Islamic city 22
Islamic Institute of Civil Justice (IICJ), Ontario, public review of 219, 220, 221
Islamic Intellectuals Association of Indonesia (ICMI) 214, 216
Islamic Religious Council of Singapore (MUIS) 214
Islamicate 51–3, 54, 55, 64
Islamization 52, 59–63, 68–70, 71
isonomia (equal justice) 166, 224
Ivy, Marilyn 3
Izutsu, Toshihiko 60

jannat al-firdaus (gardens of paradise) 22
jawanmardi (youthful ideal) 68–9
jawari 77–8

Kant, Immanuel 18, 134, 153, 159, 184, 185,
    187, 196, 203
Kasaba, Resat 178
Kavakçi, Merve 17, 124–8, 132, 177
Kaviraj, Sudipta 121
Kelly, John 5
Kemal Bey, Namik 216
Khan, Sayyid Ahmed 15, 28, 29, 30–5, 37, 39,
    49
Kharja (poetic form) 75, 92
Khomeini, Ayatollah 56
Khudoberdiev, Sultonali 109
Kiarostami, Abbas 1, 23
Kristeva, Julia 240, 242, 243, 265
Kymlicka, Will 164, 170, 195, 196

Laborde, Cecile 174
Lacan, Jacques, real, imaginary and symbolic
    orders 82, 85
laïcité/laicism 173, 174, 175, 176
laiklik 176
Laroui, Abdellah 76
Lash, Scott 134–5
Lerner, Daniel 187
Lewis, Bernard 186–7
Lister, Ruth 165
Locke, John 7, 204
Lyotard, J.-F. 143

Maalouf, Amin 216
Maaruf, Shaharuddin bin 67–8
MacLeod, Arlene 198
Madjid, Nurcolish 214, 216
madrasas 188, 195, 214
Mahmood, Saba 200–1, 202, 205
mahrem (gendered space) 121, 133
Majlis Ulama Indonesia (MUI) 216
Makhmalbaf, Samira 1, 23
maqtal (story of martyrdom) 64
Mardin, Şerif 11
Markell, Patchen 204
Marx, Karl 6, 142
maslaha 25
Mawdudi, Sayyid Abul A'la 192
Mbele, Joseph 68
Meddeb, Abdelwahab 194
Menocal, María Rosa 74, 91, 218
Mernissi, Fatima 82, 83
Migdal, Joel 157
Milbank, John 203
modernisation 4, 8, 9, 21, 26, 120, 122, 135, 154,
    168, 176, 186, 187, 191, 192, 195, 197–8
modernism, authoritarian 122
modernities 5, 11, 16, 25, 74, 95
    alternative 13, 28, 74, 95, 117, 223
    civic 9, 18, 224
    plural 3, 9, 11–13, 14, 16, 17, 74, 100, 136,
        163, 215
modernity, as techno-scientific 9, 162, 225
Moosa, Ebrahim 216
Moriscos (post-Inquisition Spanish Muslims) 77,
    89

Mosque movement (Egypt) 200
Mudejar 76–7
Muhammad 32, 33, 36, 39, 45, 47, 48, 56, 62
mujahideen 71
multiculturalism 141, 143–5, 147, 148, 153, 156,
    157–60, 170, 180, 196
muruwwah (manly virtue) 57, 60
Music of Central Asia (CD-DVD anthology)
    107, 113–14
Muwashah (poetic form) 75, 92
Muzzafar, Chandra 214

Nafisi, Azar 216
Nasrid 76–7
Nasser, Mervat 198–9
Navaro-Yashin, Yael 178–9
neo-*ijtihad* 211
Norris, H. T. 58
Nyshanov, Nurlanbek 114

Olmsted, Frederick Law 22
oral tradition 73, 75, 91
Osama bin Laden 15, 29, 41–9
Oum Kalthoum 15

Pamuk, Orhan 216
Panahi, Jafar 1–3, 23
performative reflexivity 129
piety
    embodied 199–202
    movements 202
    practices 200–2
planetarity 73, 92
pluralism 25, 147, 170, 196, 207, 208, 211–13,
    217–18, 223, 224, 225
    cultural 99–100, 116, 140, 180
    plurality 181–2, 212
    religious 159, 218, 223
    social 149, 218
    value pluralism 179–80
political Islam 13, 14, 27, 120, 192–5, 209, 216, 222
post-industrialism 141–3
postcolonialism 15, 27, 90, 215–16
Protestantism 140, 153, 187, 189, 213
public Islam 17, 119–36
public reason 25, 26
public sphere 27, 82, 84–5, 119–36, 153, 162,
    168, 171, 173, 179, 183, 192, 199–202,
    207, 208, 210, 216
Putnam, Robert 166–7, 171

Qabbani, Nizar 55–6
Qur'an 15, 27–9, 31–4, 36–49, 64, 150, 189, 191,
    192, 200, 212, 216
Qutb, Sayyid 193, 194

Rahman, Fazlur 15, 216
Raimbergenov, Abdulhamit 104
Ramadan, Tariq 216, 226
Ras, J. J. 66
rationalism 6, 15, 20, 28, 33, 133, 173, 184, 185,
    196, 203

Rawls, John 12, 25, 140–1, 145, 147–8, 149, 152, 158, 170, 185, 196, 208, 210, 212, 214
religious grammars 19, 202–5
revivalism 14, 139, 140, 143, 150, 181, 190, 210213
   see also salafi movement
Ringgren, Helmer 60
rituals of intimacy 18, 20, 148, 150–5, 156, 158, 212
Roy, Olivier 184, 189
rule of law 141, 144, 145, 148, 207, 208, 209, 217
Rumi 37, 38

Sachedina, Abdulaziz 216
Saefuddin, Ahmad 214
Said, Edward 211
Saint-Simon, Claude H. 142
Saladin Ayyubi 22, 46
salafi movement 14, 190–2, 195
Salvatore, Armando 189
Santoso, Soewito 60–1
Sassen, Saskia 138
scapes 8, 137
Schabert, Tilo 4
Schluchter, Wolfgang 122
science 15, 28, 29–31, 35, 39
   Islamic science 15
secularism 3, 6–7, 14, 15, 18, 19, 25–6, 119, 122, 124, 126, 127, 128, 129–32, 134, 136, 142, 145, 162, 168–9, 171, 172–9, 185, 187, 192, 197, 203, 205, 207, 208, 212, 216, 220, 221–2, 224
Sen, Amartya 19, 161, 181, 218
Sennett, Richard 134
September 11 5, 8, 11, 20, 41–2, 73, 138, 161, 175, 182, 207, 208, 210, 211, 216, 217, 223, 224
Shah Walliullah 216
Shahnama (Book of Kings) 65
shari'a 25, 26, 27, 151, 194, 212, 213, 219, 220, 224
Shu'aib 43–4
Simmel, Georg 125, 126
Skocpol, Theda 167
social capital 164, 167–8, 170, 212, 214, 215
social imaginary 13, 14, 20–1, 73–4, 75, 82, 84–6, 87, 90, 91, 120, 121–3, 127, 128, 129, 130, 131, 135, 155, 162, 176, 180, 213, 215, 217, 225, 226
Soroush, Abdolkarim 216
Spellman, Kathryn 146

Spivak, Gayatri Chakravorty 73
sunna 27, 28, 216

Tabari 31, 32, 37
Taylor, Charles 12, 26, 73, 74, 86, 87, 122, 136, 195, 203, 215
Tocqueville, Alexis de 8, 170, 204
Torpey, John 138
Touraine, Alain 132
tradition 14, 186, 190–1, 195, 198, 199, 204
   musical 100–13, 115–17
Turkey, modernity in 122–8, 130–1, 135, 136, 176–9, 221–2
Turkish Economic and Social Studies Foundation (TESEV), poll 221
Turkish Penal Code 222
Turkishness 222
Turner, Victor 129

ulama 32, 47, 149
ultra-orthodoxy 147
umma 11, 45, 47, 149–50, 151, 175, 196, 207, 212
Universal Declaration of Human Rights 7
universalism 9, 18, 20, 165, 174, 211
   Kantian 18, 185
Urry, John 137
ustâd-shâgird (master-apprentice) (also *ustat-shakirt*) 101–5, 109, 110, 111

van der Veer, Peter 187
veiling 129, 131, 133–4, 135, 186, 197–9, 200–1
   see also headscarf/*foulard*

Wadud, Amina 216
wahdat-al-wujud (unity of being) 214, 218
Wahid, Abdurrahman 214
Wallada 75
Walzer, Michael 165
War on Terror 42, 138, 152, 182, 207, 208, 225
Weber, Max 6, 10, 153, 168, 210
Werbner, Pnina 196, 197
Wittgenstein, Ludwig 25
women
   in heroic milieu 68–70
   narratives of 73–92
   see also headscarf/*foulard*; veiling

Yack, Bernard 9

Zajal (poetic form) 75, 92
Zarcone, Thierry 187–8, 202